EDITH
&
WOODROW

Also by Tom Shachtman

The Day America Crashed

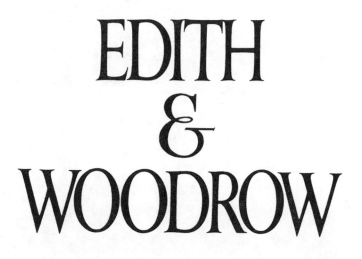

EDITH & WOODROW

A Presidential Romance

TOM SHACHTMAN

G. P. Putnam's Sons, New York

Library of Congress Cataloging in Publication Data

Shachtman, Tom, date.
  Edith and Woodrow.

  Bibliography: p.
  Includes index.
  1. Wilson, Woodrow, Pres. U.S., 1856–1924.
2. Wilson, Edith Bolling Galt, 1872–1961.
3. Presidents—United States—Biography.
4. Presidents—United States—Wives—Biography.

I. Title.
E767.S32   973.91'3'0922 [B]   80-16430
ISBN 0–399–12446–2

For Harriet
in admiration and affirmation

CONTENTS

"O, Edith, this is our golden time!
Tarnish it not by any pensive shadow
of the mind; for it may be that
nothing of futurity will be brighter
than the mere remembrance of what is
now passing."

"That was the very thought that saddened me! How came it in your mind
too?" said Edith, in a still lower
tone than he, for it was high treason
to be sad at Merry Mount. "Therefore
do I sigh amid this festive music. And
. . . I struggle as with a dream, and
fancy that these shapes of our jovial
friends are visionary, and their mirth
unreal, and that we are no true Lord
and Lady of the May. What is the
mystery in my heart?"

Nathaniel Hawthorne
"The Maypole of Merry Mount"

1

A WEDDING IN THE WHITE HOUSE

AT FIVE O'CLOCK in the afternoon on the beautiful and sunny spring day that was Thursday May 7, 1914, the guests for the wedding of Eleanor Randolph Wilson, daughter of the president of the United States, to Secretary of the Treasury William Gibbs McAdoo, began to gather in the Blue Room of the White House. Here, where Lafayette had embraced James Monroe, where Theodore Roosevelt and Prince Henry of Prussia had grasped hands, the fourteenth White House marriage was to take place. It was the second White House wedding in six months. Last November, sister Jessie had married Francis B. Sayre, who was now assistant to a college president. This day was both a happy and sad occasion for President Woodrow Wilson and his wife Ellen, for Nell, their youngest and in many ways most cherished daughter, was about to marry a man more nearly their contemporary than hers, a man they had come to call "dear Mac." Backstairs, the older retainers whispered "Nelly Grant" to one another and recalled an earlier May, another president's daughter. This Wilson bride's nickname, too, was Nell.

The courtship of Mac and Nell had begun in the early days of the administration. One evening the black doorman Brown, a man of large proportions, appeared at the entrance of the Oval Room where the family had gathered after dinner, and announced in his booming voice, "De secretary of de treasury." The president had not expected McAdoo, and the family had a moment's consternation as to what crisis might have caused his call, before Brown added "For Miss Eleanor." They had all laughed as Nell went blushingly to greet him. The next time Mac called, Brown marched into the room a bit before a similar announcement, made this time in a slightly lowered voice. As the visits became more frequent, Brown became increasingly quieter and more discreet. Finally one night he appeared, approached Nell silently, and merely rolled his eyes in the direction of the door.

McAdoo was tall and thin and southern; he had achieved success and celebrity as the builder of the first tunnels under the Hudson River between Manhattan and New Jersey. His first wife, always sickly, had passed on before he became secretary of the treasury. As a cabinet member and a bachelor, Mac was considered a good catch, and one of the best dancers in Washington, even if gossips did snigger at the thought of a man of his distinguished station in life doing that new dance, the tango. He and the diminutive captain Cary Grayson, the White House physician, had been seen in many places, a Mutt and Jeff team cutting up a storm. When Mac had begun to call seriously on Nell, she had been engaged to young Benjamin M. King, whom she had met on a trip to Mexico. It took her a long time to break that prior engagement. Ellen Wilson helped Nell decide in what true strains her heart was beating. By the time of the Sayre wedding Mac would hardly let anyone else dance with Nell, saying it was not etiquette to cut in on a cabinet member on the dance floor, and in the early spring the two had become secretly engaged. The president was philosophically opposed to the match because of the difference in the ages, but consented anyhow. For his part, not wishing to embarrass the president, McAdoo offered to resign from the cabinet when his engagement was announced—a proposal the president was glad to have, but just as glad not to accept.

They did keep the engagement secret for a while. Then one of Mac's letters to Nell was stolen before it was delivered to her—it was steamed open and then remailed—and the secret was out. The president was livid at this invasion of privacy, had instructed his secretary Joseph Tumulty to follow the matter up. He spoke to Postmaster General Alfred Burleson about it, and Burleson started an investigation which resulted only in insipid reports about mail-tube failure. It seemed not even the president was immune from red tape or mail mishaps.

The family was about to announce a wedding for the immediate future when Ellen Wilson had taken a nasty fall on her way out to church in early March. Pending her recovery, which was unnervingly slow, the date had to be left uncertain. One of the president's chief worries—the near-war in Mexico—contributed also to the initial vagueness of the date. It was only in the past week that Ellen Wilson had felt well enough—and the president safe enough from the threat of all-out war—to have the wedding. Nell and Margaret and Jessie did most of the work in getting ready for it, even issuing many invitations over the telephone at the last minute.

For these reasons, and also because the Sayre wedding had been so huge, the McAdoo wedding was rather small. Over a thousand guests had come and had sent expensive gifts when the first Wilson daughter was married in November, and the Wilsons felt it wouldn't be fair to all those people to seem required to cough up again in like manner so soon. So Nell's marriage was primarily a family affair, with the added guests of the "official" family, the cabinet. The other cabinet secretaries gave their fellow officer a last-minute stag luncheon and all was ready.

In the late afternoon the White House was abloom within as well as without. Flowers were one of Mrs. Ellen Wilson's passions, and the roses which she had planted a year ago were ready for Nell's big day. Inside, there were annunciation lilies and dogwood blossoms set off by ferns. As guests arrived they were shown to places in the Blue Room. Cabinet officers and their wives had to be seated in order of precedence. Ordinarily the first place among them would have gone to Secretary of State and Mrs. William Jennings Bryan, but since Vice-President Thomas R. Marshall and his wife were here, they took the places of honor. At the head of the room was a small dais with a *prie-dieu* set upon a startling white vicuna rug which had been given as a gift by the Chilean ambassador to Jessie, who lent it to Nell. At 5:45 the family came in, led by Mrs. Ellen Wilson, who although somewhat pale from her recent fall and illness, seemed to the guests to be much her old self, sweet and retiring, the perfect wife.

In the family party were McAdoo's five younger children, including nineteen-year-old Nona, who, not half an hour before, had thrown a terrible tantrum upstairs and almost spoiled the day, unwilling to bear the sight of her widowed father marrying a girl only five years older than herself. Fourteen months earlier, on the eve of her own father's inauguration, it had been Nell who had thrown a tantrum: seeing her mother have a moment of teary panic, Nell had hidden herself under a bed and screamed about the White House, "It will kill them both!"

That moment of torment had passed, and so did Nona's, as she took her place in the wedding party. At five minutes to the hour the bride-groom entered, looking tall and nervous next to his impeccable best man, Cary Grayson in naval uniform. Reverend Sylvester W. Beach, who had been the Wilsons' pastor most of the their years at Princeton, had come to perform the ceremony. At six on the dot, the music began, quite loud, and Nell and the president came down the hall from her room upstairs. Her gown of ivory white satin, trimmed with real old-point lace and sprays of orange blossoms, had a train several yards long; she wore about her neck a fiery string of diamonds, the gift of her bridegroom. Always considered homely, she looked beautiful today. She and the president went down the stairs. As she was about to enter the Blue Room, Nell's train turned over. Seeing it out of the corner of her eye, she whispered imploringly to the White House head usher, Irwin "Ike" Hoover, and he sprang to the rescue. Then she and her father were in the room, all eyes upon them.

In contrast to some of the new-fangled ceremonies being tried out by suffragettes, Nell promised, in the old style, to obey, serve, and love her husband. Watching her mother's tears, her own eyes filled as she and McAdoo exchanged simple and elegant circlets of gold. They knelt on the *prie-dieu* for the blessing, and Nell could see, in the dusk, the Washington Monument and the blue Virginia hills beyond. When the solemn part was over, the fun began.

After a reception in the Red Room, the guests proceeded—to the music of the Marine Band—into the state dining room. The place of honor was held by a forty-two-pound wedding cake made by the juniors of the National School of Domestic Arts and Sciences, a masterpiece that had been two weeks in the baking. The top layer had a garden of roses and lilies of the valley with Cupid joining two large silver hearts raised above the head of a miniature bride; similar excesses adorned two lower tiers. Following White House custom, the bride cut the cake with a military sword loaned to her by Dr. Grayson. There were six treasures buried in the cake. Helen Woodrow Bones, first cousin of the president, discovered a tiny ring embedded in her piece, the symbol of being next to wed. Franklin Houston, son of the secretary of agriculture, was fated to be a rich man when he found the penny. The charms further foretold that Miss Nancy Lane, daughter of the secretary of the interior, would have the best luck in the world, that Miss Sally McAdoo would be a great belle, that Miss Anne Hamlin, daughter of McAdoo's assistant, was doomed to spinsterhood, and that Secretary of the Navy Josephus Daniels was consigned to perennial bachelorhood. Mrs. Daniels and the secretary's four sons laughed heartily over that one.

Music for dancing had been personally selected by the unmarried Wilson daughter, Margaret, who aspired to a singing career. Among the guests were a half-dozen young military officers whose duty it had been these past fourteen months to squire the Wilson daughters about Washington. Nell had almost lost her heart to one of them. Tonight the young men had quite a bit of work, for there were many cousins and school chums of the Wilson girls and daughters of cabinet members. The bridegroom extracted a promise from twelve-year-old Sally that even if she had received the token that said she would be a great belle, she would consent to wait at least a year or two before marrying. Sally McAdoo nodded, and was swept away in a whirl of gold braid.

The bride and her sisters left the dancing to go upstairs so Nell could change to her going-away outfit. (The privacy of the family quarters was jealously guarded. Once the girls had disguised themselves and joined a White House tour, asking to see the Wilson girls' bedrooms. They were delighted when no one would let them in.) All had separate rooms on the second floor. At first Margaret had been given a large room where she could have her piano. Looking on the mantel over the fireplace, the girls had discovered a small plaque which read:

> In this room Abraham Lincoln signed the Emancipation Proclamation of January 1st, 1863, whereby four million slaves were given their freedom and slavery forever prohibited in these United States.

Margaret, afraid of ghosts, had wanted to change her room then, but had been persuaded not to.

Living in such a historic house was difficult. The servants insisted it was haunted by ghosts, most importantly that of Lincoln, whose brooding presence the girls felt they could sense in many spots throughout the mansion. One story the servants told affected the whole family deeply: two weeks before his death, Lincoln had "seen" his own body lying in state, had been "told" that he would shortly be assassinated. The enormous Lincoln bed was still in the White House somewhere, but Ellen Wilson would not have it in her bedroom; before the Wilsons, the Tafts had not used it either.

"Mr. President," the orotund Taft had said to Wilson on inauguration day fourteen months ago, "I hope you'll be happy here."

"Happy?" Wilson had inquired incredulously.

"Yes, I know," said Taft, "I'm glad to be going. This is the loneliest place in the world."

Nell came down the stairs, dressed for going away. Times past she and her father had folded their arms, bumped and pushed each other up and down the White House stairs playing "chicken," with each attempting to be more outlandish than the other, while Jessie or Marga or Mother would smile at their antics. Now at the bottom of the stairs, the unattached girls and women lined up to catch the bouquet. In November, Jessie had flipped hers to Nell with the accuracy of the

world's current baseball star, Ty Cobb. Today Nell tossed hers careless-
ly, as Marga had no beaux, and it was grabbed by a midair leap of
twelve-year-old Sally McAdoo. Her father the bridegroom gave a groan
audible to the whole party.

To escape the reporters, Mac had planned a ruse. His own car and
White House autos were drawn up in several spots front, back, and side
of the mansion, with the shades on the windows drawn. A dozen people
came out at once, and the reporters didn't know which way to turn.
Jessie and Frank dived into one car, Marga and Cary Grayson into a
second, two other couples into the third and fourth, and all left rubber
as they roared out the gates, pursued by wild-eyed reporters. After the
decoys had drawn out the newsmen, Mac and Nell slipped into Mac's
inconspicuous little car and got away clean. They had planned a sojourn
in Europe, but because of the still-worrisome situation in Mexico, had
decided on a nearer and shorter trip.

The president was unable to bear the sight of Nell going away, and
asked Colonel House to remain inside with him as the others traipsed
out to the south portico. The guests drifted out of the White House and
the party was over. Ellen, who had summoned up her strength for this
day, went wearily upstairs. So did the other family members. Then
Wilson and House sat out on the porch away from the street, in the
moonlight.

Edward M. House, a small, frail man from Texas with an independent income, was Wilson's adviser in things political, philosophical, and
personal. He had helped devise Wilson's campaign strategy and had
chosen three cabinet members. He was the man to whom—just a few
days ago, for instance—Ellen turned for financial advice in Wilson
family matters. He was the man to whom, almost alone among men,
Wilson felt he could unburden his whole heart. There was between them
something mystic, an unshakeable bond, and Wilson had known it from
the first time they met. Within weeks of that first meeting they were
exchanging confidences. "My dear friend," Wilson had told House
then, "we have known each other always." To others, Wilson said that
House was his second personality, his independent self, that "his
thoughts and mine are one."

The Colonel reciprocated, making Wilson's purposes in life his own.
House knew he could never be president, but he could be the *eminence
grise* and exercise, through Wilson, great power. During the campaign,
when he thought Wilson was in personal danger, he telegraphed home
to Texas for a famous ranger to come and guard the campaign party.
Both House and the ranger carried guns from then on, providing the

candidate with their own security patrol. (A few years earlier, the same duo had played a pistol-packed charade with Mark Twain at the old author's home in New York, chasing Twain up and down the stairs with guns drawn.)

This evening, in the moonlight, House thought the president distressed. Nell had been the one who had always laughed the loudest at Wilson's corny limericks, his imitations of July Fourth orators and heavy-footed Englishmen and, lately, of Cary Grayson approaching a golf putt. Wilson had rejoiced in Margaret's eager, impulsive conversation, and in Jessie's love of serious discussion, but Nell had been his frolicsome chum. "She was simply part of me, the only delightful part," Wilson wrote to a friend.

Tonight, the president rambled. He couldn't bear having Nell leave altogether. He wondered: in the summer when he and Ellen were away, would it be all right if Mac and Nell lived in the White House? The Colonel demurred; that might give a bad impression of Mac as heir apparent. Wilson spoke of having no real home anymore, said he felt unsettled, bothered by the endless streams of office seekers and people with gripes to air. The women suffragists, in particular, were insufferable. The president wished aloud that Champ Clark had been nominated by the Democratic party at Baltimore instead of Woodrow Wilson.

Listening, House wondered if he could detect signs of what Dr. Cary Grayson had told him privately a few days before, something even the president did not know: that an eye doctor in Philadelphia had detected Wilson's arteriosclerosis advancing under the strain of his work. As early as 1913 one of the president's recurring illnesses had been concealed from all but the family. No one knew of the arteriosclerosis. House looked but could see nothing more than tiredness in his friend, and tried to bring him out of his depression. Whenever they had no pressing business to discuss, Wilson tended to recall the troubles he had had when he was president of Princeton University—showing, House wrote in his secret diary, "how deeply the iron entered his soul."

To avoid such recollections, House on this evening channeled the discussion to consideration of Federal Reserve matters, to the imbroglio with Mexico, to his own forthcoming trip to Europe which he had been planning for some months. House was due to leave in a fortnight. It would be, House thought, "the great adventure," an attempt to head off a more and more threatening concatenation of forces in Berlin, London, Paris, and Vienna. Although virtually no one believed war to be imminent, all knew the forces now opposed on the continent were dangerous. House was to go and see if the foreign leaders would be interested in

joining with the United States in as-yet unspecified steps toward disarmament and a turning of their power to the upgrading of undeveloped
nations in the world. Think of it: if the power of the United States,
Germany, and Great Britain could be used to lift the industry and
economy in, say, Central Africa, or the vast and unused stretches of
jungles in South America—why, the character of the world could be
changed!

It was a grand scheme, and outlining it helped to lift the president's
spirits. When at last he went up to his bedroom, he seemed, if not happy,
then reconciled to the losses and gains of the day.

2

A SOLDIER'S WIFE

In May of 1914, the world seemed new. A nickel paid for carfare, a phone call, coffee, a shoeshine, a Hershey's bar, chewing gum, or a beer. Ragtime had come and was fading. Pope Pius X had banned the tango as evidence of the new paganism. There was the new poetry: a magazine called *Poetry* had just come out, with Ezra Pound proclaiming "To Hell with *Harper's* and the Magazine Touch." There was the new art: Marcel Duchamp's *Nude Descending a Staircase* had been a sensation at the Armory show not many months before. There was the new woman: Isadora Duncan had announced after the birth of her second illegitimate child that marriage was an oppressive superfluity. Greenwich Village was discovering Sigmund Freud, and a magazine to be entitled the *New Republic* was taking shape at the edge of the Village, next door to a home for wayward girls and across the street from a theological seminary. One of the new editors of that journal, young Walter Lippmann, was writing in his first book,

> We are unsettled to the very roots of our being. There isn't a human relation, whether parent and child, husband and wife, worker and employer, that doesn't move in a strange situation. We are not used to a complicated civilization, we don't know how to behave when personal contact and eternal authority have disappeared. There are no precedents to guide us, no wisdom that wasn't made for a simpler age. We have

changed our environment more quickly than we know how to
change ourselves.

America was industrializing at a rapid pace. Though technology had
not yet invaded every home and garage, it was making heavy inroads:
there had been 300,000 new automobiles produced in the last year.

On a balmy May day shortly after the McAdoo wedding, the handsome forty-one-year-old widow of the head of Washington's oldest and
most prestigious jewelry and silver store, Edith Bolling Galt, was touring the city in her electric car. She was the first woman in the city to
own one, and she delighted in driving it, sometimes with her young
friend Alice Gertrude Gordon, called Altrude by everyone, the
orphaned heiress to a mining fortune. The girl, whom Edith loved as a
daughter, would come down from New York, and often they would go
out together gallivanting in the electric. Over a period of months, Edith
had developed a special relationship with the uniformed officer at the
corner near the White House. He would see her perking along in her
vehicle, and stop traffic so she could make her left turn, then give her a
smart salute. He was positively charming. Altrude thought that, as with
most men, he was secretly in love with Edith.

Last summer Altrude and Edith had gone to Europe together, but
they thought they wouldn't go again this year—too much of a strain.
Besides, Altrude was being pursued by a number of suitors, among
them the dashing White House physician Cary Grayson. Rather than
leave town, this summer they would hang about Washington and take
only a few side trips, to be available if there were a call from the White
House, for instance. Today the mansion seemed less busy. The president
was in New York, speaking at a funeral of Americans killed in Mexico.

Wilson had not gone to New York easily. There were serious threats
on his life if he should appear to eulogize the men. Grayson and House
had urged him not to go. Mayor Mitchel of New York, who had
recently been shot at himself, also asked the president to stay home. But
there would be Secret Service guards, and Colonel House with his trusty
six-shooter—and the president felt that having sent the young men to
their death, he must pay them his respects at the very least. "When the
people of the United States elected a President," Wilson told his
secretary, Joe Tumulty, "they had a right to expect that they had
chosen a man and not a coward." Tumulty went to Ellen Wilson, whom
he loved as a mother, and pleaded with her to dissuade the president

from going to New York. Ellen demurred, saying, "a soldier's wife has no right to interfere with his duty."

Such remarks were characteristic of both Ellen and Woodrow Wilson.

Thomas Woodrow Wilson had grown up surrounded by the stress of war. Born in Virginia in 1856, his earliest times were shadowed by the Civil War and Reconstruction. Once, a small spectator in a large crowd, he saw General Robert E. Lee pass by on a horse; years later he wrote that Lee had a character too large ever to be contained upon a stage, that men could write about Lee but they could never explain his greatness. It was said of Lee that he was a man without intimates, that he talked as a friend only with God. The same would later be said of Wilson.

The young boy grew up as a Scotch Presbyterian, God-fearing to the extreme, the son and grandson of ministers, surrounded by religious men who commanded through the power of their oratory, and by women whose virtues and strengths sustained their men and made those men's contributions worthy by their own attitudes. Wilson's family was neither poor nor wealthy. A story—perhaps apocryphal—was told of Wilson's father, Joseph Ruggles Wilson: a man stopped him on the street and observed that the minister's carriage was run down while his horse was well-groomed; that, the minister explained, was because while he himself took care of his horse his congregation took care of him. Father Wilson was stern, a diligent teacher who made the boy write and rewrite his sentences until they said precisely what he meant. Wilson adored his father; in later years he wrote essays for the minister's church newspaper. When his father grew old, Wilson took him into his own house and cared for him until his death. His mother, whose gentleness was widely known, he also worshipped.

As a boy Tommy ran and played with other boys, but spent much time growing up in a house full of adoring females. He read, wrote constitutions for little clubs, dreamed of the sea—lived a life where permutations of the mind were perceived as being of great moment, wherein complexities and contradictions could exist in the elastic web of an expanding consciousness. Man was perfectable, yet predestined; women were purer and greater creatures than men, yet inferior; the South had lost the Civil War, yet had emerged morally triumphant.

He went to religious Davidson College in 1873, soon came back because he was homesick and could not stand the loneliness occasioned by separation from his adored mother. At home he read widely and conceived of himself as a future statesman; the vocation of minister seemed less attractive than it had in former years. In 1875 he went north to Princeton College. Here he discovered, as he wonderingly wrote to his father, that he had a mind. He organized a debating club, became managing editor of the *Princetonian*, read Bagehot and Burke and called them his masters. He formed a solemn covenant with a classmate to "school all our powers and passions for the work of establishing the principles we (hold) in common; that we would acquire knowledge that we might have power." He wrote an article on cabinet government in the United States and sent it off to a small national magazine edited by young Henry Cabot Lodge of Harvard, who published it in August of 1879, a few months after Wilson graduated Princeton.

It was an auspicious time to come to manhood. Thomas Alva Edison had just perfected the electric light; the world was changing at a rapid pace. Wilson knew politics was his profession, but he entered law school at the University of Virginia, where he debated a lot and wrote another club constitution. Romantic and bookish, he pressed a suit on his cousin Harriet Woodrow, whom he had always known. She rejected him in as kind a way as possible. In 1882 he formed a law partnership in Atlanta, but his practice languished. He was more interested in writing articles, did some for the *New York Post*. Then, on a visit to Rome, Georgia, he saw and met the daughter of a local Presbyterian minister, Ellen Louise Axson.

She was a beauty, and one with a fine mind. Already she was mature enough to be caring for the house of her widowed father and her three younger siblings. In addition she was a painter, a great talker when her enthusiasm was up, and as much a romantic as he.

The South at that time still believed that Sherman's marches had been directed mainly against a society of women and children. Southern females never forgot the war or the devastation of the postwar era; this colored the fabric of their lives completely. Ellen, as much as Woodrow, was a child of the Civil War and Reconstruction South. Her aims were characteristic of those of her background and age: to be a good mother; to assist her husband; to aid the poor, especially individual blacks, by acts of kindness. Southern women who grew to maturity in the 1870s and 1880s were overwhelmingly influenced to press for peace, a high and feminine ideal in a low and masculine world. Women of the North might agitate for suffrage, but southern states overwhelmingly voted against such innovations. Peace was the only true cause to which a southern woman could aspire, the only one appropriate to her upbringing. Southern women were used to being put upon pedestals by their men, but being up there, says Ernest Groves, "tended both to maintain chivalry and also to shut off from the life of the women the influences coming out of modern life." Ellen was old-fashioned; her attitude reflected her background completely.

In 1883 she had many suitors, but none so ardent or imaginative or needful of her as Woodrow Wilson. Within moments, it seemed, he was declaring his love for her. This was the right and proper thing to do in those days: the boy asked the girl to marry him, then started the formal courtship. Wonder of wonders, Ellen accepted Woodrow's overtures.

A few days after declaring his love and being accepted, Wilson arrived at Johns Hopkins to begin graduate work in government. Toward the end of his term at Hopkins he completed a book about *Congressional Government*, which he sent off to Houghton Mifflin, who agreed to publish it on what Wilson deemed quite favorable terms. The book was acclaimed as an insightful analysis of the problem of leadership; it contended that we lacked a strong executive branch and that power had shifted to congressional committees.

Wilson received an offer from the newly formed Bryn Mawr College for Women, outside Philadelphia. Ellen wrote him that

> perhaps the greatest circumstance in its favor to my mind, lies in the fact that you would be the *first* professor—that you would enter on the work untrammeled by precedent. . . . *But*, do you think there *is* much reputation to be made in a *girl's school*—or, an it please you, a "Women's College?" Can you be content to serve that sort of an institution? . . . If they are going to have "prudes for proctors, dowagers for deans" it would be more consistent to follow Tennyson's scheme to the bitter end and exclude men altogether—on penalty of death!

Wilson thought that Ellen knew so much more about literature and life than he did; she was always teaching him. He knew only politics and history and government, nothing elevated. He worried that their marriage would mean Ellen might have to give up opportunities for serious painting, and was distressed. She was living at a boardinghouse in New York, studying bravely at the Art Students League. Was she sure marriage was the right path? Yes, she said, because

> when head and heart unite in telling me that this is the man whom I most honor, admire and look up to as well as the only one I can love, it would be strange indeed if I did not wish to spend my life with him—and for him. The really strange

thing is that you should choose to spend your life with *me*.
You know Carlyle says that "let but the rising of the sun or
the creation of a world happen twice and it ceases to be
marvellous." But this is one great mystery that even use and
wont cannot make less marvellous . . .

They were married in June of 1885, and moved to Bryn Mawr. While he
taught, Ellen raised a family. Two daughters were born during the years
at Bryn Mawr. Ellen painted seldom there. Tiring after a while of
teaching girls, Wilson moved with his growing family to Wesleyan in
Connecticut, where he taught men as well as women, and coached the
football team. Ellen painted more; she had a studio and spent much
time in it. Her young sister would find her at the studio, paint in her
hair, lost in another world and reluctant to go back to a demanding
husband and—now—three little girls. She always returned home on
time, despite the feeling that her own promise was not being fulfilled
even as her husband's star was rising. She painted a madonna after an
Italian master. Woodrow hung it near the center of the house, vowed he
would take it with him always. In 1890, it went with them to Princeton.
Here Woodrow grew steadily in stature, writing several books, lecturing
to nonacademic groups. By 1896, when the college became a university,
Wilson was the most popular and magnetic teacher on staff, and was
chosen to give the address at Princeton's sesquicentennial celebration.

At Princeton, from time to time, Ellen became ill at ease and
depressed. Then she would recover and be her old self, retiring but not
unhappy. Painting provided some avenue of personal pleasure and
accomplishment.

Woodrow's biography of George Washington was published in 1897
(as was a competing one by Henry Cabot Lodge) and a period of intense
work was capped in 1902 with the publication of his five-volume
History of the American People. He was forty-five. In June of that year
he was selected nearly unanimously to succeed the retiring Dr. Patton
as president of Princeton University. He had reached a peak of success.
If long ago Ellen had chosen a man whom others had thought beneath
her aspirations, he had now fulfilled the promise of her dedication, the
submergence of her career for his. He knew what he owed to Ellen.
Away on a trip, he wrote her,

My delight in you is so complete, my loneliness without you
so irremediable, all satisfying companionship so impossible! I
literally never know what it is to have either heart or mind
satisfied, or even at rest, away from you. . . . My love for

you released my real personality, and I can never express it
perfectly either in act or word away from you or your immediate inspiration. . . . Love unlocks everything within me
that is a pleasure for me to use. I never used my mind, even,
with satisfaction till I had you.

As president of the university, Wilson had some early success in
introducing the preceptorial system, and in raising Princeton's admission and disciplinary standards. During this time, Ellen grew ever
calmer, was sweet and cultured, and seemed to live in a world removed
from workaday reality. Visionary, idealistic, she let her husband mix
with the soiled clay of the world, while she kept out of it. To come home,
for Wilson, was not only to relax, it was to find a pure, bracing, uplifting
atmosphere. In the family, when Wilson would say something with
which she did not agree, Ellen would respond, "Oh, Woodrow, you don't
mean that, do you?" "Madam," he would answer, "I ventured to think I
did, until I was corrected."

It was a ritual to go along with others: no business talk at the dinner
table, quiet reading together, standing with legs up on the table to drink
a toast to the New Year. The Wilson daughters could not recall ever
hearing a cross word or argument between their parents.

But there were some bad times. In 1907, in the midst of one of her
recurrent depressions that lasted for over a year, an incident occurred
that could have broken the marriage. While alone on vacation in
Bermuda, Wilson had an affair with the woman who would be known to
history as Mrs. Peck.

Mary Allen had made an early marriage to a man named Hulbert,
who died, and then another to a man named Peck, which ended in
divorce and later in her reassumption of the Hulbert name. To Woodrow Wilson, at a time when his own wife was in acute depression
following her brother's death, Mary Hulbert was charming, quick of
tongue, sensitive, flirtatious, overdramatic—and available. (It is worth
noting that Mrs. Hulbert's charms captivated at least briefly several
other interesting men of the age.)

As a woman, Mary Hulbert was nearly the complete antithesis of
Ellen Axson Wilson. People who knew them both felt Mrs. Hulbert
filled a need on Wilson's part for gaiety, verbal dalliance, and play that
Ellen Wilson could not or would not fill. In any event, the Wilson-
Hulbert correspondence, which went on for many years, shows that the
two were intimate, though just how intimate and for how long is not
known.

Ellen found out about the affair, though this, too, is shrouded in uncertainty. From Woodrow's letters to her and from hers to him, and from the absence of certain letters which ought to be in such a series but which seem to have been destroyed at a later date, the conclusion that Ellen knew is inescapable. What is also clear is that the intense phase of this affair passed quickly, and that the Wilsons were reunited as lovers as well as marriage partners, and Mrs. Hulbert faded into the background. However, Wilson continued to write to her faithfully, and she to him, for many years. In fact, Mary Allen Hulbert was invited to Princeton to stay, and the Wilsons together to Bermuda to stay, in the intervening years. Over the course of their marriage, Ellen graciously allowed Mary Hulbert (and a few other women) full access to Wilson's mind (if never to his body), as if she knew they satisfied for him certain yearnings which she did not share.

By the time the initial breach with Ellen was healed, and Mary Hulbert thrust only to the role of long-distance correspondent, Wilson was having problems with Princeton. Trying to get academic excellence firmly established, he backed a plan to abolish the old-style eating clubs and have undergraduates housed and taking their meals with faculty advisers in a new quadrangle of buildings. Here instruction would be continual and Princeton would become a hothouse for the mind, not simply a place to nurture friendships that might later prove useful. The faculty loved the plan, the alumni hated it.

Taking it all personally, Wilson toured the country, appealing to the alumni on the plan's behalf. He couched the conflict in terms of democracy versus autocratic and elitist institutions. It was a losing battle: he would not compromise, and the plan went down the drain.

Then he became embroiled in another controversy, this one for virtual control of Princeton. Dean Andrew West of the graduate school wanted a lavish residential graduate college and more autonomy; Wilson wanted the whole university to grow—not just one part of it. Again he labeled the battle as democracy versus special privilege, and even the newspapers saw it that way. When at last an alumnus died and left his estate to be administered by West for the graduate college, Wilson told Ellen, "We have beaten the living, but we cannot fight the dead. The game is up."

If Princeton no longer seemed to want him to lead them, others did. Colonel George Harvey, a conservative magazine publisher, and Boss Jim Smith of the New Jersey Democratic machine entered Wilson's book-lined study at Princeton in June of 1910. Smith asked in wonder, "Do you read *all* these books, Professor?" "Not every day," Wilson answered, and laughter broke the ice. The men assured him he could be nominated for governor of the state, that he would win handily—and, moreover, his win would make him a leading contender for the Democratic nomination for the presidency in 1912. On condition that he would be beholden to no one once nominated, Wilson agreed. Thinking Wilson insincere in such a naïve pledge, Smith agreed.

However, as soon as he was nominated, Wilson broke publicly with Smith and the other bosses, and they found they had to support him or lose everything. He campaigned as a reformer, plotting out each speech with Ellen, who would often suggest changes and important ideas; he found it was her ideas that generated the most applause and comment. Campaigning taught him that he could speak the language of the people as well as he had spoken that of academia. The training he had gotten at his father's hands in saying things simply and directly was again bearing fruit: a newspaper columnist wrote during the gubernatorial campaign that Wilson was the only man he'd ever heard who could be confidential with a crowd. He won the governorship—and started thinking of the presidency.

As in all great political victories, the times and the man seemed to be as one. Reform was the key to the day, and Wilson held that key. In 1911, Wilson's work as governor was characterized by a reform leader as "the most remarkable record of progressive legislation ever known in the political history of this or any other state." Tumulty, House, McAdoo, and others who would be prominent figures in later years gathered about the man who could voice the innermost wishes and thoughts of the people in electrifying manner.

In early March of 1911 Wilson was convinced that his chance was near at hand. The Democrats had no clear front runner for the presidential nomination, and Taft was running the country weakly. What Wilson had to do was woo William Jennings Bryan, three times the Democratic standard-bearer and the conscience of the reform spirit in America. Bryan decided to give a speech in Princeton at a time when Wilson was away in the South giving a speech of his own. Ellen Wilson on her own invited the Great Commoner to the house, and telegraphed Woodrow to change his plans and get home quickly. Wilson complied. The two leaders impressed each other with their Christian ideals. Next year at the convention in Baltimore, in a matter of principle, Ellen helped persuade Wilson to back Bryan against the party's regulars— and this support led eventually to reciprocal support by Bryan, and Wilson's nomination. Woodrow told Ellen that once more she was responsible for getting him where he was in life.

Wilson campaigned across the country against the incumbent William Howard Taft, whose lackadaisical administration had been hopelessly discredited, and against ex-President Theodore Roosevelt who was running on the Progressive (Bull Moose) platform. It was a wild campaign. When TR was shot on the campaign trail, Wilson refused to attack the Rough Rider while he recuperated—people liked that. Conversely, Roosevelt was vilifying Taft, whom he'd practically appointed to the presidency—and people *didn't* like that.

It was whispered in the campaign that Wilson and a Mrs. Peck had had an affair. Wilson denied it, told people that southerners just liked to write "mush notes." Roosevelt, informed of the scandal and offered the opportunity to smear Wilson, refused to do so, because no one, he said, would believe such sexual skullduggery of a man who looked like an apothecary's clerk.

Wilson was not only new, he had in him the clergyman people had always respected, the teacher they'd always listened to; and he spoke a vision in colors and cadences that straightened the spine and stirred the mind. In an age of orators, he was the best one many had ever seen or heard. There was a crisis upon us, he said; America was about to forget

> the ancient time when America lay in every hamlet, when America was to be seen in every fair valley, when America displayed her great forces upon the broad prairies, ran her fine fire of enterprise up over the mountainsides and down into the bowels of the earth, and eager men were everywhere captains of industry, not employees; not looking to a distant city to find out what they must do, but looking about among their neighbors, finding credit according to their character, not according to their connections.

The coming election, Wilson said, was an epic battle, a struggle for emancipation, for a new American revolution: either we would have free enterprise, or we would have no freedom whatsoever.

Wilson drove hard at the Progressive vote as well as the Democratic. As Roosevelt and Taft split what had been the majority party down the middle, Wilson won the presidency with a minority of the popular vote but a great majority in the electoral college. As with Lincoln and Jefferson before him, he profited from the schism in the opposing party. His victory speech showed no exultation:

> There is so much to reconstruct . . . that a generation or two must work out the result to be achieved. . . . I summon

you for the rest of your lives to work to set this government
forward by processes of justice, equality and fairness.

His appeal was emotional and passionate; at times he could hardly hold
back his own tears when he spoke, so great was his conviction. In his
inaugural he spoke of the emotions:

> The feelings with which we face this new age of right and
> opportunity sweep across our heartstrings like some air out of
> God's own presence, where justice and mercy are reconciled
> and the judge and the brother are one. . . . Men's hearts
> wait upon us; men's lives hang in the balance; men's hopes
> call on us to say what we will do. . . .

And while he plunged into the whirlwind of the White House and the
responsibilities of the presidency, his wife adjusted to the big mansion.
She refused the social whirl, worked to create an atmosphere helpful to
Woodrow's work and well-being. She planted gardens, made the house
comfortable; the staff thought her wonderful. Black maid Maggie Parks
said she seemed like an angel, and she acted like one as well when she
brought the Parks family the Wilson girls' old clothes—Mrs. Parks's
daughter was crippled, Ellen knew. Housing in the black community,
Ellen saw, was atrocious, unsanitary; she dragged congressmen to view
the slums, and prodded Woodrow to help public employees by putting
restrooms in government buildings. A bill to help change Washington's
housing was known as hers; its passage languished.

Five of Ellen's paintings were included in an exhibit of notable
women artists: had she devoted her life to the canvas, knowledgeable
people said, she might have ranked with the great portraitists of the age.
She sold the paintings for high prices to obtain money for a charity for
the education of southern mountaineers, which she helped foster.

The bond between Ellen and Woodrow continued to grow in the
pressure-laden White House. When, in the summer of 1913, Ellen left
Woodrow alone to go with the girls to Harlakenden, an estate in New
Hampshire, the elder Wilsons wrote love letters as they had done thirty
years before, Ellen every day, Woodrow mostly on Sundays. Her letters
warmed his heart, he said, and gave him

> so constant and vivid a realization of you that even this
> barren house seems full of you, my heart is serene and strong
> for every turn of the day, and even loneliness is tempered

with a delightful sense of moving in an atmosphere of assured love and comradeship. . . . It seems to me that I never loved you as I do now! . . . So long as you continue to feed me with the sweet affection upon which I live, I shall fare excellently, just as well as a man could who was never intended to be a bachelor for so much as seven days together. . . . I adore you! No president but myself ever had *exactly* the right sort of wife! I am certainly the most fortunate man alive! . . . The real source of youth and renewal for me is my love for you, the sweetheart I picked out the moment I laid eyes on her and who has been my fountain of joy and comfort ever since. . . .

To which the lady replied,

Your wonderful, your adorable Sunday letter has just come and has made me fairly drunk with happiness. I would give anything to be able to *express* my love as perfectly as you do, dear heart, for then indeed I might hope to make you as happy as you make me. But then no one else in the world can express anything so perfectly as you—so there's no help for it, unless when you write those "great heart words" you will say to yourself "her heart is as great as mine and it echoes all I say, though she has not the genius for expression." . . . I am perfectly sure that you are the greatest, most wonderful, most lovable man who *ever* lived. I am not expressing an opinion, I am simply stating a self-evident fact. . . . God bless you, my darling, my darling. . . .

As the summer wore on, they summed up more and more their lifelong feeling for each other. "It is very wonderful how you have loved me," Woodrow wrote,

The soul of me is very selfish. I have gone my way after a fashion that made me the centre of the plan. And you, who are so individual, who are so independent in spirit and in judgment, whose soul is also a kingdom, have been so loyal, so forgiving, so self-sacrificing in your willingness to live *my* life. Nothing but love would have accomplished so wonderful a thing. If I have not justified it, I have been deeply grateful. I at least have sense enough to know what treasure I have enjoyed and lived upon, and how pitifully poor I should have been without it. . . .

Some of the letters were graphically intimate; Wilson was highly sexed, and Ellen was his lover in every way still in the golden summer of 1913.

One of the matters often discussed in the Wilson family was what to do about Mexico. Ellen, who had made a study of that country for Woodrow, hated its dictator, General Victoriano Huerta.

A month before the Wilson inauguration, Huerta had violently deposed Francisco Madero, who was later shot while trying to escape on the way to prison. When Huerta's government had demanded world recognition, President Taft simply did not act, but bequeathed the problem to Wilson. As there were many interests at stake, recognition was no simple matter. Mexico was one of the world's leading producers of crude oil, and American, British, French, and German companies vied for concessions; along both sides of the river at Tampico, oil storage tanks sat like huge mushrooms. American oil interests wanted Huerta recognized, but Wilson was more interested in the morality of the situation than in the oil. As far as he knew, Madero had been working for democracy and Huerta was not. Wilson told the press, "We can have no sympathy with those who seek to seize the power of government to advance their own personal interest." Within the family circle he spoke of Huerta with a grimace. "I will not recognize a government of butchers," he said when nobody was around who would quote him. (Stockton Axson, Ellen's brother and a close friend of Wilson's, noted that the president almost always had had a pet hate; it was his way of directing anger.) As 1913 wore on, the task of preserving American interests in Mexico seemed to be resolving into a choice between recognition of Huerta and armed intervention, neither one of which was palatable to Woodrow Wilson.

The president sent envoys, replaced the ambassador (Henry Lane Wilson, no relation), and did what was called "watchful waiting." Huerta promised an election, then reneged, then held one and disavowed the results. In early 1914 word reached Wilson that Huerta was about to declare war on the United States—in an effort to unite the disparate Mexican factions—and was just waiting for two shiploads of guns from Germany to start shooting. Meanwhile the other factions were sniping away, one headed by the aristocratic Venustiano Carranza, the other by the bandit Pancho Villa. By early April 1914 Villa had

routed Huertaista forces in the north and was rapidly approaching the
center of the country where he hoped to link up with Carranza for a
showdown against Huerta's men at Tampico. The situation was a
powder keg and everyone knew it. American warships were dispatched
to stand off shore; correspondent Jack London went down to cover the
fracas for *Collier's*, John Reed was having tequila toasts with Villa, and
Lincoln Steffens was arguing philosophy with Carranza. Jingoistic
slogans flew through the United States and not a few people lamented
that Teddy Roosevelt was not around to lead the cause. Everything
waited on the German arms.

Then an American whaleboat landed without permission—they were
looking to buy gas for small boats—and the crew was captured. Within
hours they were released and a personal apology given to Admiral
Mayo, but Mayo took the incident as an affront to American dignity
and demanded a formal apology, punishment of the offenders, and the
firing of a twenty-one-gun salute to Old Glory. He exceeded his authority and escalated thereby a minor incident into a *casus belli*.

How, said Huerta cunningly, could he salute a country that hadn't
recognized him? Promising the offenders would be punished, the dictator asked Mayo to withdraw the ultimatum. Mayo would not do so,
which produced a dilemma for Wilson: though the president personally
deplored the admiral's actions, he must now back him up or lose to
Huerta. Wilson quickly consulted with cabinet and Congress, dispatched additional warships to Tampico, and demanded Huerta accept
Mayo's terms. Ellen had already taken her fall and was recuperating at
White Sulphur Springs, West Virginia, and Wilson was there. As the
cabinet drew up contingency plans for war, Wilson told Tumulty, "The
people seem to want war with Mexico, but they shan't have it if I can
prevent it."

The president had brought Ellen back to the White House. Then, at
2:30 in the morning of April 21, 1914, he was awakened by Tumulty to
take a call from Secretary of State Bryan. The German steamship
Ypiranga was about to land at Veracruz and deliver Huerta considerable guns and ammunition—what did the president want done? The
president asked Bryan's recommendations and called for those of Navy
Secretary Josephus Daniels. All argued for action. Tumulty thought to
himself that it was one of the ironies of the age that these men, all
pacifists, should be contemplating action that might well precipitate the
country into war. Finally Wilson told Daniels to order seizure of the
customs house to prevent the guns from reaching Huerta—or Carranza
or Villa. After finishing with Bryan and Daniels, Tumulty was still
there. Did Joe agree with the decision? He did. Wilson reiterated his

own belief in it, his voice husky with emotion. In the morning the president told valet Arthur Brooks never to awaken him at night again: one never made the best decisions at such a time.

Part of the reason Wilson agreed to intervene at Veracruz was because he thought the episode would be bloodless. The American and Huertaist commanders had been talking, and the Mexican was willing to pull his forces back before shooting began, but it didn't work out that way. As the Marines fanned out toward the customs house, they were sniped at from many sources, among them a school for young Mexican naval cadets. Both the school and the cadets were destroyed by the navy's guns; other snipings brought similar retaliation, and the final death toll reached several hundred Mexicans and nineteen Americans—but Veracruz was taken. (Absurdly, when the *Ypiranga* was actually intercepted it was found to be carrying, not German arms, but Remington rifles which Huerta had purchased in New York and had shipped through Germany as a ruse.)

Wilson heard of the American deaths from dispatches which were terribly graphic:

> Henry Pulliam . . . gunshot wound through chest, abdomen, spinal cord had caused paralysis lower half of body; would have been totally helpless cripple.

The news went through him like a knife. At a press conference he appeared pale, his skin thin as parchment. He could not get the idea "off his heart . . . that it was I who had to order those young men to their deaths."

In the days that followed, American reinforcements arrived, and Huerta struck back. Through four days the United States lived in real—if undeclared—war with Mexico. Then, as if by God's hand, the countries of Argentina, Brazil, and Chile (the "ABC powers") offered their services to mediate between the United States and Mexico. Wilson agreed instantly to the idea and so, in a few days, did Huerta. A few hours after Huerta had accepted the offer, Wilson sat down with Samuel G. Blythe of the *Saturday Evening Post* and said that his ideal for Mexico was an orderly and righteous government, "but my passion is for the submerged 85 percent of the people of that republic who are now struggling towards liberty."

Days later, he had to go to the funeral of the Americans killed in this terrible affair.

New York suspended all business and the streets were jammed with hundreds of thousands of people, all silent as each coffin was borne on a gun caisson, sailors on either side, Marines behind. Church bells pealed as Wilson and Daniels rode with the parade to the Brooklyn Navy Yard where the relatives had gathered. Daniels read the roll of those who had died: Boswell, Defabbio, De Lowry, Fisher, Fried, Frolichstein. . . . Noting the diversity in these names when he came up to speak, Wilson told the crowd

> they are not Irishmen or Germans or Frenchmen or Hebrews anymore. They were not when they went to Veracruz; they were Americans, every one of them. . . . The flag under which they served was a flag in which all the blood of mankind is united to make a free nation.

And he spoke of himself, as well.

> I never went into battle, but I fancy that there are some things just as hard to do as to go under fire. I fancy it is just as hard to do your duty when men are sneering at you as when they are shooting at you. . . . The cheers of a moment are not what a man ought to think about, but the verdict of his conscience and of the consciences of mankind, so when I look at you I feel as though I also, and we all, were enlisted men.

Many in the press sniped at Wilson for having equated bravery in office with bravery under fire. He was too pacific, people thought. Many still preferred Teddy Roosevelt, who, a few days later, showed up in Washington, back from the Brazilian jungle, thirty pounds lighter and with the boil of tropical diseases still in his blood. Roosevelt went to the White House, and he and Wilson made small talk for a while out on the porch. The bitterness that had been between them during the campaign seemed to have faded. The presidency being an exclusive club, only members really knew the difficulties of the office.

The ABC powers were due to meet on the twentieth of May. Wilson demanded of them that Huerta must go, and that whatever government took over Mexico would have to promise to progress toward democracy. Such ideals must be upheld, else the lives lost at Veracruz would have no meaning.

In his letters at this time to friends, Wilson reiterated a prediction he had made just before taking office: that the presidency would kill him. But it wasn't he that was dying, it was Ellen.

After Nell's wedding, Ellen Axson Wilson seemed to slip swiftly into ill health. There was nothing Grayson could find really wrong with her at first, few outward manifestations. Mrs. Elizabeth Jaffray, the White House head housekeeper, thought Ellen was just in a depressed mental state. The president was most solicitous, trying with his own hands to get her to take nourishment, encouraging every hopeful sign, believing the best and never the worst. Ellen was his inspiration, a sort of mother to him as well as a wife, a woman who assured the continuity of his past and his future.

As May turned to June, and Ellen complained that she was "tired," Grayson realized she was more than that. He diagnosed her condition as Bright's disease with the complication of tuberculosis of the kidneys. He even called in specialists who confirmed his sad findings. Ellen's condition was fatal, but Grayson did not yet dare tell the president. Conscious of Wilson's advancing arteriosclerosis, he did not want to worry him. There was little either of them could do for Ellen, anyhow.

Despite all hints that the progress of the disease was inevitable, Wilson still wrote to friends that Ellen was improving slightly.

In mid-June Grayson put the First Lady permanently to bed. Woodrow made time to take tea with her; she conversed with him intelligently, wanted to know details—for instance, on Mexico, one of her pet subjects.

While ABC powers had been meeting, Carranza and Villa and their armies had defeated Huerta's forces on several fronts, taking the second most populous city of Guadalajara. Spurred by Wilson's demands, the ABC powers recommended a transfer of the government to the Constitutionalists (Carranza's party). Huerta seemed on the way out. Ellen was cheered by this news even as her condition worsened: Woodrow's moral force, to which she had contributed so much, seemed to be prevailing.

Mid-June brought the thirty-fifth reunion of Wilson's Princeton class of '79. Jack Hibben, currently president of the university and formerly Wilson's best friend, invited the president to lead the "Pee-rade." Wilson refused. Hibben had supported Dean West in the old controversy, and the wound still smarted. The old alumnus's bequest that had been Wilson's undoing—originally estimated at from two to four million—had since been revealed as amounting to only $600,000. Wilson had been right on other matters, too: his educational reforms were being instituted by other colleges around the country, and, after Princeton no longer wanted him to lead, he had gone on to be the country's leader. He did agree to at least walk in the "Pee-rade" with his former classmates, but for him the reunion was saddened by the fact that Ellen was not strong enough to be there.

As Ellen faded in ways hardly visible to the daily observer, a small event in Europe began to take on large ramifications. On June 28, Austrian Archduke Franz Ferdinand and his wife were reviewing some troops in a provincial capital. It was their wedding anniversary. The archduke had been heir to the throne of Austria until he renounced his claim to marry this woman; the right to review troops was one of the few prerogatives he retained. During the day, the archduke and his wife were killed by Serbian assassins. On July 5, Germany agreed to support Austria in punishing Serbia, even if that meant war with Serbia's ally, Russia.

Colonel House, in Europe at the time of the assassination, had been trying to arrange a meeting between Germany and Great Britain to discuss commonality of aims. Six months earlier, House had told Wilson that the fall of 1913 was too early for such a meeting. Now it was too late. The archduke's death aborted House's mission, and he hurried home.

Ellen Wilson was helped to sit out on the White House lawn among the flowers in a garden she had started. "It will be so lovely," she whispered to gardener Charlie Hemlock, "but I'll never live to see it finished." In a less resigned mood she wrote indignant notes to senators who were attacking Woodrow's policies; the notes were never sent. People came to see her; she lay on a white sofa in an upstairs room and refused to let them talk of her condition. On the fifteenth of July the glad news was received at the White House that Huerta had fled Mexico and was on his way to Spain. Huerta gone! Ellen rallied at the news, then sank still deeper.

Grayson brought more specialists in, but all they could say was that, more than the disease, there was an ebbing of the will to live. Ellen grew weaker. She urged Woodrow to go out and play golf. He said he would, made as to leave, and then didn't go, but sat unbeknown to her just outside her room, silently going over his papers. The whole house functioned at a hush. In the middle of the night he would wake up and go to her bedside to gaze at her, trying to will her to revive.

On July 23, Austria delivered an ultimatum to Serbia, and, on July 26, rejected the Serbian reply. The stage was set for war. Wilson said that he felt as if he had malaria or some other dread disease. These were the most momentous events in the world since Lincoln occupied this house, he wrote to a friend. At lunch on the day Austria declared war, he asked Nell not to tell her mother anything of the conflict. Nell agreed, then asked him if he thought the United States would become involved. He stared at her as if dazed, put his hands over his eyes, and said, "I can think of nothing—nothing, when my dear one is suffering."

Nell tried to cheer Ellen by telling her of the absurdities of the Washington social round; making thirty calls a day, leaving cards, saying nothing. Thursdays she and the other cabinet wives were at home to callers between three and six. Ellen listened politely but did not seem amused.

The family were all hiding their secret fears from one another; all knew in their hearts Ellen could not last much longer.

On July 29, Austrian forces bombed Belgrade, and Russia mobilized her armies along her Austrian frontier. On July 30, both countries ordered general mobilization. On July 31, Germany sent an ultimatum to Russia to demobilize within twelve hours or face all-out war. The world went wild. Repercussions were felt as far away as the United States, where the New York Stock Exchange was closed to avoid panic, and people worried about a run on the banks. In Germany the government had already made up its mind. Kaiser Wilhelm II declared "the sword has been forced into our hands." Germany's Chancellor Bethmann Hollweg ended a speech with "If the iron dice roll, may God help us." The German military ponderously swung into all-out war. France, Russia, and England were allies—they would all have to be attacked.

The German master plan called for attacking France through Belgium; once France was on her knees, the armies could then be brought to bear on Russia. Even while Germany's armies secretly crept up to the border, German diplomats asked whether France would remain neutral in a war between Germany and Russia. When at the last moment there seemed to be a glimmer of hope that France would indeed remain neutral, the kaiser was told that the railway schedules could not be changed, and that the plan to invade had to go forward. At seven in the evening, German troops thus crossed into Luxembourg on their way to Belgium and thence toward France.

At midnight, the French were mobilizing, crowds in the Place de la Concorde were tearing off the black mourning that the statue of Alsace-Lorraine had worn since the last German war, and they were singing the "Marseillaise." In London, Admiralty First Lord Winston Churchill put the great British fleet on alert.

As World War I began in earnest, Admiral Grayson told Wilson he should notify all members of the immediate family to come to Ellen Wilson's bedside. Jessie, brother Stock Axson, and others who were away from Washington were sent telegrams. The news went out to the preoccupied world that the First Lady was seriously ill. Theodore Roosevelt sent a note hoping the news of Ellen's illness was exaggerated: he knew only too well the complications of Bright's disease, which had killed his own first wife. The president's friend, Colonel House, just back from Europe, had glimmerings of how serious Ellen's health was, but stayed away from Washington nonetheless.

On August 2, a Sunday, newsboys in Washington shouted that Germany had given an ultimatum to Belgium: let us through to France, or we will conquer you as well. The Belgian answer thrilled the Allies: "If we are to be crushed, let us be crushed gloriously." At the White House, Wilson received the Belgian news in a dispatch from Minister Brand Whitlock with a sort of helplessness. There was nothing he could do, he thought.

In London, Edmund Grey, the government's foreign secretary, quoted to Parliament Gladstone's words about 1870: "Could this country stand by and witness the direst crime that ever stained the pages of history and thus become participators in the sin?" The answer in 1870 had led to France's defeat. It must be a different answer now. Hours after Grey finished speaking, Germany declared war on France, though German armies had been attacking in the direction of France for days.

On August 4, Wilson told Ellen that Jessie had arrived. "I understand," she said, knowing full well that she was dying. Woodrow did not tell her about the crisis in Europe. But sitting by her side, holding her hand in one of his, with the other he wrote out a penciled note to the belligerents offering the good offices of the United States in an attempt to avoid total war. All over Europe, United States embassies were being asked to take over the usual channels of diplomatic exchange between the countries already at war. Wilson hoped that before the conflict got too large, there could be some mediation. Perhaps there was still hope. There were, however, no immediate replies to his notes. In England, Grey stood at a window at dusk and uttered the immortal line, "The lamps are going out all over Europe; we shall not see them lit again in our lifetime." In Belgium, the battle of Liège raged. All over Europe, the armies of a half-dozen nations marched to war on a scale never before imagined. The battles thus joined, German militarist von Moltke thought, would change the character of the earth for the next hundred years.

* * *

On the morning of August 6, Dr. E. P. Davis, Princeton classmate and long-time friend of Wilson's, arrived from Philadelphia to visit the White House. He took a look at Ellen, then asked Woodrow to come into a downstairs room with him, and there told his friend that the end was only hours away. There was no longer any use in the family's deluding themselves. Wilson cried, then recovered enough to go into the bedroom and see Ellen. Barely conscious, she asked about her slum-clearance bill: was there any movement on it? Wilson had word sent to the Senate and House that his wife was dying, and would like knowledge that the bill had been passed before she died.

Throughout her last day Ellen was calm, peaceful, and lucid. She recognized Mrs. Jaffray, who looked in; she whispered to Cary Grayson to take care of her husband, and to tell him at the appropriate time that he must marry again; when Woodrow came in she smiled at him. The family sat waiting. After lunch, word came from the Senate that the slum-clearance bill had been passed; Wilson told her this and she smiled again. As the afternoon wore on Ellen's breathing grew fainter. The president and her daughters sat in her chamber as Frank Sayre and William McAdoo paced in an antechamber just outside.

Jessie, Nell, and Marga knelt at the foot of the bed and prayed. Looking up, Nell saw a smile on her mother's face she thought was "divine." Woodrow sat, immobile, holding Ellen's hand as she lapsed into unconsciousness. Downstairs a clock chimed five times.

"Is it all over?" the president asked. Grayson checked, and nodded. Wilson's head fell toward his chest. He walked to a window and, looking out, said, "Oh, my God, what am I going to do?"

3

A TRAVELLER
BETWEEN LIFE AND DEATH

WILSON WAS SO devastated moments after Ellen died, that Grayson worried for the president's health. Wilson was not a very well man. The vision in one eye was permanently impaired; there was arteriosclerosis; there was asthma and other respiratory difficulties. He had had a handful of strokes—some of them severe—dating from his fortieth year. The cumulative strokes had been hidden from the public because Grayson (and Wilson) thought it should be nobody's business but the family's.

"I must not give way," the president muttered, and tried not to. There were things that had to be done. Ike Hoover, long-time employee of the White House, told the family that custom dictated that the body should be put in a casket and held in state. Wilson could not bring himself to agree as yet. With the help of others, he lifted Ellen's body from where it lay and laid it out on the white sofa, where she had received visitors during her illness. He folded her hands over her breast, placed a white silk shawl about her shoulders. With her golden brown hair braided and plaited around her head, she looked much like the madonna she had painted long ago, which hung nearby.

During the next two days, Wilson spent very little time in the executive offices, mostly dictating telegrams about Ellen's death. With his daughters he sat near Ellen's body, praying, trying to control his shock and grief, observing the rather formal Scottish mourning custom of his family. For the next two nights he sat up alone by the white sofa, the sole living person in the chamber of death. It was only on the third day that Wilson would permit his wife's body to be placed in a coffin for a ceremony. Thousands of messages of condolence poured into the White House. Dressed in a white suit with a band of black mourning, the president read some of them.

On Sunday a short funeral service was held in the East Room, where Lincoln, Garfield, and McKinley had lain in state, and where just a few months ago Jessie had married Frank Sayre. After the service, the coffin was taken to the special train waiting at Union Station. The train left Monday afternoon for Rome, Georgia. The funeral was to be private; nevertheless there were small delegations from the House, the Senate, the cabinet, as well as White House employees, relatives, and friends. Pleading his well-known inability to suffer the heat of the South in summer, Colonel House didn't make the trip. As the train passed through the countryside, church bells pealed along its route. At several stops, the funeral party was joined by additional family members. Wilson kept Ellen's casket in the parlor car; he couldn't bear to have it travel with the baggage, sat with it all the time.

The train pulled into the station at Rome, Georgia, Tuesday mid-afternoon. The town was a place of almost overwhelming memories for Wilson. Here he had first caught sight of Ellen, and by the banks of the Etowah River they had taken long walks and courted. Eight hundred relatives, friends, and officials gathered at the First Presbyterian Church for services. Enormous amounts of flowers surrounded the catafalque. Ellen's father had been pastor of this congregation for many years; the service was conducted by the man who succeeded him.

Tumulty, Grayson, McAdoo, and Sayre sat by the president and his daughters. Stock Axson, Ellen's brother, had managed to arrive from Oregon; he stayed close to Woodrow, who had let him know how much he needed such friends. Ellen's sister, who was ill, could not attend. During the ceremony, two hymns which had been favorites of the First Lady were sung.

As the cortege wound its way to Myrtle Hill Cemetery, passing the house where Ellen had lived as a child, it began to rain. Torrents came down. The thousands of bareheaded spectators were without protection, but a tent had been erected over the gravesite for the family. As the simple rites were read, the president broke down. His body was racked with sobs, shaking visibly before the enormous crowd. Ellen was buried beside her mother and father, in an unadorned casket, wearing her wedding ring. For minutes after the service was concluded, Wilson stood by the grave, silent and unmoving, as wind and rain swept into the tent. Attendants suggested he could now leave the cemetery, but he would not do so until the casket had been completely covered with earth.

On the way back to the station, the president told one of Ellen's cousins that he wished space to be made alongside her grave for his own. He ordered a stone of Italian marble, and for the inscription chose a favorite verse from Wordsworth:

> A traveller between life and death;
> The reason firm, the temperate will,
> Endurance, foresight, strength, and skill;
> A perfect woman, nobly planned,
> To warn, to comfort, and command
> And yet a spirit still, and bright
> With something of angelic light.

When he reached the train, the president, after conversing for a few moments with some of Ellen's schoolmates, took to his berth and went to sleep. He had had scarcely any rest in the preceding five days.

After his deep sleep, the president rode the rest of the way to Washington on the observation platform. Thoughts of war and death commingled. Many times during his career, Wilson gave himself over to solitude, and out of it came his deepest, most mature moments. Ray Stannard Baker, attempting to understand the man, felt that on that observation platform the president descended, as Emerson said, "into the secrets of all minds. . . . In utter solitude, remembering his spontaneous thoughts and recording them, he is found to have recorded that which men in crowded cities find true for themselves also."

Wilson's first step back in Washington was to urge passage of twenty "cooling-off" treaties which Secretary of State Bryan had signed with the various nations; the Senate ratified eighteen in a day on his recommendation. A week later, Wilson had formulated what he thought must be the country's attitude toward the European war: "We must be impartial in thought as well as in action, must put a curb upon our sentiments as well as upon every transaction that might be construed as a preference of one party to the struggle before another."

Most Americans believed the European conflict could and would proceed to its end without unduly involving the United States. Wilson's phrases were seconded by Henry Cabot Lodge, Theodore Roosevelt, and William Howard Taft, and were universally lauded in the press. Those that urged coming in on the side of the Allies, such as President

Eliot of Harvard, soon had to eat their words when fresh evidence surfaced that Germany had not been the only aggressor. Despite the fact that we were deeply immersed in world trade, that we had troops recently involved on the soil of other nations, that our liners were stranded and citizens economically hamstrung—despite all these signs—America was perceived by its citizenry as isolationist to the core, a country concerned with its own affairs, not with those of the squabbling Europeans.

As the country struggled to comprehend the onset of the faraway war, Woodrow Wilson remained trapped in grief. He displayed all the characteristic signs. He lost weight. He was preoccupied with images, talk, and mementos of the dead Ellen. He suffered immense guilt, telling Grayson that he felt the presidency had had to be paid for with her life, that she would be alive now if they had continued in their old ways at Princeton. He wrote thank-yous for condolences only, at first, to the more casual of acquaintances; he could not yet deal with the sentiments of those who had really known Ellen or were close to him. He begged Stock Axson to stay with him in the White House, asked the cousins not to leave. McAdoo told Helen Bones, the cousin who lived at the White House and who had herself been ill, to get up and be well, because there was no one else to be official hostess. She tried.

Woodrow Wilson's behavior at this time resembles greatly that of the English writer and deeply religious lay theologian C. S. Lewis, who lost an adored wife and chronicled in a diary the stages of his own grief. In the acute phase, Lewis observed:

> No one ever told me that grief felt so much like fear. I am not afraid, but the sensation is like being afraid. The same fluttering in the stomach, the same restlessness, the yawning. I keep on swallowing. . . . There is a sort of invisible blanket between the world and me. I find it hard to take in what anyone says. Or perhaps hard to want to take it in. It is so uninteresting. Yet I want the others to be about me. I dread the moments when the house is empty. If only they would talk to one another and not to me.

Wilson felt much the same way. The fundamental impulses of grief are to return to the time before death, and to simultaneously reach into the future to a state of mind wherein the past will be forgotten. The conflict between the two is profound. Reality is that death is final. The struggle to resolve the impulses reaching towards past and future at once, drains the grieving person of vitality. He withdraws, yet often simultaneously throws himself into his work, seeking solace therein. C. S. Lewis did so, and so did Woodrow Wilson. At this time Wilson's work was to shape the last phase of the grand reforms he believed his administration had been elected to achieve.

Reform, progressive reform, had been coming for twenty to thirty years. William Jennings Bryan had announced it; Roosevelt had embodied it before the rest of the country was willing to accept it. Now Wilson felt it was up to him to finally implement its promise. And reform was badly needed.

During the great leap westward fifty years earlier, some people became hugely rich while the agrarian life began to wane and the cities to explode. New organizations for structuring economic life sprang into being. Unions ballooned to five times their earlier size in the first decade of the new century. Where before the middle class had been individual shopkeepers, now these men were going to work for larger and larger corporations, becoming junior engineers or clerks. They felt that opportunity no longer knocked for them as it had for their fathers. People believed that the doors to the clubs of power were closed, that price increases were stifling their enjoyment of life as well as their prospects for striking out on their own. Trusts seemed to be inching up the prices of food, fuel, and rent while squeezing out the little guy who tried to compete in these fields. People had never thought of themselves before as *consumers*, but now intellectuals were calling them that. Economic man—as opposed to social man—had been born. And was worried about surviving.

The average person with such worries tended to idolize the clean-cut, scholarly yet exciting presidential candidate Woodrow Wilson, who campaigned for office saying, "The high cost of living is arranged by private understanding." Wilson's words had the ring of truth.

He let people know—he'd gotten the idea from Louis D. Brandeis, the "people's attorney"—that the J. P. Morgan Company, through interlocking directorates, commanded more than twice the assessed value of all the states west of the Mississippi—monopoly on a grand scale. But hadn't Teddy Roosevelt busted those trusts? No, Wilson implied, branding Roosevelt—who was running against him—not as the trust buster, but as the man who would legitimatize monopolies and then try to regulate them. Regulation was nonsense, Wilson told the people, "If monopoly persists, monopoly will always sit at the helm of government. I do not expect to see monopoly restrain itself. If there are men in this country big enough to own the government of the United States, they are going to own it."

The facts bore him out: twenty millionaires sat in the Senate. Teddy, said Woodrow Wilson, was old hat, in the pocket of the trust interests (more or less). He had "promised too often the millennium," had spoken too loudly and had carried too small a stick. Now it was time for a new man.

As governor, Wilson had chased the trusts out of New Jersey with his "seven sisters" laws. He'd championed progressive tenets such as referendum, initiative, and recall, pushed them through a balky legislature by the power of his personality. He repudiated Wall Street, took campaign contributions only in small amounts; he told factory workers they should have the right to organize.

Wilson's first actions as president were to restructure the economy. He insisted that the tariff pushed through by Republicans in 1909 had to be changed. It hampered small producers, gave windfalls to monopolies, made enemies abroad, and made consumers pay in the form of higher prices. Wilson hammered through a downward revision averaging twenty-nine percent and gave free entry to clothes, shoes, steel, sugar, and wool. To compensate for the loss in government revenues, he agreed to enact the small, first permanent income tax.

Then he got to work on the currency and credit system. In return for raising cash to run the Civil War, private financiers had been given the pursestrings of the country. In 1907, J. P. Morgan had personally stopped a money panic in New York—but would he do so in the future? Everyone agreed reform was fifty years overdue. But how to accomplish it? The Republicans' suggestion, a gigantic central bank controlled by private bankers, seemed to Democrats like legitimatizing the "money trust." Wilson's Federal Reserve System would issue an elastic currency based on the commercial resources of the country, and was to be controlled by a presidentially appointed Federal Reserve Board. Bryan got his agrarian faction to go along, House and McAdoo brought in the skeptical but essential New York banking community. Carter Glass and Albert Burleson were to shepherd reluctant congressmen—along with Wilson. Of the president's methods in the persuasion department, a Democratic congressman wrote, "Here are the facts, he says; here are the principles; here are our obligations as Democrats. What are we going to do about it? He has a curious way of making one feel that he, along with the rest of us, is perfectly helpless before the facts in the case."

Democrats were in line, and after Senate Republicans had finally been convinced by public outcry to do something, the Federal Reserve Act was passed and signed into law in December of 1913. The *New*

York World called it a "Magna Carta of political and industrial liberty under a government by law." It was the greatest achievement in financial legislation in fifty years.

In early 1914 Wilson unleashed his Justice Department. Attorneys there forced several monopolies to divest themselves of companies which precluded competitive practices. Then Wilson started a second round of legislation aimed at the trusts: a strengthening of the Sherman Act, and the creation of the Federal Trade Commission. Senator Lodge agreed in principle with this legislation; ex-President Taft was quoted as saying the Democratic party had fulfilled its campaign promises.

Teddy Roosevelt, mapping the River of Doubt in Brazil, had no comment. His monument, the Panama Canal, was due to open in August of 1914. Before it had been built, we had promised all countries would pay tolls equally, but the Republicans had sneaked in a toll exemption for United States coastwise shipping. Great Britain sent up a howl. Wilson pronounced the issue as moral obligation versus special privilege—and got the exemption repealed. He believed that this "fair play" victory would long be remembered as one of his greatest accomplishments.

At the time of Ellen's illness, Wilson had incorporated much of Roosevelt's New Nationalism into his New Freedom. His idealism had become tempered with the necessity for practical solutions. An article in *Collier's* suggested he had enormous capabilities, but

> There is in him something of the fanatic and the stuff of martyrs. . . . When he makes up his mind what he wants, no man in our public life has ever wanted it so hard or known better how to get it. Power—power—power—is his desire— *to be exerted, it must be admitted, solely in behalf of the common good as he sees that good.*

Wilson, the article said, had singlehandedly resurrected the Democratic party after a generation of desuetude. Would his ascendancy over the nation's imagination pass?

> The answer to this is that already it begins to pass. The President is causing his own shadow to recede. . . . His voice will sound less and less like the oracles of God. But by the same token it will sound all the more like the oracles of man. . . . Woodrow Wilson himself will not fail—his genius is too practical, his patriotism too lofty, his mastery of his party too complete, and his passionate devotion to the

popular cause too obvious. It is his ideas, principles, policies, and party which may fail.

By late July 1914, nearly all the Wilson programs had been pushed through and, in between reports of Sarah Bernhardt receiving the Legion d'Honneur, the ads for Cluett-Peabody collars, and the plan to grow pygmy hippos in the Louisiana swamps for meat, one found "Bradstreet's" grudgingly admitting that business was looking up.

Then the war came, and Ellen died, and everything seemed to go wrong at once. The stock exchange panicked and closed, cotton piled up and started to rot on wharves, railroad presidents frantically petitioned for emergency increases in rates, and Morgan petitioned to be allowed to send money out to Britain and France. The entire economy was in trouble. More than that, the New Freedom was threatened. For instance, Colonel House wrote (by way of McAdoo) that they should shelve the remaining New Freedom legislation to allow business to work itself out of the nose dive. Wilson feared for his domestic reforms. Sadly, he told Josephus Daniels the whole edifice might be undermined because "War is autocratic . . . Big Business will be in the saddle. More than that, Free Speech and the other rights will be endangered."

War, which wreaked havoc in his childhood, might ruin everything in his maturity. It was a time of crisis, and Wilson faced it with a mind disrupted by a loss for which he had not been prepared. The fundamental crisis of bereavement, writes Peter Marris, comes not from the loss of others, but from the loss of portions of one's own self:

> When the dead person has been, as it were, the keystone of a life, the whole structure of meaning in that life collapses when the keystone falls. . . . To say that life has lost its meaning is not, therefore, just a way of expressing apathy. It describes a situation where someone is bereft of purpose and so feels helpless.

Could Wilson maintain the balance in his soul between expectations of the future and the excruciating remembrances of the past? He had to. Else everything would fail. He sought help from the only friend he had whom he thought capable of seeing the whole picture, Colonel House. On August 30, Wilson arrived at Harlakenden with Grayson, primarily to be with House, who met him there. The dead Ellen was the center of the visit.

The men played pool (equally badly), walked, talked of golf, told stories, and dwelt on the past. Wilson put House in Ellen's bedroom, even rose a half-hour earlier than necessary one morning so that his friend might have uninterrupted use of their common bathroom.

As they sat on the terrace overlooking the broad valley of the Connecticut River, Wilson showed House photographs of Ellen, read some of the dozens of poems printed in newspapers which he thought caught her spirit, wondered how he could continue without her. House recorded in his diary how

> Tears came into his eyes, and he said he felt like a machine that had run down, and there was nothing in him worth while. As far as he could see, he was still doing good work and his mental capacity had not been impaired by the trouble he had gone through, and yet, he looked forward to the next two and a half years with dread. He did not see how he could go through with it.

In reply, House appealed to his idealism, speaking of the work there was to be done on humanity's behalf when the war ended and Wilson could have a hand in the "readjustment of the wreckage." The diary continues,

> I spoke of the world having started wrongly, with brute force dominating. Later this was recognized as unjust and for the first time the beginning of law was established. It was equally wrong for the mentally strong to oppress the mentally deficient, and when that was recognized, another great step forward would be made, and I hoped he might prove an instrument for doing this. I laid stress upon the power of public opinion and of the advantage of having it enlisted on our side. Reforms of this sort came too slowly, and he did not have a hopeful outlook.

After this idealistic talk, when the president retired for the night, House sat up with Grayson, who told him "all the mischievous, petty White House gossip." House knew most of it, because the principals in it were writing to him as well. There was a feud between Tumulty and McAdoo: the former thought the latter might be a grafter, the latter thought the former too close to certain Wall Street interests. House lamented to his diary that everything the president did, felt, and thought came in for terrible scrutiny.

If House's views on what needed to be done in the cause of international peace were fuzzy at this time, as the diary entries indicate, Wilson's perceptions were not. In this he was, perhaps, influenced by Ellen's recent death, by the necessity of keeping the peace which had been so precious to her—peace, a value—when the flesh was gone. Peter Marris writes that when a great loss has occurred,

> There must be a reinterpretation of what we have learned about our purposes and attachments. . . . The loss must be insisted upon, otherwise the value of the lost relationship may seem disparaged. . . . But . . . while the dead must be dismissed, the values they represented in all their relationships must be preserved.

Evidence of Wilson's determination to uphold Ellen's values comes from a conversation Wilson had with his brother-in-law Stock Axson, a talk so startling that Axson took the liberty of writing it down right then and there. It was perfectly obvious, Wilson argued, that the war would vitally change the relationships among nations, and so four things would be essential to the reestablishment of the world's equilibrium after hostilities ceased. First, no nation should ever be allowed to acquire an inch of land by conquest. Second, the rights of small and large nations must be recognized as equal. Third, war munitions must henceforth be made under public control, not by private hands for profit. Fourth and last, "There must be an association of the nations, all bound together for the protection of the integrity of each, so that any one nation breaking from this bond will bring upon herself war, that is to say, punishment, automatically."

In September of 1914, all the average American could think of about the war was, as a newspaper quipped, "We never appreciated so keenly as now the foresight exercised by our fathers in emigrating from Europe." Having no part of it was a hard goal to attain, for a battle for America's public opinion was already underway.

Our language and much common heritage linked us with England, though vast areas of the country, especially the Midwest, had been settled by German and Scandinavian immigrants. If the English could point to the immortal poets, Germans could point to social reforms, character traits such as orderliness and discipline, and Christmas carols. All were admired by Americans. Many Americans were anti-British—the Irish, for instance, were emotionally involved in a struggle for autonomy in their old homeland. Others did not believe the "selfless motivation" of the Tommies going to aid Belgium; they felt the British had ulterior motives—in particular, the aggrandizement of their colonial empire. Yet most of the information that came into the United States was pro-British and pro-French, since these nations controlled the seas and since most of the newspaper stories emanated from the Allied side. An example were atrocity stories circulated about what the "Huns" had done in Belgium: the vast majority of these stories were later disproved, but they disturbed and influenced Americans when they were first read and heard.

Wilson found life increasingly difficult. Neutrality was growing harder to maintain, and there were other problems with a Congress finally getting balky. His personal life was swallowed up, blotted out; he wrote to Mary Hulbert:

> It is very strange. I feel almost as if I had lost my sense of identity and were living in some new, unfamiliar world. . . . The place [of the presidency] has brought me no personal blessing, but only irreparable loss and desperate suffering. . . . I have succeeded so far, I believe, only because I have not sought my own pleasure in the work of the office, and have, more than my predecessors, devoted my entire time and energy, alike of body and mind, to work of the administration and of leadership to be done from day to day. And now self is killed more pitilessly than ever—there is *nothing but the work* for me.

As the midterm congressional elections neared, Wilson worked tirelessly, for he knew that an adverse reaction at the polls might cut his slim majority in the Senate and doom his programs for reform. Most sitting presidents lose congressional ground two years after they have been elected, and Wilson knew it could easily happen to him. He pushed the sitting Congress hard. September 26, he was able to sign the Federal Trade Commission into law; October 15, the Clayton Act strengthening the anti-trust statutes; October 20, the Alaska coal lands leasing bill; October 22, an additional taxes bill. All of these were considered to strike at "the interests," and were the last great and unhampered blows of the New Freedom. Already the foreign war was changing our economy, and would perforce provide the economic directions of the next several years. The experts still predicted a short war, but that was not at all certain. On October 24, 1914, Congress was released from a session that had lasted a year and a half, and that had produced more far-reaching legislation than ever in a similar session in the history of the country.

The midterm election came. As with the rest of the country, Wilson went to his voting place. He used Stock Axson's apartment in Princeton in order to keep his name on the rolls. When he arrived at the station he chatted with some old acquaintances. Jack Hibben appeared, and said that he had been told by a student that Wilson wanted to see him. Wilson thought Hibben was the victim of a hoax, but nonetheless, with the memories of the graduate school imbroglio still vivid, he looked his old friend straight in the eye and said, "No."

The results of the election were far from clear cut. Republicans claimed victory because, without a lot of money being spent and without a leader of national scope, the party had rolled up a vote that had come close to wiping out the Democratic control of the House of Representatives. The margin there was reduced from 73 to 25. On the other hand, Democrats claimed victory because in 1912 they had won with a split Republican party, but this time they had won fair and square with the Republicans united—in an election following on the heels of tariff reform and other stiff and unpalatable measures.

On the whole, support for progressivism seemed to have weakened. An eight-hour workday bill was defeated in Washington, Oregon, and California; workmen's compensation failed to pass in Montana (even though a nationwide figure showed one out of sixteen workers a year had a disabling accident on the job); a full-crew law was repealed in Missouri; ten progressive constitutional amendments were defeated in Wisconsin. Reform, Wilson told McAdoo privately, was over. He had come to do certain things, and he had done them. Now he looked to other horizons. He wrote that he was tired of having to take action on

> troubles of trades or regions or commodities that one must lend the influence of the government to lessen or relieve; problems of trade that must be worked out in spite of the war; credits that must be strengthened and put upon their feet again; alarms that must be quieted; errors that must be corrected; plans that must be made upon a great scale out of uncertain elements; controversies that must have the sting and danger taken out of them; businesses that must be encouraged or got out of a tangle. Government is become a sort of special providence, and we dare not stop to think how unfit or inept we are to be Providence at all.

In another letter, he told Mary Hulbert of the loneliness pouring back in on him as the work slackened a bit. He was losing spirit and vitality because "Washington is a hideously empty place, a desolated lonely place. There is no human intercourse in it,—at any rate, for the President. God pity him!"

In the midst of such feelings, Wilson hurried to New York to be with House. They held discussions on several matters of pressing importance, and then, at nine in the evening on a mid-November night, went for a walk from Fifty-third Street west to Seventh Avenue, then down Seventh to Broadway. At several places along the route, crowds had gathered to hear soap-box orators. House and Wilson stopped too, but were soon recognized; as they moved on, segments of the crowd followed, making the Secret Service nervous.

By the time they reached Herald Square, a great throng was behind them. They ducked into the opulent lobby of the Waldorf-Astoria at Thirty-fourth and Fifth. Here, fountains spurted champagne, and the elegant of New York and a dozen foreign countries came to cavort. House and Wilson quickly went up one elevator, traversed the building on an upper floor, and came down on the Thirty-third Street side. Having eluded the crowd, they continued a quarter-mile more down Fifth Avenue, then took a bus back to House's brownstone. Wilson was exhilarated and wished he could walk about the city more often. House suggested whiskers. The president initially agreed, but then said there would be an awful scandal if it were found out. The loneliness closed in again, and he told House his life had become sad, that he could not help wishing when they were out just before that someone would kill him.

His eyes were moist; he spoke of not wanting to live longer, of not being fit to do the work at hand. He was a mere human being, "a traveller between life and death" as any other, and surely as frail. Yet, he felt, he knew himself to be so perfectly disciplined that unless someone assassinated him, he would go on doing the best that he could until the end.

4

MY HEART IS VOICELESS

Dr. Cary Grayson's pursuit of Altrude Gordon was stalled in the late fall of 1914. She was of several minds—on the one hand the thought of marrying him was wonderful, on the other she was young, rich, and footloose, and there were other suitors. She led Grayson on a merry chase but she knew that should he tire of it, though, there were plenty of attractive young ladies in Washington waiting to take her place.

Cary Grayson was an extraordinary young man. His family could be traced back to the Revolution, and he was a proud Virginian. As a doctor, his training had included a period in a Washington hospital as an assistant in obstetrics, after which he went into the navy. While treating a friend of Theodore Roosevelt's, he came to the president's notice. Roosevelt took a shine to him, and invited him on an all-day ride which sapped the endurance of most of the other officers who went along. Grayson kept up with TR, and his future was made. When Roosevelt's mantle passed to Taft, Grayson attended the Taft family.

At the inauguration in 1913, Grayson was called to minister to Wilson's sister, which he did smartly; Taft then commended him to Wilson with the comment that the doctor was both a Democrat and a Virginian, neither of which could be helped. Grayson observed the new president's physical health, which was shaky. Years before, Wilson had relied on a stomach pump he used himself, and on "powders" to treat his various conditions. Grayson shuddered at these ideas. He put Wilson on a diet which would give the president more strength and less stomach upset—for a while, a raw egg in orange juice every morning (which the president compared to eating an unborn thing)—and insisted he play a round of golf a day. Grayson himself golfed with Wilson, carefully letting the president win about half the time. The two became good friends, the younger man serving in part as the son Wilson had never had.

Once, after golfing in Pass Christian around Christmas 1913, the two men were walking back home with their clubs when they spied something amiss on top of a nearby house. "Oh, Mr. President," said the lady who opened the door, all aflutter, "it's so good of you to call on me. Won't you walk into the parlor and sit down?" "I haven't got time to sit down," Wilson said, "your house is on fire!" Then he and Grayson climbed to the attic and put out the fire before the fire company arrived; the Secret Service men were apoplectic when they found out.

The following summer Grayson was called in to minister to Altrude's summer companion, Edith Galt. She had fallen ill on their trip to the New England mountains and was slow recovering. Grayson wrote steadily to his old friend Mrs. Galt for support in his suit, telling her in his letters, as an aside, how lonely and bereft the president was. Now, in the fall, he took to visiting Edith Galt for moral backbone and to speed her progress toward recovery. Helen Bones was also ill at this time. In an effort to have all his female charges get better, Grayson introduced the pinch-hit mistress of the White House to Mrs. Galt, and told them to take bracing constitutionals together in Rock Creek Park. They accepted the suggestion, got along well, and often stopped afterward for tea at Mrs. Galt's house.

As to Wilson's own health, physically he was all right, but there was little life in him. Helen Bones wrote to a relative, "I cannot tell you how terrible this house seems without Cousin Ellen; and it simply grows worse every day . . . no one can offer Cousin Woodrow any word of comfort, for there is no comfort." Wilson wrote to a friend that "Even books have grown meaningless to me. I read detective stories to forget, as a man would get drunk!" His hair had gotten much whiter; he spent more time visiting relatives—Jessie and Frank, for instance, at Thanksgiving. Jessie was pregnant.

So was Nell. The McAdoos were having a difficult time. Nell moved daily between the White House and her own residence, Ellen's death depressing her as well as Woodrow. McAdoo was in a bind; the president's loss of initiative at this time, and the situation of the country, brought him more to the fore than ever. Mac was the leading cabinet member after Bryan, involved in the Federal Reserve Board, the emergency financial legislation, the federal building programs, War Risk

Insurance, the shipping bill. Cary Grayson thought McAdoo over-worked and heading for a possible breakdown—while the very industry and sweep with which McAdoo acted was making his name a household word.

The bind was, as Colonel House noted to his diary, "McAdoo has the Presidential bee firmly fixed." That was not unreasonable for a cabinet member, but for Mac it meant mixing loyalties. His own finances had been seriously depleted by his cabinet service. The Metropolitan Life Insurance Company had offered him its presidency at a salary of $85,000 a year. Should he take it? The decision hinged largely on whether he could be a viable presidential candidate from such a spot. If Wilson were to run in 1916, Mac couldn't do so himself, but if Wilson chose *not* to run, that was a different story. And there was a glimmer of that possibility: Grayson had told him that the chief was not a hundred percent, and that he considered the president might find it either impossible or unpalatable to run in 1916, especially if his depression continued. That was hopeful. Then Mac asked Colonel House. The counselor thought it would be disastrous for Mac's chances if he were in the pocket of an insurance company, but if Wilson didn't run in 1916 (and House wasn't sure he would), House wasn't averse to being privy counselor to yet another Democratic president. He advised Mac to stay put and keep quiet. Privately, House thought it would be better for the cabinet if the disputatious Mac would resign, but he wasn't going to say that to McAdoo.

Mac would not, however, act behind Wilson's back. He told the chief his problem, and Wilson said he'd always believed that the "interests" would try to ruin his administration by buying people away. That was enough for Mac. He decided to remain in harness and let time decide whether or not 1916 would be the moment to toss his hat into the ring.

It was dinner conversations such as these that gave Wilson indigestion. Yet he would rather die, he told House, than say so to his son-in-law. Ever tactful, House told Mac that Grayson had asked all intimates to refrain from talking shop with the president at meals.

By the late fall of 1914 Teddy Roosevelt had begun to change his views on the war. When it had broken out, TR had backed Wilson's neutrality policy. Now he grumbled to Lodge that what we should have done at the war's outset was protest the invasion of Belgium as a violation of the Hague Convention and join with the Allies to crush Germany and Austria. Perhaps, he intimated, Wilson was a coward.

When questioned as to his earlier position, Roosevelt insisted he had always favored war. Evidently Belgium seemed more virginal in retrospect after she had been violated for a few months.

Strict neutrality was running into problems in any case. Both sides were provoking us, Britain at this time more than Germany. The English navy was routinely stopping and searching neutral ships for contraband cargo, which we felt was a fundamental violation of the freedom of the seas (at that time an undefined and fuzzy concept). We wanted the British to sign the pre-war Declaration of London which would have kept searches to a minimum and allowed us commerce with both sides. At this time the British would sooner have signed the Declaration of Independence. On October 29 the British declared new and larger contraband lists, and on November 3 declared the entire North Sea to be a war area which neutral ships might enter only at their peril. This outraged Wilson, but he forced himself to remember the lessons of history: as he had written in his five-volume *History of the American People*, there had been as good cause in 1812 for us to go to war with Great Britain as with France. Madison had allowed himself to become angry with England and to declare war on the British rather than (as he should have in Wilson's view) on Napoleon, "the enemy of the civilized world." Wilson wasn't going to allow his temper to lead him into a similar error.

He might have struck back by denying war monies to England unless more free trade were allowed. Bryan, an arch-pacifist, had written searingly that money was "the worst of all contrabands because it commands all others." In August, Wilson had accepted that reasoning; now, he rejected it. Our economy demanded trade with the Allies, and the realist Wilson knew this. He decided to ignore the British provocations.

Right after the election on November 3, Bryan pushed Wilson toward a bold step: calling on each belligerent to state war aims and possible peace terms. House, shown a Bryan letter to this end on December 3, called the suggestion "entirely footless," and said that it would get European powers' backs up. Wilson evidently agreed, for the two friends began to work out a plan for House to privately pursue peace negotiations through the ambassadors—Bryan was considered too heavy-handed and naïve for this delicate task.

Wilson was looking beyond the New Freedom to broader horizons, then, when Congress opened on December 8. He told the legislators, "Our program of legislation with respect to business is virtually complete. . . . The road at last lies clear and firm before business."

It was a time of change in everything. Samuel Gompers, president of the American Federation of Labor, was advocating free schools, free textbooks, an eight-hour day and six-day week for all workers, the abolition of sweatshops, women's suffrage, and a guaranteed minimum wage. (Wilson regarded him as a visionary, considering such goals beyond the purview of federal legislation.) Freud's *Psychopathology of Everyday Life* appeared for the first time in English. Billy Sunday drew enormous crowds for a ten-week stand in Philadelphia. Henry Ford was firming up plans to give ten million dollars of his profits to his 22,000 workers, and called on other employers to "recognize the unequal distribution of earnings and endeavor in their own way to make a better division." Medical science had just proved conclusively that chewing gum was not an aid to digestion and that alcohol, rather than being a stimulant, was actually a depressant. Many states had already gone dry. Bohr and Rutherford debated the structure of the atom. The women's movement had advanced to the point that when a misogynist told Ethel Barrymore, "There isn't a woman alive who'd rather be intelligent than beautiful," the actress could reply, "That's because so many more men are stupid than blind."

Yet by the end of 1914 the war was causing the country to slide toward depression. New York estimated 400,000 people were out of work. Relief agencies claimed they were overwhelmed and that people were sleeping on docks and in warehouses. Such conditions were giving rise to agitation from the Industrial Workers of the World, the "Wobblies." Immigrants, who had been arriving at the rate of a million and a half a year until the war's beginning, put more pressure on the economy. Thousands of boxcars of cotton, wheat, and lumber languished in seacoast yards because there were not enough ships to carry them to neutral countries. Private capital was not buying or commissioning vessels, even with War Risk Insurance that would reimburse them if the ships were seized or sunk. Wilson wanted his new shipping bill passed by Congress, but Congress was dilatory. It contained, one magazine said, too many lawyers. A lawyer, noted the *Literary Digest,* was a man who induced two other men to strip for a fight and then ran away with their clothes. Most people believed the European mess would never come over here: the *Literary Digest* found two-thirds of the newspaper editors didn't think we needed any strengthening of our army or navy at all. The only people who disagreed were on the West Coast and feared an invasion from Japan.

If Congress was dilatory, Wilson seemed no longer as persuasive as he once had been. He trumpeted about past accomplishments. Why, he asked, didn't Congress connect the re-opening of the New York Stock Exchange and the fact that banks were returning emergency currency issued them in August, to the opening of the Federal Reserve System? He knew what he was doing. People ought not to disagree with him. His temper shortened. Not only was he angry at Congress in general, but at Senators Root and Lodge who were holding him up. Once he thought these men had consciences; now, he wrote, he found they had none.

The worst was that while his anger was rising, she who used to be able to defuse that anger was gone—and along with her, it seemed, had gone that part of himself willing to grant charity and goodness of motive to those who disagreed with him. He denied himself pleasures such as going to vaudeville and the theater, continued to wear a mourning band on his suit. The death of someone important to you, writes Glenn Vernon, means a cessation of certain behavior patterns:

> Without doubt, part of one's way of behaving dies or is no longer possible when [the] individual with whom the behavior has been integrated is no longer there to react. . . . If an individual is, in part, what he does, and if he knows himself by the manner in which others respond to him, he loses something of himself in the death.

As a result, there is a crisis. There is pain. There is despair. In this period C. S. Lewis felt

> There is spread over everything a vague sense of wrongness, of something amiss. Like in those dreams where nothing terrible occurs—nothing that would sound even remarkable if you told it at breakfast-time—but the atmosphere, the taste of the whole thing is deadly.

Peter Marris points out that there is a profoundly conservative impulse to this period, that we ignore or avoid events that don't match our understanding, that we refuse to innovate, that we refuse to deviate from codified behavior in order to defend our very ability to make sense out of life. For Wilson, the real Ellen was receding into memory, mere images of affection which were no substitute for the real person. C. S. Lewis spoke of his dead wife thus:

> The reality is no longer there to check me, to pull me up short, as the real H. so often did so unexpectedly, by being so thoroughly herself and not me. . . . The most precious gift that marriage gave me was this constant impact of something very close and intimate yet all the time unmistakeably other,

resistant—in a word, real. . . . The rough, sharp, cleansing tang of her otherness is gone.

In his darkest moments, C. S. Lewis, whose faith was one of the most thoroughly searched and articulated in modern times, cursed God for being implacable, a "Cosmic Sadist"—then, ashamed, decided it was himself who was lacking. His loss was like that of a man whose leg had been cut off: he would never walk normally again, he felt. And even when he felt better, that feeling in itself gave rise to shame, because he was under an obligation "to cherish and foment and prolong one's unhappiness." A similar tone can be discerned in Wilson's letters at this time. People he had known for many years hesitated to bother the busiest man in the world: of the newer intimates, McAdoo had become a son-in-law, Daniels a cabinet member who would not presume to mix friendship and business, and House was an infrequent visitor at best though he was the most doggedly persistent in his attentions. The letters find Wilson flailing out wistfully for friends:

How jolly, how wonderful it would be if . . . the friends I love best were within call and I could go to them and sit for long familiar talks and the interchanges of sympathy that are better than oxigen and are fit to keep alive on!

The friend to whom he wrote this was Mary Allen Hulbert.

After Ellen's death Wilson poured out much of his grief to Mary Hulbert, explaining often how he was "dead in heart and body, weighed down with a leaden indifference and despair." Because of their special relationship he seemed able to say things to her he could never say to others. By fall and early winter of 1914, Wilson's letters were containing pleas for her to put in an appearance at the White House—there was always a room for her here, that sort of hint. She was unable to come to Washington, held at home by difficult personal problems: her money was running out, she had no prospects of making a living in her new city of Boston; most seriously, her son had just lost a great deal of money in a venture and was not well. When Wilson was told of this in great detail, he responded generously, writing to five friends in Boston, asking them to help get work for Mary as an interior decorator. She thanked him, then complained to him further that the *Ladies' Home Journal* had "lost" some articles she had written. It was, she intimated, wrong and weak of her to ask, but could he intervene? Wilson wrote to the editor, and the magazine not only found the articles but agreed to print them.

Wilson was never one who liked to be asked for favors; when petitioned, he was usually generous to a fault, but he didn't like to be asked.
It was apocryphal that the best way to lose your prospects for a job in
the administration was to ask for one. House, McAdoo, and Daniels—
who hadn't asked—were prized by Wilson for their "selflessness." As
Mary Hulbert continued to ask small favors, Wilson grew more and
more courteous, and more and more distant. In asking for his influence,
just at the time when Wilson wanted her sympathy, she alienated him.
The throbbing need he had tried to convey to her, she was too busy with
herself to understand.

In December 1914, the president found a breeze of hope. House came
to Washington with a letter from German Undersecretary for Foreign
Affairs Arthur Zimmermann requesting that Wilson renew his calls for
peace discussions. Wilson was so excited that he wanted House to leave
instantly for Europe. Suddenly Christmas didn't seem so dreary.

At about this time, Mary Hulbert's intellectual place was filled
briefly by Mrs. Crawford Toy, the very bright and lettered daughter of
a Virginia clergyman and wife of an ancient Harvard professor. Nancy
Toy wrote Wilson of the heady ferments of Cambridge and was not
above telling him precisely how the academics disagreed with his views.
And she sent him for Christmas one of the greatest gifts he said he'd
ever received, a Scots horned spoon, such as used in the old country to
eat porridge. It cemented their friendship brilliantly, for Wilson had a
deep wellspring of Scot in him: at New Year's, it had been family
custom to stand upon chairs, with one foot each on the dining table, to
toast the changing year.

Nancy Toy came to dinner shortly after the first. It was a heady
atmosphere, run through with talk of history and philosophy. A portrait
of Wilson by Seymour Thomas was unveiled. The crowd being equally
divided as to its merits, Nell McAdoo insisted that her father stand in
front of it for comparison's sake. In an impish mood, the president
wouldn't stand still, but twisted his mobile face about in horrendous
contortions, sticking out his tongue, rolling his eyes, letting his jaw go
slack. Not to be outdone, Nell acted as sculptor, molding his features
with her hands, when she let go of his chin it would sag to his shirtfront,
when she tipped it up he'd reel backwards until they were all laughing
and Nell gave up in mock despair. As they went up the marble staircase,
Wilson and Mac walked bowlegged and pigeon-toed; when they got to
the study, the president read from A. G. Gardiner's *Pillars of Society*.

At one point in the evening somebody mentioned the newspaper reports that Daniels had forbidden naval personnel to sing the pro-British ditty "Tipperary." Wilson's fist came down on the table; Mrs. Toy had never seen him angry before, never wanted to see him angry again. Wilson was livid; Daniels, he said, had not given the order. As usual it had been a subordinate who had done something silly, and Daniels had had to back him up as Wilson had Mayo. Daniels was ". . . surrounded by a network of conspiracy and lies. His enemies are determined to ruin him. I can't be sure who they are yet, but when I do get them,—God help them!"

Wilson's anger was being healthily vented. But his interest in Mrs. Toy was quickly fading. The daughter of a clergyman had ceased to have faith in a personal God, and Wilson told her passionately that

> My life would not be worth living if it were not for the driving power of religion, for *faith*, pure and simple. I have seen all my life the arguments against it without ever having been moved by them . . . never for a moment have I had one doubt about my religious beliefs. There are people who *believe* only so far as they *understand*—that seems to me presumptuous and sets their understanding as the standard of the universe. . . . I am sorry for such people.

No one could trample on his—or Ellen's—deeply held values.

In Congress, Senator Lodge tied Wilson's shipping bill to a string of "bad" foreign policy ideas which had resulted in the "unnecessary" fighting and dying at Veracruz. It was another blow at a value Wilson had deeply held. He could, he wrote, no longer "fight rottenness with rose water." Two days later he came out swinging in his Jackson Day speech to the Democratic faithful in Indianapolis:

> The trouble with the Republican party is that it has not had a new idea in thirty years. I am not speaking as a politician; I am speaking as an historian. . . . The Republican party is still a covert and a refuge for those who are afraid, for those who want to consult their grandfathers about everything.

Here we were, Wilson said, living at an extraordinary moment: half the world was aflame, many millions were starving, we had the food to succor them, and at the same time we could make a decent profit in selling it. But, alas, we had no ships and the usurious businessmen who ran the few that were available were charging ten times what decency would allow. Wilson had the only solution that made sense, his shipping bill—and what was happening to it?

> I hear it said in Washington on all hands that the Republicans in the Senate mean to talk enough to make passage of that bill impossible. . . . Some of them are misguided, some of them are blind; most of them are ignorant. . . . May we not look forward to the time when we shall be called blessed among the nations, because we succoured the nations of the world in their time of distress and of dismay?

The Republicans insisted on crying foul until Wilson had to admit (privately) that portions of the speech showed "a palpable lapse of taste." But, he insisted, there was a real fight on: the Republican forces of pro-business conservatism were opposing his ideas of democracy and the chances for peace.

Secretary of State Bryan found out about House's proposed trip for the first time on January 12, and he too cried foul. Bryan felt *he* should go. Had he not been agitating for peace for thirty years? Did he not go about giving people swords beaten into plowshares with quotations on them from Isaiah and from himself? It was monstrous that House should be going in his stead! Bryan lusted after the Nobel Peace Prize as if it were the Holy Grail, and here was House stealing his opportunity to get it.

The president worked hard to calm the Great Commoner. House, he said, going as a private individual, might be able to do things a secretary of state could not. The official attitude of the United States had to remain uncompromised. Bryan reluctantly agreed.

House and Wilson devised a secret code for their correspondence, and Wilson gave him letters of introduction to use as he saw fit. It was not necessary, said the president—or even possible for him in this case—to give House precise instructions because they both knew what had to be done. House recorded their parting in graphic detail in his secret diary:

> The President's eyes were moist when he said his last words of farewell. He said "Your unselfish and intelligent friendship has meant much to me," and he expressed his gratitude again and again, calling me his "most trusted friend." He declared I was the only one in all the world to whom he could open his entire mind. I asked if he remembered the first day

we met, some three and a half years ago. He replied, "Yes, but we had known one another always, and merely came in touch then." . . . He insisted upon going to the station with me. He got out of the car and walked through the station and to the ticket office, and then to the train itself, refusing to leave until I entered the car.

As House was about to sail on the *Lusitania* on January 30, he sent Wilson a final letter:

Good-bye, dear friend, and may God sustain you in all your noble undertakings. When I think of the things you have done, of the things you have in mind to do, my heart stirs with pride and satisfaction. You are the bravest, wisest leader, the gentlest and most gallant gentleman and the truest friend in all the world.

If it sounded like a valedictory, perhaps that was because House was a bit afraid the *Lusitania*, the pride of the Cunard line, might be torpedoed by one of the *unterseebooten*, because she was the biggest target afloat. It almost happened. On February 5, nearing the Irish coast, fearing for his liner's life, the captain raised the American flag (perhaps mindful of his distinguished passenger) and so made it into port unscathed. Although this practice had some precedent and was not illegal or even particularly immoral, the incident caused a bit of scandal: a foreign belligerent using the United States flag as a cover for its own operations was unthinkable! Still the American outcry was muted. People realized that American finances were increasingly intertwined with those of the Allies. And many believed that the Allies were in effect fighting for western civilization, and therefore for the freedom and continued existence of the United States.

Neutrality vis-à-vis the Germans was also difficult to maintain. Berlin announced that after January 18, 1915, the area around the British Isles would be considered a war zone, and that neutral ships might suffer accidents therein—especially if British ships continued to "misuse" neutral flags. Exasperated, Wilson on February 10 sent notes to both Germany and Great Britain warning them strongly that they would be held to "strict accountability" for violations of our neutrality, and hoped Germany wouldn't enforce the war zone idea.

The president was losing his leisure hours in an epidemic of cipher dispatches. He would write and type virtually all of his messages himself; he also decoded House's telegrams himself when they came in. Foreign messages kept him up late at night, and ate into the time he had previously devoted on Sundays to letter writing.

Outside the administration, ex-President Roosevelt and other important Republicans were beginning to make angry noises about America's military preparedness. TR wrote to Lodge on February 15 that he was going to smite Wilson "with a heavy hand" in some new articles, because "I think this administration is the very worst and most disgraceful we have ever known." Henry Cabot Lodge agreed with Roosevelt completely.

Before Woodrow Wilson had entered the arena, it had been Lodge who held the distinction of the scholar-in-politics. Now it was Wilson, and Lodge reigned only as the gadfly of the Senate, a man continually quotable since the time of the last Democratic president, Grover Cleveland. "I was opposed to our good friend Grover Cleveland," Lodge wrote to TR in early 1915, "but never in such a way as this. I never expected to hate anyone in politics with the hatred I feel towards Wilson." At the opening of the Wilson administration, Lodge had held his ire in check; then, as the ranking Republican member of the Foreign Relations Committee, he began to become an increasing thorn in Wilson's side. Mexico had awakened him; Europe irked him as Wilson (in his view) had refused to act; the shipping bill convinced Lodge's quicksilver mind that Wilson was becoming definitely dangerous and possibly dictatorial. When Lodge raised the specter of the shipping bill being turned to dastardly ends—such as the wholesale interference by government in private business—the answer he got was that Woodrow Wilson would never use legislation in such a way. That, Lodge felt, was Wilson saying "trust me." And Lodge would not do that.

Wilson, by asking people to trust the president and being mostly unable to say why, since the peace feelers had to be kept hushed, was out on a limb with the shipping bill. It passed the House of Representatives on February 16, but then Lodge organized a filibuster against it in the Senate. More than once Lodge himself had said that filibusters were unethical, but now he saw one was necessary to head off what he called Wilson's encroaching monarchism. Lodge was the most masterful user of senatorial tactics alive. Cots were set up in cloakrooms, Senators passed all previous records for continuous speaking. To Wilson's angered dismay, seven Democratic members joined Republicans in the maneuver, and Congress adjourned on March 4 without completed action on the shipping bill. It was a clear defeat for Wilson.

* * *

Above, The Wilson family in 1913. *Left to right:* Margaret, Ellen, Nell, Jessie, and Woodrow (*Library of Congress*)

Left, Inauguration Day, March 1913, at the White House. "I'm glad to be going," said Taft, "this is the loneliest place in the world." (*Library of Congress*)

William Gibbs McAdoo, Secretary of the Treasury and son-in-law (*Library of Congress*)

Colonel Edward M. House, The Sphinx in the Soft Felt Hat (*Library of Congress*)

Joseph P. Tumulty, Presidential secretary (*Library of Congress*)

Thomas Riley Marshall, Vice-president, "What this country needs is a good five-cent cigar." (*Library of Congress*)

Captain Cary Travers Grayson, M.D., "The outside of a horse is good for the insides of a man." (*Library of Congress*)

Edith Bolling, *above, circa* 1892; *right, circa* 1910; *below,* in her electric runabout, the first in Washington
(*The Woodrow Wilson House*)

The President with his first grandchild, early 1915 (*Library of Congress*)

The President and Mrs. Galt are engaged: a collage by a Washington newspaper (*Library of Congress*)

Attending a World Series game; Mrs. Bolling beams at her newly engaged daughter
(*Library of Congress*)

Edith as First Lady, early 1916
(*Library of Congress*)

Colonel House, separated from his old friend by Mrs. Wilson, returns to give a report (*National Archives*); Below left, Ex-President Teddy Roosevelt and General Leonard Wood. "Well, at least he kept *us* out of war!" (*Library of Congress*); Below top right, Senator Henry Cabot Lodge (*Library of Congress*); Below, bottom right, Senator Albert Bacon Fall (*Library of Congress*)

The Big Four: Orlando, Lloyd George, Clemenceau, Wilson (*Library of Congress*)

All Paris turns out to celebrate Woodrow Wilson (*National Archives*)

The Hardings and the Coolidges
on Inauguration Day, 1921
(*Library of Congress*)

Last portrait, 1924
(*Library of Congress*)

As Wilson entered upon the last phase of his personal grief, both Jessie and Nell were pregnant, and as Mac was in the hospital for an operation and Frank Sayre was busy in Williamstown, Jessie came home to stay at the White House. She went to church with her father and sat up with him a bit in the evenings. Nell came often for visits. Somewhat ahead of schedule, but not unexpectedly, Jessie went into labor. The ubiquitous Dr. Grayson was called, and attended her with several nurses and women relatives in the small Rose Room. In the absence of the father the president had to be the worried male of the entourage. He stalked the corridor outside. When he heard a baby's cry, it seemed so loud that he excitedly whispered "Twins!" It was a single boy, later dubbed Francis B. Sayre. Cary Grayson washed the baby off, then handed him to housekeeper Maggie Parks and asked her to take him into the large Rose Room by the fireplace and keep him warm. Mrs. Parks hurried in with her bundle and there found the president. He looked at the baby and tears came into his eyes. Neither he nor Mrs. Parks spoke as they stood by the fireplace, but she knew that unvoiced thoughts of Ellen were in Wilson's mind. These were echoed in a letter to Jessie shortly after they had gone back to Williamstown:

> I felt so dumb when you were here, dear. I did not know how to *say* the things that were in my heart about you and the baby and all the crowding thoughts that made my heart ache with its fulness. I had to trust you to *see* them. . . . I can talk about most things but I always have been helpless about putting into words the things I feel most deeply, the things that mean the most to me; and just now my heart is particularly voiceless. But I do love you and yours, my dear, more than words can say, and there *is* added to my love now the mother tenderness which I know the depths and beauties of in *her* heart. She was beyond comparison the deepest, truest, noblest lover I ever knew, or ever heard those who knew the human heart wish for!

The president had placed Ellen firmly into his treasured past, while maintaining in his own life the values she had cherished most. His tragedy had driven passion even deeper into his soul. Henceforth he would be both angrier and more loving, think more grandly and concern himself with more petty matters. He was willing to delve more deeply into his heart to say those gentle and ennobling words which are the emblems of human love—the letter to Jessie is among the most tender he could muster in a lifetime of correspondence to his daughter. Wilson's disabling grief was reaching an inevitable and healthy conclusion. He was discovering—as do all who mourn—that sorrow is not a state, but a process, a constant evolution. One reaches for affirmation. As C. S. Lewis put it:

> God has not been trying an experiment on my faith or love in order to find out their quality. He knew it already. It was I who didn't. . . . Heaven will solve our problems, but not, I think, by showing us subtle reconciliations. . . . We shall see that there never was any problem.

For Wilson, mourning had begun in a deep and specific hurt, had come in time to that generalized state in which purposes and attachments associated with Ellen were retrieved, and had progressed to where his personal identity had been again reestablished. Death had given more meaning to life. The process had been difficult, necessary, and inescapable. Now the normal desires for emotional security, for personal achievement, for meaning in the world, could again be pursued.

How? In a startling observation, Peter Marris says that the opposite of this process of bereavement is the process of courtship—which winds the stair from general desires up to the establishment of certain values and requirements for a mate, and thence to deep and specific attachment to one special person.

On a blustery day in early March of 1915, when Woodrow Wilson and Cary Grayson were out playing their usual round of golf, Edith Bolling Galt and Helen Bones were out tramping through Rock Creek Park. All were getting their shoes muddy. When it began to rain, Helen insisted that Edith, for the first time, come home with *her* for a spot of tea. They would not have to worry about appearances because Cousin Woodrow and Cary wouldn't be there. However, the mud had also cut short the golfing, and the foursome—quite disheveled—met in a corridor by accident. They all laughed. When informed of the ladies' plans, Cary Grayson chortled and said to Helen Bones, "I think you might invite us to tea."

5

THE KNIGHT AND HIS LADY

EDITH BOLLING WAS born on October 15, 1872, in the small county seat of Wytheville, Virginia, the seventh of eleven children of Circuit Court Judge William Holcombe Bolling and Sallie White Bolling. Her grandmother seven times removed was the Indian princess Pocahontas, who had married Captain John Rolfe in the seventeenth century. The Bollings were an old Virginia family, part of the aristocracy of the South.

Prior to the Civil War, the family had been reasonably well-to-do plantation owners. The war was terrible to people of their sort. After it, there were no slaves to work the Bolling plantation, and no money to pay those old retainers who did not want to leave. Shortly after the war, William Bolling had to shutter the plantation's doors, take his growing family, and move to Wytheville, where an old house that had been in the family for some time awaited them. It was badly in need of repairs, having been used as a Confederate hospital; the family patched it up slowly over the years.

The house was filled to bursting with relatives of many generations by the time Edith was three: several grandmothers, aunts, and other relatives, as well as the Bollings and their children. Most of the money went for food. Even so, there were a few servants, and life was not unpalatable. The very young and very old diverted each other.

Edith's greatest early influences were the people in her family. Chief among these was Grandmother Bolling. This old woman, who always wore black, had been confined to her room for many years because of a spine injury she had suffered when young. Even so, she was indomitable. She had been brought up to believe that idle hands were the cradle of the devil; that the family had once been great and was still aristocratic even if reduced in circumstances; that southerners of their class were the only true repositories of manners and morals in the country. She transmitted these beliefs to her children and grandchildren. In Grandmother Bolling, the ante-bellum South lived on and influenced even those children born years after the Civil War.

Grandmother Bolling's room was the center of the house. For Edith, it was the school to which she went. It taught that the past was to be revered and treasured, that having strong likes and dislikes was natural, that religion was essential for life, and that you either were among the chosen or you were not and there wasn't much you could do about it. Grandmother Bolling, Edith remembered, "never relaxed her vigilance."

Being an invalid, the small old woman required care of an extraordinary sort. She used Edith as her eyes and ears to learn and report about the state of the household and what was happening in the town and in other people's minds. Under her tutelage, Edith learned to be a diligent observer of the world around her, and to report in accurate detail what she had seen or had been told. For such services Edith was rewarded with attention and with personal lessons in reading, writing, the Bible, French, dressmaking, crocheting. Edith slept in Grandmother's room. For recreation the family replayed the Civil War in tableaux and in stories written by a cousin: in these the rebels always won.

Until the age of thirteen, Edith had never been out of the backwater town of Wytheville and had never been to a formal school, though she knew her letters and had been reading for some time. There were nine surviving children in the Bolling family, and not all of them could go to school at one time because it was too expensive. The judge would not send his children to schools he thought inappropriate—rather, he would keep several home, help them himself with their lessons, or occasionally hire a tutor or governess. This was commonly done in the South at the time. Not yet thirteen, in May of 1885, Edith went on a trip to a larger town with her father, and took several side trips alone—trips which provided Edith with her first glimpses of a wider world. She loved every minute away from home.

Judge Bolling was stern but caring. In the evenings he would read Shakespeare and other classics out loud in a strong, mellifluous voice; he would also lecture the children on religion and ethics. His Episcopalian church sought him out often as a lay reader, and rather than sending his children to Sunday school he taught them religion at home.

Edith's small, gentle, frail mother had married when young, and bore many children to her older husband. Her primary quality was loyalty. She was always, Edith later wrote, "radiantly happy . . . despite personal privations." If mother's life was sheltered, it seemed to need sheltering: she had left home to be married before she was eighteen, and had been under the strong protection and influence of her husband ever since. The addition of seemingly innumerable children had only served to make her more loyal and coping. Judge Bolling was the be-all and end-all of her life. And he shielded her from the world.

In 1885 Edith's oldest sister Gertrude married Alexander Hunter Galt of Washington and moved away. In early years the family had been close; now it began to spread out. The judge felt it was time that Edith went to school to be "finished." In 1887 she was packed off to a small boarding school, the Martha Washington College of Abingdon, Virginia. The place and headmaster were Dickensian. Edith felt nearly starved on the food, and she froze in underheated and drafty halls. In the music rooms the girls had to practice the piano in such cold that their fingers refused to strike the keys. By Christmas holidays Edith's clothes no longer fit; she was tall and slender.

At home for a bit, she practically stole another sister's gentleman caller out from under her nose. He was thirty-eight, a wealthy New Yorker who plied her with candy and flowers and moonlight picnics. In the fall she did not return to school, being subject to "terrible colds" and not wanting to bear the drafts again—and also because there were now numerous callers hovering about. In the fall of 1889 Edith went to a new school, Powell's, in Richmond. It was not only a distinct antidote to her earlier bad experience, but in two months severed whatever ties she had had to the New Yorker.

At Powell's, Edith worked hard. Her friends were of the "better sort" of woman: two of them married Senators. In May of 1890 the school year came to an abrupt halt when Mr. Powell had an accident and was forced to close the place. Edith never went to classes again; by the next winter, when she wanted to go, the money had to be used for the three younger boys. Edith was eighteen, tall, and strikingly handsome, could read and write and do numbers and play the piano and sing, and had a fine background in morals and in the household arts: she was considered ready for the world.

So in 1891 Edith went to Washington to stay with Gertrude, who had married a Galt. This was an entirely new world: they went to the theater, the opera, dinner parties. Edith stayed four months. The week before she was to go home, after attending a concert by Adelina Patti, Edith came in breathless with excitement and found a cousin of her brother-in-law, Norman Galt, having supper at the house. Norman, twenty-seven, was immediately taken with Edith, visited frequently during the week before her departure, and discussed coming down to Virginia soon.

Edith spent the summer at home, but was back in Washington at her sister's house the next fall. It was clear she was there to catch a husband. It was just as clear that Norman was quite interested in having her as his wife.

Norman Galt was a rather junior partner in his family's jewelry and fine-silver store, which had been in business since the early years of the nineteenth century. Wedding presents for those of the middle and upper classes had been bought there on a regular basis since Lincoln's time. Galt's was a proper, elegant, and money-making establishment, with something of the "grand institution" about it.

If Norman was ardent, Edith remained cool. For four years she said no to him; however, he was always around, was a member of her brother-in-law's family, was reasonably well-to-do, and had prospects of greater wealth. Edith stayed in Washington and kept him at arm's length. No one better seemed to come along, and as the 1890s rolled by and Edith changed from being nineteen-going-on-twenty to twenty-four, marriage to Norman Galt became inevitable. The wedding took place in 1896.

In her autobiography, Edith never says she loved Norman, but says rather that they had a close friendship and that he was marvelous to her family.

It was the spirit of the times. Many marriages were not entirely for love; though young women such as Edith were unfailingly romantic, they were also practical. A woman's place in the world was judged by her husband's status; the most important choice in a woman's lifetime was that of a husband, and such a person must have qualities that would lead to a reasonable degree of comfort in life—if at all possible—because it was not attainable by any other means, especially if one's own family fortune was close to nonexistent. Norman fit Edith's bill of particulars reasonably well. There was between them, though—as their years of correspondence reveal—no spark of excitement.

After the wedding, Edith and Norman moved in with Norman's father until they were able to afford their own small house. They had been married for less than two years when a series of deaths and illnesses plagued the Galt family. Norman's brother-in-law died; twenty-four hours later, Norman's father died; within months, Norman's older brother Charlie became a hopeless invalid. The combination of these tragic instances left Norman Galt in charge of the family business at the age of thirty-five. The Norman Galts were now, if not wealthy, at least more than respectably well off. In 1899 Edith's adored father died. Most of her family, after this death, was quite dependent on Edith. By the early years of the new century Edith's mother and the three younger children were all being supported by the store.

In September of 1903 a son was born to Edith and Norman. He lived only three days. Edith's birthday cards in October of 1903 are mixed with letters of condolence. After this death, Edith was unable to have children. She was also hospitalized for some time with the complications resulting from the birth and bereavement.* Edith Bolling Galt kept the existence and the death of her infant son a family secret throughout her life; it is only now, with the opening of her private papers, that it finally became public knowledge.

There is evidence that Edith took this blow quite hard, though she did not talk about it. Norman was forty; she was no longer able to conceive and have a family; her father was dead, and her mother did not want to make decisions because they made her "nervous and unhappy." Edith began to take frequent trips to visit relatives, to order dresses from New York, to go to the theater. She was in her early thirties, and virtually independent.

In 1908, after a brief illness, Norman Galt died and left her sole owner of Galt's. It seemed unwise to liquidate the business, so, with the assistance of the store's managerial employees, Edith began to run it herself.

She proved herself a capable businesswoman. Her soft manner hid the proverbial iron fist: debts were paid off, retiring employees were not replaced, others were regretfully but firmly dismissed to trim the work force to a minimum. Day-to-day management was left to trusted managers, but Edith, with the assistance of an older lawyer, Nathaniel Wilson, went over accounts on a regular basis. Though not schooled in traditional business ways, Edith had intelligence and the sensitivities of a quick learner—a sort of "street smarts." She followed her conservative instincts, and when she once made a mistake she took care not to make it twice. With the Galt family thinned by early deaths, Edith drew a good income to support herself, her mother, and three brothers.

Thirty-six, attractive, widowed, moneyed, she now became more cosmopolitan, took a trip to Europe every year. She learned much on her journeys and was prized as a guest at dinner parties for her ability to converse easily on many topics. She had a few women friends her own

---

*It is possible that she met Cary Grayson at this time, when he was taking a residency in obstetrics and gynecology.

age, but men liked her greatly. While she was an old-fashioned woman in charm and appearance, she seemed to men less cloistered than other women of her class who never had much to do with anything outside their homes.

Edith enjoyed the role of surrogate mother to a series of young women relatives and friends: a niece who moved to Panama, her younger brothers' girlfriends, and others. Among these "daughters" was, in 1911, Alice Gertrude Gordon, the recently orphaned daughter of a wealthy mining engineer. Altrude was seventeen, attractive, rich, and smart. She and Edith went to Europe together for five months, and after this trip they were lifelong friends.

In 1912 Edith's sister-in-law Annie Litchfield, the wife of her brother Rolfe, became a fanatic Wilsonian. She went to the Baltimore convention at which Wilson was nominated and worked for him in the campaign. She got Edith to read Wilson's collection of speeches, *The New Freedom*, before Wilson took office. Edith commented archly that the sentiments expressed were fine, but how was anyone ever to accomplish such visionary aims? Annie dragged Edith to the theater to catch a glimpse of the great man; then she wangled an invitation for them both to meet Wilson personally—but Edith merely drove Annie to the White House in her electric car and rode around the block while Annie had her appointment. When Wilson made his first and famous address to Congress in person in 1913, Edith was in the audience.

Edith spent the summer of 1914 with Altrude in Maine, chosen because of its proximity to Harlakenden, where Cary Grayson, Edith's old friend and the White House physician, had planned to stay with the president and his family. Ellen Wilson's illness and death held Grayson in Washington for most of the time, but he wrote to Altrude and to Edith. On August 25, he painted for Edith a sad portrait of the mourning president:

> For several days he has not been well. I persuaded him yesterday to remain in bed during the forenoon. When I went to see him, tears were streaming down his face. It was a heart-breaking scene, a sadder picture no one could imagine. A great man with his heart torn out.

When Grayson's arrival kept getting put off, the intrepid ladies went on a hiking and camping trip in the wild without him. This was when Edith ate a questionable chicken and got ptomaine poisoning; in the absence of other medicine she took pills marked as "cholera cure," which, if they did not cure her, at least seemed to make her no worse. Returning to

Washington, she proceeded slowly through a convalescence guided by Grayson. Notes in the autumn of 1914 between the two show Edith urging restraint and patience in Grayson's pursuit of Altrude; once he complimented her on being a "good prophet" in her political perceptions. She predicted McReynolds's elevation to the Supreme Court and his replacement as attorney general by Thomas Gregory.

In the fall, Grayson had brought her in touch with Helen Bones, recommending the walks that resulted in Edith's initial face-to-face meeting with the president. Forty-five years later, on a courtesy visit to the White House, Edith would point out to a delighted Mamie Eisenhower the exact spot where she—in her words—"turned a corner and met her fate." At the time of the meeting with Woodrow Wilson, though, all she could think of was she was lucky that, despite her muddy footwear, she still looked presentable in a smart black tailored suit which Worth had made for her in Paris.

They all had an hour of talk around a fire in the oval sitting room on the second floor. Edith's "Shenandoah twist" accent was delightful, and she was a good listener as well as a woman with a fund of stories. A man who had traveled extensively with her once swore that being with Edith made a man think of perfumes, flowers, "of all the things made to give pleasure." She was asked to dinner but declined, taking a raincheck for an evening on which she could get herself more suitably attired for dinner at the White House.

There is some evidence that the president had seen her before, had been at least faintly intrigued by Edith Galt. Out on a "motor" with Grayson one day earlier in the year, he had asked who he was writing to. Another time, Grayson had followed Edith's car (when she was driving with Altrude) and the president looked on in interest and amusement as the good doctor carefully memorized the license plate of Edith's electric to show Altrude how much he cared.

With Wilson's obvious approbation, the dinner was set for the following Tuesday, March 23. In between, Helen and Edith walked together several times in the park. On that Tuesday evening the red-carpet treatment was much in evidence: a White House car was sent to pick Edith up from her home. At dinner Edith sat between Wilson and Grayson; Colonel Edward T. Brown (Ellen Axson Wilson's first cousin) and Helen Bones were the only other guests. Immediately after dinner Grayson excused himself to see the ailing McAdoo, Colonel Brown retired early, and Wilson, Edith, and Helen sat having coffee around the fireplace. Woodrow was persuaded to read several English poems. It was a lovely evening. After being delivered home in the White House car, Edith feverishly wrote a note to her sister-in-law, the fervent

Wilsonian Annie Litchfield, describing the evening and the president who was "perfectly charming and one of the easiest and most delightful hosts I have ever known."

A similar evening followed two weeks later, with Helen, Edith, and Woodrow. That evening Wilson explained in great detail his relationship to his father, and how he had to write things over several times until they said what he really meant them to say. Edith, whose own father had also been a perfectionist and a preacher, felt a bond growing between herself and the president. From fathers they went on to the post-bellum South that had formed the core of both their childhoods, and told the Negro dialect stories which passed for humor among southerners. Lonely, mature, intelligent, of the gentility, both were religious and incurably romantic. The romance picked up speed. Edith was invited to go on walks not only with Helen, but also with Nell McAdoo and with Margaret Wilson. She was being looked over. The threesome of Helen Bones, Edith, and Woodrow went to a baseball game and took numerous open-car automobile rides in the spring air. On the rides, the president often talked of the rapidly developing situation in Europe. It seemed to clarify his own thought to tell Edith about the conduct of the war as they sped through the cool April nights, a driver trying not to hear in the front seat, a car full of Secret Service agents behind.

For one thing, House's mission to Europe for peace seemed to have run into a quagmire. Edward Grey delayed House in London and nearly completely convinced him that the Germans did not want peace. House finally got away, but went first to Paris where he heard similar sentiments before going at last to Berlin. There he tested the waters thoroughly and, in consequence, never asked directly about the kaiser's interest in negotiations. As he was returning to London, the spring offensives started in Belgium.

Sir John French broke through German lines at Neuve Chappelle, but having no reinforcements was soon shoved back. Fifty thousand Frenchmen died for five hundred yards of Champagne, sixty thousand for no yardage at Saint-Mihiel. Politicians compounded the generals' insufficiencies by having Commonwealth forces try to take the Dardanelles. The Germans blundered as well. Mired in the west, they pushed east into Russia, which was a mistake because now the tsar's forces were roused from lethargy to defend their native land. Both sides courted Italy; an early pact was to have brought Italy in on the German side, but the Rome government reneged—not enough spoils. On April 26, in a secret treaty, the Italians agreed to come in with the Allies for post-war territoriality considerations. Within days, Italians were being killed on the front.

As Charles W. Eliot put it then in an issue of the *New York Times Current History of the War*,

> The destructiveness of war waged on the scale and with the intensity which conscript armies, the new means of transportation and communication, the new artillery, the aeroplanes, the high explosives, and the continuity of fighting on battle fronts of unexampled length, by night as well as by day, and in stormy and wintry as well as moderate weather, make possible, has proved to be beyond all power of computation, and could not have been imagined in advance.

There had never been such destruction, either of people or of property, in the history of the world. The resulting dislocations of the economies of all the belligerents and of the neutral nations, Dr. Eliot concluded, would be felt for many generations to come.

All of this meant increasing difficulty for the United States. Germany and Great Britain hardened their positions on neutral ships. If Germany could break the blockade with her submarines (now being built at an increasing rate) she might outlast England and win; should England succeed in starving Germany or in effectively cutting off access to raw materials for munitions, Germany might have to surrender. Germany rationed flour, which Great Britain then placed on its own contraband list. The United States protested both the subs and the listing of flour, but neither belligerent would budge an inch.

At home the war produced an odd mixture of good and bad. We were selling so many horses to Europe that there was fear cowboys would have to start walking. The Panama-Pacific Exposition, hailed as the greatest world's fair, opened in San Francisco to great hoopla, but unemployment was rampant in other big cities. Some said the Wobblies were fomenting strikes and riots, but when defenseless strikers were mowed down in New Jersey, the *New York Sun* (generally sympathetic to business) said there was no evidence to show any justification for the employers' violence. Prices were rising; so were income taxes and the growth of the government in Washington.

Mexico was again giving Wilson cause for concern. Obregón's forces defeated Villa's in battles in early April, and by the middle of the month Villa seemed no longer a political or military factor to be reckoned with. On the other hand, General Huerta had secretly come back from Spain—with German money!—and was living at the Ansonia Hotel in

New York. He was also threatening to go back to Mexico, another headache for Wilson.

By the last week in April, Mrs. Galt was a nightly dinner guest in the White House. Nearly every evening the presidential car, with Helen Bones or Grayson or Margaret, would come and pick Edith up, then return to the White House to get Wilson, and a group would go out touring; afterward they would come back for dinner and an evening of reading and conversation. Later the car would take Edith home. For Edith the days began to be unimportant; she waited for the nights to begin. One evening Wilson mentioned a favorite book of his, Hamerton's *Round My House*; next day he sent Edith a copy of the book borrowed from the Library of Congress (until an ordered one should arrive) along with a note:

> I hope it will give you a little pleasure. I covet nothing more than to give you pleasure—you have given me so much! If it rains this evening, would it be any fun for you to come around and have a little reading . . . (or) are you game for another ride?

Unfortunately Edith had promised her mother the evening, and had to send regrets; but, she wrote back,

> Your wish to give me pleasure has been so abundantly fulfilled already, that for you to take time to send a personal note is only generous good measure with which you fill my goblet of happiness. Thank you. I am very tired tonight, and can think of nothing more restful than to come and have you read to us, or—in case it clears, blow away the cobwebs in another way, by another life-giving ride. . . . [Your] pledge of friendship blots out the shadows that have chased me today.

These are the first in a series of love letters. Curiously, in her book of memoirs, Edith described Woodrow's letters as exquisite, touching, and completely private, and refused to quote from them—or, for that matter, from her own. In one of hers she did quote—the one above—the feelings have been almost obliterated in her sanitized version:

> I can think of nothing more restful than to come and have you read to us, or in case it clears, go for another ride, *but* (that word so often destroys plans) I have promised my dear

Mother to spend this evening with her, so cannot give myself either pleasure.

On April 30 the bookseller's copy of *Round My House* arrived with a note, flowers, and an invitation for Edith and Altrude to dine. Altrude was so flustered that, on receiving pink roses instead of an expected color, she decided at the last minute to change her gown. Knowing the president's insistence on promptness, Grayson persuaded the ladies to finish the details of Altrude's toilette in the back seat of the White House limousine.

The dinner was unusually lovely, but was over early, as the president and his household were leaving next morning for the baptism of Francis Sayre in Williamstown.

That next morning, beneath an advertisement announcing the *Lusitania*'s departure for Liverpool, was a stark warning printed in the New York dailies by the German embassy. It said all vessels in the war zone were "liable to destruction" and that those who sailed on British or Allied ships in that zone did so "at their own risk."* Only one of the 1257 passengers and 667 crew members, evidently, felt the slightest nervousness about embarking, and he changed to a different liner.

When the Cunard line had launched the *Lusitania* it was the largest vessel in the world, the first to be propelled by four turbines, the first to steam for twenty-four hours at an average speed higher than twenty-five knots (26 ⅓). It was the fastest ship afloat. Although not commissioned in the Royal Navy, the ship sailed under the express protection of the British fleet. The first days of its voyage were smooth, sunny, and unexceptional, and in Washington no one worried about its safety.

Woodrow and Edith did not see one another for several days as he was out of town, but Woodrow wrote to her (in a note of April 30), that sharing

> any part of your thought and confidence . . . puts me in spirits again and makes me feel as if my *private* life has been recreated. But, better than that, it makes me hope that I may be of some use to you, to lighten the days with whole-hearted sympathy and complete understanding.

This last, because Edith had already begun to reveal to Wilson—the

*On May 1 the American tanker *Gulflight* was torpedoed in the Irish sea and three American sailors died. At nearly the same time German planes dropped a bomb on the American ship *Cushing* in those same waters.

most sensitive, most intelligent man she had ever met—the vacuousness of her life in Washington. Yes, of course, she had money, a lovely house, family from whom she could derive some emotional sustenance; but she was a comparatively young woman of forty-two who had had an unsatisfactory marriage and who had been widowed since thirty-six; more, she had tastes for conversation about literature and politics which her present circumstances and circle of acquaintances could not satisfy. The more time she spent with Wilson, Grayson, and Helen, the less attractive her own environment seemed.

For Wilson, the value and specific longings toward comfort, companionship, and the satisfaction of spiritual and physical needs were coming to have a specific focus. When the president returned to the White House on May 3, Edith was immediately called to come to dinner. There were other relatives present during the meal, but afterward they discreetly left Edith and Woodrow alone on the south portico. The president drew his chair close to hers, told her that he had asked Helen and Margaret to give him an opportunity to tell her what he had already told them: that he loved her.

Such a simple and early declaration was as characteristic of the times as it was of the man. Correct behavior did not allow for any indication of encouragement on the part of a woman toward a man until he had declared his complete intentions toward her; before such time, she was to remain reserved and pleasant, unprovocative, and basically unresponsive. After a declaration was made, then the woman was released from her bonds of reticence.

In her memoirs, Edith said she was shocked by Woodrow's declaration, and said the first thing that came into her mind: "Oh, you can't love me, for you don't really know me; and it is less than a year since your wife died."

"Yes," she reports him as saying, "I know you feel that; but, little girl, in this place time is not measured by weeks, or months, or years, but by deep human experiences; and since her death I have lived a lifetime of loneliness and heartache. I was afraid, knowing you, that I would shock you, but I would be less than a gentleman if I continued to make opportunities to see you without telling you what I have told my daughters and Helen: that I want you to be my wife. In the circumstances of the spotlight that is always on this house, and particularly on me as the Head of the Government, whoever comes here is immediately observed and discussed; and do what I can to protect you from gossip, it will inevitably begin. If you can care for me as I do for you, we will have to brave this."

They talked on in this mode for another hour. Edith told him that if it had to be yes or no right this instant, it would have to be no—but that they should keep talking. Conversely, she also threatened to go to Japan that summer, since Europe was out. At ten o'clock, Helen and Woodrow drove her home in silence. Edith sat in a big chair in her room for hours, then wrote and rewrote a note to the president. She copied from memory a poem she had learned long ago.

> Since you exalt me thus, I must not
>   prove your wisdom vain,
> Unto these mighty heights, oh help me
>   wondrous love I must attain.*

She wished he were there so she could talk to him; the written word was inadequate and cold, and she did want so much to help. She thrilled to her fingertips to remember the tremendous thing he had said to her earlier,

> and how pitifully poor I am, to have nothing to offer you in return. Nothing, I mean, in proportion to your own great gift! I am a woman, and the thought that you have *need* of me—is sweet! But, dear kindred spirit, can you not trust me and let me lead you from the thought that you have forfeited anything by your fearless honesty to the conviction that, with such frankness between us, there is nothing to fear. We will help and hearten each other. There will be no subterfuge. You have been honest with me, and perhaps I was too frank with you—but if so, forgive me! And know that here on this white page I pledge you all that is best in me—to help, to sustain, to comfort—and that into the space that separates us I send my spirit to seek yours. Make it a welcome guest.

If she were conciliatory, it was perhaps because she knew she had said some tough things; among them, that Woodrow should hold his emotions in check. He could not. He, too, copied out a poem—Shakespeare's thirtieth sonnet, composed another, and begged her not to go to Japan, and

> . . . did my best to do your bidding, for it is in pleasing you; but grief and dismay are terrible companions in the still

*The origin of this poem is unknown. Dr. Arthur S. Link suggests Edith wrote it herself.

night, with hope lying dead and I could not endure them
beyond the dawn. I will do better. They shall not conquer me.
I shall get used to them, as I have so many others like them,
and be by degrees stronger than they are—with God's help,
and yours! I wonder what God means to do with me, having
cast me off?

This is the only time in the long history of Wilson as a mature man,
when he ever doubted that his purposes and God's were one.

Next day, walking in Rock Creek Park, Helen Bones was cross with
Edith because she hadn't said yes right away and relieved the pressure
on Woodrow. Edith, however, felt secure in her convictions about both
the speed and the warmth of the burgeoning feeling between her and the
president. The chill that had been on her heart for a long time was
thawing rapidly, but the pace was so quick that she dared not trust it.
Time, in this instance, would have to wait.

Helen brought Edith's note to Wilson; the next night, he answered it.
Something had happened between them: he had put his happiness to the
test, and it had not been rejected as he had first thought, but merely put
off for a while. There were some things, he wrote, that he had to try to
say

. . . before the still watches come again in which things
unsaid hurt so and cry out in the heart to be uttered. It was
this morning—while I lay awake thinking of you in all your
wonderful loveliness and my pitiful inability to satisfy and
win you, to show you the true heart of my need, and of my
nature—that you wrote that wonderful note . . . with its
fresh revelation of your wonderful gifts of heart and mind—
the most moving and altogether beautiful note I ever read;
and I must thank you for that before I try to sleep—thank
you from the bottom of my heart that your words touch as if
they knew every key of it. I am proud beyond words that you
should have thought of me in such terms and put the
thoughts into such exquisite, comprehending words.

Woodrow Wilson—whom newspapers often described as enigmatic,
cold, and austere—had an overweening desire for his close friends to
understand that he was very different from his public image. Now, a
woman was responding to the display of his most private emotions, and
he was grateful:

* * *

God has indeed been good to me to bring such a creature as
you into my life. Every glimpse I am permitted to get of the
secret depths of you I find them deeper and purer and more
beautiful than I knew or had dreamed of. If you cannot give
me *all* that I want—what my heart finds it hard now to
breathe without—it is because I am not worthy. I know
instinctively you *could* give it if I were—and if you understood—understood the boy's heart that is in me and the
simplicity of my need, which you could fill so that all my days
would be radiant. Browning speaks somewhere of a man
having two sides, one that he turns to the world, another that
he shows a woman when he loves her.

He wanted her to open her eyes and see that private side, warts and all.
These were, he wrote, the supreme years of his life, when minutes
counted more than days would at some future time. But she was still
seeing the president, not the man Woodrow Wilson,

> whose heart must be satisfied if his life is to tell for all it
> might tell for and who would want you—oh with *such* a
> longing—whether he had ever been heard from or
> not. . . . Here stands your friend, a longing man, in the
> midst of a world's affairs—a world that knows nothing of the
> heart he has shown you and which would as lief break it as
> not, but which he cannot face with his full strength or with
> the fullest of keen endeavour unless you come into that heart
> and take possession, not because it is exposed but because
> simply and only because, you love him. *Can* you love
> him? . . . Will you come to him some time without reserve
> and make his strength complete? . . . Whatever happens,
> you will have the companionship, the gratitude, the loyalty,
> and the devoted, romantic love of
> > Your devoted friend,
> > Woodrow Wilson

> What would I not give for words that would really make you
> see and feel what is in my heart. You could not shrink!
> > WW

> How much of my life has gone into this note you will never
> know unless, someday—

> Do not misunderstand. What I have now at your generous
> hands is infinitely precious to me. It would kill me to part

with it—I could not and I hope you could not. And I will be patient, patient without end, to see what, if anything, the future may have in store for me.

A staggering letter. And not alone, for in the early morning of May 6, Wilson got up to write more, thinking he had not adequately answered her note in his own. He berated himself for last night's note which he thought too egocentric. He read and reread her note, his "little charter of liberty" which brought tears to his eyes, "tears of joy and sweet yearning." For her beautiful spirit,

> I will be its knight—serve it, not myself, and feel myself grow a better, purer man in the service! . . . You have had too little joy in your life; I shall try to add to its stock, not take away from it! The wonderful woman I recognized and loved, and sought selfishly to claim, I shall seek to enrich, not impoverish . . . I seem to have been put into the world to serve, not to take, and serve I will to the utmost, and demand nothing in return.

These notes came together to Edith at her home. All of the courting was done at the White House or in neutral surroundings; the president thought it would not be wise to visit her house, though he wanted greatly to see a space she had made her own. Men at this time believed one could read a woman's character by seeing a woman's space, by learning to some degree how a woman decorated a place and, by inference, how she might design his space. Edith answered Woodrow's notes as best she could, found the one written that morning full of tenderness and yet

> vibrant with *strength* and the blessed surety that you have *found yourself!* This is what makes me so proud of you, and so sure that all's right with the world! You could not *be* yourself and not feel as you do today. . . . My heart is tingling with the wonder of your revelation of yourself. . . . On my heart rests a golden rose, and in my heart is a treasure of purer gold. May I never tarnish this pure trust, but guard it with my life—and leave the rest to God.

In Wilson's era, gentlemen regarded women as purer and finer creatures than themselves, the repositories of moral and spiritual worth. Courtliness was more than a pose, it was part of the respect accorded to womankind in general and a chosen lady in particular. Women expected to be treated in this way—especially southern women—and, when they were, responded with what was best in them. Looking through Edith's correspondence prior to the spring of 1915, one finds much less tenderness, depth of psychological observation, attempts at beautiful turns of phrase. But for Wilson it was all there: if he was being her knight, she was determined to be his perfect lady.

After these exchanges, they had dinner together, and Woodrow tried to tell Edith his conception of public duty. It was an emotional trial for him to describe a feeling which he had spent his entire life shaping. When he saw an answering light in her eyes, he felt wonderful: it was, he thought, an omen that he might (eventually) receive from Edith solace to ease the burdens his high office had brought to him. In the morning, his letter was shot full of religious grace: he had prayed for her to accept his love and knew if she did, if she agreed to be his mate, it was because God willed it: "God comes to a man, I think, through the trust and love of a sweet, pure woman. Certainly God seems very near when I am with you." It was perfectly possible for him, he wrote, to be captain of his fate and master of his soul well enough without her—but he no longer wanted only those goals.

A few hours later the captain of German U-20 sent a torpedo into the underbelly of the *Lusitania*, ten miles off the Irish coast. It was just three months after Colonel House had passed this point on this very ship. Within ten minutes, the liner was nearly down and the submarine's captain decided not to send a second shot through the writhing masses of humanity trying desperately to get away from the sinking ship. Nearly immediately, news of the disaster was flashed around the world. First word was only that the *Lusitania* was down. The number dead was not yet known; the total would reach 1198 out of 1924 (including 124 Americans). That this great liner had gone down so rapidly when it had been supposed to be nearly unsinkable was an unbelievable shock, and the reverberations from the attack were enormous.

The president had been about to go out for golf when the first news reached him. He waited at the White House all afternoon for further word, then in exasperation took an automobile ride to pass the time. It was after dinner when the reports came in on the great number of deaths. Before the Secret Service knew what he was doing, Wilson walked out of the White House and up Sixteenth Street, seeming oblivious to the rain. Returning after half an hour, he spoke to no one—indeed, had said virtually nothing all day—but before going to bed he wrote another note to Edith. The penmanship is less sure, the wording echoes with the difficulties to be faced, the "cruel compulsion of circumstances," the "many possibilities of infinite loss and mistake," and of keeping "the cynical world at arm's length." Not only did the tragedy of the *Lusitania* weigh heavily on him, but he was losing confidence in his wooing, and thought Edith was using her "splendid strength and conscience to determine *what is best for me*—when the only thing that is best for me is your love—and what you should *do*—what our actions and outward relations to one another should be is quite another matter."

The morning newspapers of May 8, a Saturday, provided most Americans with the first deeply shocking experience of the war. Reading of the *Lusitania*, people remembered the *Maine*, and reporters invoked the fact that the Civil War had started when the Confederates fired on a union supply ship bound for Fort Sumter. People prepared mentally for war, as they had not for a generation. For nine months Americans had read that the war on the other side of the Atlantic was pure, unadulterated hell—men dying by the tens of thousands, millions starving. In this era of religious imagery and fervor, Americans referred to the war across the water as Armageddon. Now, on May 8, they believed for the first time that they too stood at the edge of the abyss.

The *Des Moines Register and Leader* editorialized that "The sinking of the *Lusitania* was deliberate murder," a sentiment echoed by many other papers and millions of readers. Almost the entire East Coast would have accepted entry into the war on the Allied side at this moment, but in the West and Midwest sentiment was not so high. The German embassy insisted there had been definite contraband on board the *Lusitania* and, in fact, there were over 5,000 cases of rifle casings, shrapnel, fuses, and other war materiel. Secretary of State Bryan insisted that American passengers ought not to have been traveling on a British ship in time of war. Still, most people knew the *Lusitania* was primarily a passenger vessel, that the cargo was incidental.

All eyes turned toward the White House. Although it was up to Congress to declare war, Congress would probably only do so if the president requested such a declaration. Wilson kept a low profile over the weekend. To satisfy reporters, he had Tumulty issue the statement that

> Of course the President feels the distress and the gravity of the situation to the utmost, and is considering very earnestly, but very calmly, the right course of action to pursue. He knows that people of the country wish and expect him to act with deliberation as well as with firmness.

* * *

While the country's newspapers worked feverishly through Saturday on their Sunday supplements to get pictures of the *Lusitania*'s dead and rescued passengers, Wilson saw almost no one, but did communicate with Edith.

He had taken her into his confidence in state matters already, expressing to her his growing problem with Bryan; now he talked to her of the *Lusitania*. He needed emotional help. Her note answering his wondered, "Why should I be chosen to help you? . . . The thought makes me tremble and grow afraid, and I long to come and have you answer the question." Woodrow answered the question characteristically:

> There is nothing to make you tremble or grow afraid. It is all very simple and very beautiful. I have seen you, I have known you to be of my essential kith and kind (though much finer— the *woman* of all that is in me), and I have loved you beyond all power of doubt to hold back, oh, with such an instant intuition, such an irresistible power of comprehending love, and I know that no one can help me as you can. . . . Just as one knows (*how* does he know, do you think?) moving music when he hears it, or the voice of true prayer, or the tones of sympathy and affection—just as he would know that he had reached *home* the moment the door opened and he stepped within the sacred and yet familiar and beloved place where his spirit had been bred.

There was nothing bright in his thoughts these days, he wrote, except her. Next morning another note followed in his hand, which seemed shaken by emotion: "Do you think it an accident that we found one another at this time of my special need and that it meant nothing that we recognized one another so immediately and so joyously?"

He "worked" for her on the beginnings of a note to Germany. He tried to marshal what was best in him, to meet the terribly high standards he ascribed to her expectations of him. She was ecstatic over having in some small way been of moral assistance to him in this world crisis, and wrote that the thought of helping him was "so exciting, so virile" that she could hardly sleep. In her morning's service at church, there was a special prayer for the president of the United States. She had recited it, and thought not of the office, but of the man,

* * *

and then such a wave of shame came over me that I dared
think of you there, save as the choice of a great people who
had put in your keeping the destinies of millions—and that
you, in your loneliness, had offered me those same strong
hands to put my own in. . . . I hated myself, came home
humbled.

On the morning of May 10 the White House car came to pick her up
for lunch. She had in her hand another note written hastily just as the
car was coming for her, a note full of emotional dynamite. She gave it to
Wilson as he was leaving to go to Philadelphia to make a speech. In it
she told how she had thought that the possibilities of love, both spiritual
and physical, were actually dead in her, after all she had been through.
But now, she said,

> We both deserve the right to try, and if you, with your
> wonderful love can quicken that which has lain dead so long
> within me, I promise not to shut it out of my heart, but to bid
> it welcome, and come to you with the joy of it in my eyes. On
> the other hand, if I am dead (as I believe) you will not blame
> me for seeking to live, even if it means pain in your own
> tender heart when my pulses refuse to beat in unison with
> yours. Goodby, and know that you carry with you all that
> brings me happiness.

Love might be possible! Fired by Edith's promise, in Philadelphia
Wilson gave to a group of newly sworn citizens one of the finest
speeches of his life. In it were echoes of the awakening he was experiencing with his new-found lady:

> This is the only country in the world which experiences this
> constant and repeated rebirth [the naturalizing of immi-
> grants]. . . . This country is constantly drawing strength
> out of new sources. . . . You come with a purpose of leaving
> all other countries behind you. . . . It is one thing to love
> the place where you were born, and it is another thing to
> dedicate yourself to the place to which you go. A man does
> not go out to seek the thing that is not in him; a man does not
> hope for the thing that he does not believe in
> . . . you . . . imported in your own hearts a renewal of the
> belief. . . . You are enriching us. . . . A nation that is not
> constantly renewed out of new sources is apt to have narrow-

ness and prejudice . . . whereas America must be the
example . . . of the healing and elevating influence in the
world. . . . There is such a thing as a man being too proud
to fight. There is such a thing as a nation being so right that it
does not need to convince others by force that it is right.

Wilson received a great ovation, then started back by auto to Washington. As he read Edith's notes he discovered that she had signed her name, rather than her initials, for the first time; also she was letting him into her secret thoughts. It was great news. As he confessed in a note to her,

If I said what was worth saying to that great audience . . . it
must have been because love had complete possession of me. I
did not know before I got up very clearly what I was going to
say, nor remember what I said when I sat down; but I knew
that I had left the speech in your hands and that you needed
me as I needed you. . . .

They were in love; if they were not completely together, at least there were signs that they might one day be so entwined. If he held true to what was finest in himself, the knight of peace might one day prove worthy of his lady.

6

IN SUMMER AND STORM

IN THE CLEAR atmosphere of morning the president regretted his rhetorical overflow in Philadelphia: he thought he should have kept the phrase "too proud to fight" to himself, as it had not been fully developed. Later, in cabinet, he went over the note he would send to Germany. It would hold Germany to strict accountability for the *Lusitania*, and suggest that it was virtually impossible to use submarines against merchant shipping "without an inevitable violation of many sacred principles of justice and humanity." Wilson ended the draft with a call for Germany to disavow the actions of its submarine commander, make reparations, and prevent new incidents.

Almost alone among the cabinet, Bryan thought the note too strong, that it would encourage our jingoes and anger the Germans because it mentioned their violations without saying anything of repeated British violations. Instead of insisting that Americans had the right to travel anywhere in safety, Bryan wanted Wilson to be warning American citizens not to travel on ships which might be attacked. When his arguments failed, Bryan suggested the note go with a press release or announcement of interpretations which would say "administration circles" believed Germany would respond to the note "in a spirit of accommodation."

Wilson initially agreed to Bryan's postscript, but then Tumulty got hold of him and, enraged, pointed out that the press release would give the impression that the United States was going to take Germany's provocations lying down. It would sap the force of the note. Wilson agreed to table the press release. Tumulty, white as a ghost, went to join Secretary of War Lindsey Garrison for lunch. He said he had just experienced the worst half-hour of his life. On hearing the story, Garrison said, "You should receive a medal of honor for this day's work."

The country's attitude toward Germany began to change radically. In the *New York Times*, for example, the German propagandist Bernhardt Dornberg, who pre-*Lusitania* had been a "spokesman," was now labeled a "mouthpiece." Pro-Ally sentiment was creeping west and south. Though the country was mostly disposed against war, it was obvious that further incidents similar to the *Lusitania* could cause public opinion to rapidly tilt toward war.

The *Washington Post* editorialized on May 12,

> The plain truth is that the United States is in no condition to declare war upon Germany. It could not make its demands effective by force of arms, because it has no navy and no army capable of waging war on the scale that would be required.

On the other hand, it was Wilson's view that we could wage an effective peace. Ex-President Taft understood this, and wrote to Wilson that Congress ought not to be called because it would only seek to declare war, when "It seems to me that it is the duty of every thoughtful, patriotic citizen to avoid embarassing you in your judgment and not to yield to the impulse of deep indignation which the circumstances might naturally arouse." Theodore Roosevelt disagreed—loudly. He proclaimed that the *Lusitania* disaster underlined our desperate lack of military preparedness.

By and large, though, the country preferred Wilson's stance. Edith felt, as the country formed ranks in back of Woodrow, like a worm in the dust at his feet, sensed the "thrill of extacy" (sic) that came to one who had been in darkness but who now saw—even in the far distance—"the gleaming of a light." Wilson exulted:

> You have tried to crush your heart, you have left it without air to breathe, but it has broken from you and triumphed in spite of you. You must acknowledge the victory. Neither your happiness nor mine will be full until you do.

Together with a large party, they went aboard the presidential yacht

Mayflower for a trip to New York. It was the first time they had to be away from the pressure and the prying eyes of Washington. They had a good trip, were continually together. Their sense of camaraderie increased when squalls hit and they were the only two passengers who didn't turn instantly green.

As the storm worsened, Grayson tried desperately to maintain his composure and tend to Altrude, whose moans were frightful, but he could not. Wilson chided him—after all, Grayson was a navy man. Edith went to fetch Altrude some brandy; as she was coming up from below decks the boat seemed to turn upside down, and she had a wave of weakness and sat down, legs askew, blindly clutching the brandy bottle to her bosom. Wilson found her thus, and they both laughed at the absurd picture she made. Tumulty alone managed to show up to lunch with them, but then turned the same shade as the peas and did not reappear above decks until the *Mayflower* anchored in New York.

Left to themselves, Edith and Woodrow exchanged little notes, spent much time discussing Woodrow's political problems, chief among them William Jennings Bryan. The Great Commoner threatened to resign if Wilson didn't protest British as well as German attempts on our neutrality. Wilson had agreed to send a note to England but wanted to face one provocation at a time. At least the British weren't killing anyone. Also, House had wired Wilson excitedly that his private talks with Grey might result in the British taking foodstuffs off the contraband list, removing the chief source of friction. What, Woodrow asked Edith, should he do if Bryan actually tendered his resignation? Edith quoted a line from a play she had seen:* "Take it, sir, and thank God for the chance."

Bryan had greatly helped Wilson win the presidential nomination. As secretary of state in a time of peace, Bryan had championed cooling-off treaties which actively promoted peace and negotiation, and had been an asset in handling Mexico, the Panama tolls, and in restoring strained relations with Japan. Wilson could tolerate Bryan's gaffes, such as serving only grape juice at official functions, and taking money for Chautauqua talks to augment his small salary, and grumbling about not enough jobs for "deserving Democrats" in the wake of a successful election campaign, because they shared common aims.

But Wilson had been writing all of the most important State Department messages himself—or without Bryan's help—and House was doing diplomatic battle because the heavy-handed Bryan was not subtle enough to negotiate in less than clear-cut situations. By 1915 Bryan's

Rosemary, with John Drew and Maude Adams.

totally pacifistic attitude in a complicated world seemed to Wilson unrealistic; many of the causes Bryan espoused would have led to economic disaster, and still might have had no effect on stopping the war or even on keeping America out of it. In the main, Wilson agreed with Bryan that we were becoming too belligerent, that we might well be talking ourselves closer to war, but the president was sworn to be the defender of American constitutional rights, and the defense of the right to travel anywhere was now clashing with the utopian desire for peace. Wilson had now to decide what to do with Bryan. In a sense the *Lusitania* affair had put Bryan's fate in German hands: how Germany would answer the note to which Bryan objected would determine whether he stayed on or left the cabinet.

By the time Edith and Woodrow returned to Washington, they knew what it was to spend more than a few hours at a time together, and the pain of being again separated was sharp. "Back in prison," Edith called it, and wished she could be with him and hold him close: "You have been so vividly before me that I lose the sense of being alone. And find myself turning to welcome your coming if there is a noise or motion in the house."

She asked him if he remembered William James's famous essay, "On a Certain Blindness in Human Beings," which describes people as seeing but not seeing, hearing but not hearing. There was a fable of a bird singing in the woods, she said, which a monk did not hear because he was not conscious of it: "Dear Heart, I have been seeking for so long for that bird, and now I am hearing him, clear and sweet is his call each day, and if you will kiss the other eye into life, I believe I will see him."

He wrote that it was very hard to be separated from her and not to know what she was thinking at all times; he longed for them to be together, as the weeks since he had declared his love for her were ones of terrible strain.

In England, House had done something rash. In trying to get Grey to take foodstuffs off the contraband list, House had conceived a deal: if Britain would allow shipment of food to Germany, House would ask Berlin to halt submarine warfare against merchantmen. Without permission from Wilson, House cabled Gerard, our ambassador in Berlin, to get him to ask the German government to delay answering the *Lusitania* note and to try to make the deal. This did just what Wilson had tried to avoid doing—link the German and British violations of neutrality. Wilson swiftly chastised House, and the affair blew over without further trouble, but it did not help speed the German note and exacerbated, not calmed, international tensions.

As Wilson waited for the German reply, he received a note from Edith which described that forbidden place, her room. She imagined him lying on the sofa, calling to her. She charted her moods, tried to match his rhetorical ardor which seemed unflagging. He sent her flowers from the National Arboretum, told her she was the only woman who could wear an orchid—usually the orchid wore the woman. She described a sunset in lyrical colors.

Nell McAdoo gave birth to her first child, a daughter she named Ellen. Pleased and touched at the gesture, Wilson mentioned it to friends to whom he wrote on May 23. It was unsettling, though, to be reminded of Ellen when his mind was caught up with Edith. In between obligatory birth announcements he dashed off an agitated note to Edith: "What is it, dear Heart? Is anything the matter? Do you *wish* to be left to silence and your own thoughts? I confess I feel embarrassed and fear to intrude. . . ."

Then it was back to the desk to write to Mary Hulbert that there was no use in her stopping at the White House now, because he was so busy he would only be able to see her at meals. Later in the evening Wilson arrived on Edith's doorstep for an unexpected visit, just a glimpse and a quick kiss. How wonderfully disciplined lovers they were, he wrote a few days later,

> held apart not only by extraordinary circumstances but by thoughtful love itself—the love proved and tested by the self-restraint which is our chief pain and yet our chief proof that we are of the patriciate of love and live with a gallantry that is above self-indulgence.

He went over proofs of pictures of her, chose several to have by his desk and bed. Her spirit presided now over his workspace, since she had come and watched him struggle over some state papers there. The best hours of the day, he wrote to her, were the ones when he composed his notes to her in the early mornings or late evenings. He might as well try to define his life as his love; it was too complex and too simple. Therefore to dissect it would seem "like picking a flower to pieces to discover its perfume." There was no longer a barrier between them, and he ventured to say

> that never in your life before have you looked so wonderfully beautiful as I have seen you look when the love tide was

running in your heart without check, since you came to understand yourself and me. I have seen a transfiguration, and it has filled me with as much awe as ecstasy.

It also filled him with desire. On the evening of the twenty-seventh, they went out riding. For once Helen and the driver sat in front, Edith and Woodrow in back, the divider curtain drawn. Evidently Wilson became more ardent than Edith could then bear, and they had a difficult time, for at dawn, after dual sleepless nights, they wrote each other painful notes. Edith apologized for hurting him—apparently by being unable to meet his advances—and said she knew he was right in every word he said, "But, try as hard as I can, *now* it seems the only way. If this can be changed it will be because you are the master of my heart and life . . . but *you* must conquer." Wilson's note—in pencil, the handwriting agitated—entreated her to

find out whether you really love me or not. You owe it to yourself and you owe it to the great love I have given you, without stint or measure. Do not be afraid of what I am thinking, but remember that I need strength and certainty for the daily task and that I can not walk upon quicksand. I love you with all my heart.

Quicksand—that hurt her, and she let him know through Helen that it had. All day long he struggled with the knowledge, and then the German answer to the *Lusitania* note arrived.

It was absurd and evasive, saying that the liner had sunk so quickly because illegal ammunition in its hold had exploded—and that therefore the sinking was the fault of the Cunard line: in short, Germany claimed it had merely acted in self-defense. Wilson knew he would have to write a stronger note in return.

He went to bed and had another sleepless night, hours of depression and "exquisite suffering" which brought on an illness that neither he nor Grayson could decipher, and then, in the early morning hours, a new insight to offer to Edith: it was *he* who had been blind, who had been afraid of love; he had told her the truth and himself had acted as if he had not believed it. Did she want him to conquer? Very well, because his weakness was gone. "I not only believe love is supreme but that it is *creative. . . . I shall win*, by a power not my own, a power which has never been defeated, against which no doors can be locked, least of all the doors of the heart." Her own note was conciliatory, and the squall was over.

Two days later, at 7:30 in the morning, despite warnings to stay away, Mary Hulbert arrived at the White House. Before she got there, Wilson had written a note to Edith which told her she was the "loveliest in womanhood," that she had great "dignity and reserve," and that her beauty was of the "noblest type." Mary Hulbert's primary purpose this day was to extract from Wilson a loan. Her son's business dealings had left them in debt; would Wilson buy the mortgages on some properties she owned in California, in exchange for $7,500? Faced with such an urgent request, Wilson could hardly refuse, and arranged to have the money forwarded to her in exchange for the liens. Mary Hulbert departed at four, but the consequences of this visit were later to haunt her and Wilson, and Edith as well.

That same day Edith spent a few hours with her lawyer, Nathaniel Wilson, a diehard Republican who had become enthusiastic about the president (to whom he was not related). He knew nothing of how deeply the pair were entwined, knew only that Edith had been going to the White House lately, and suggested to Edith that she school herself in national and international problems, else she would eventually bore the president. The president's interest in her could be either a *surface* right—something superficial—or a *permanent* right—which went down into bedrock. It all depended on her.

As May turned to June the president seemed increasingly determined to turn his back on the past, in both his private and public life. He struck out in new directions.

First, he issued a warning to the warring Mexican factions that unless they were able to stabilize their government in the very near future the United States might have to take some action "in order to help Mexico save herself and serve her people." The period of watchful waiting which had characterized the administration's Mexican policy was ended.

Wilson's second decision was to give Edith a present, a beautiful ring. It was not, he told her, an engagement ring, for they could not think of a public announcement yet (and Edith had not agreed to be engaged), but it was a generous gift. She was all the world to him, giving him the strength to go on:

> The German note must be answered and answered very soon. But when I see your eyes alight to-night with the sweetest, holiest thing in all the world and hold you close in my arms and kiss you with pledges as deep as my soul, I shall be made fit for that and more.

* * *

Such pledges made her speak boldly: would he please not see German Ambassador Johann von Bernstorff alone? Would he work further "for her" on the draft note of reply to Germany because there was "nothing of himself in it?" Would he play a charade of noninterest when her sister came to a White House reception? He did all of these things.

The reworking of the note to Germany resulted in a third major decision. When Bryan read it and insisted it would result in war, declared he would not affix his signature to it and would resign rather than sign, Wilson did not try to convince him to stay. Instead he asked his son-in-law to intervene. Mac spent hours trying to persuade Bryan to stay, even suggesting that the secretary and his wife go away for the weekend before rendering a final decision. Nothing, however, would change Wilson's decision to send the note as he had rewritten it. Bryan remained adamant, and insisted he must resign even if, as Mac told him, the resignation would destroy him. The Great Commoner felt strongly that the note meant certain war, and that "I must do my duty according to my conscience." At a cabinet lunch Bryan said sadly, "I go out into the dark; the President has the power and prestige on his side. . . . I have many friends who would die for me."

On the day of his departure, Bryan wandered the halls of the State Department, trying to find people to shake hands with, and leaving behind tracts on peace and prohibition for the moral edification of his successor. He and the president clasped each other warmly: they both wanted peace, but had differing ideas on how to achieve it. Publicly Wilson was fulsome in his tribute; privately he was hurt. Sustained only by the thought of Edith, he sent her three letters on the day of the resignation. The newspapers, he wrote, "do not express the real feeling of the country for that strange man. . . . He suffers from a singular sort of moral blindness and is as passionate in error as in the right causes he has taken. There are deeper waters than ever ahead of us."

Public opinion seemed to agree. Bryan was branded a quitter and a deserter, and effectively lost his sway over public sentiment: afterward he was a gadfly for peace, but never again a serious challenger for the moral leadership of the country. The people's reaction furthered Woodrow's conviction that "with your hand in mine, your life linked with mine, my incomparable Darling, *nothing* will hurt me *too* deeply."

Edith was fiercely happy and proud that her advice had turned out to be politically and morally accurate and helpful. She hoped that Bryan would expire from an overdose of either peace or grape juice. She and Woodrow cried in each other's arms, chased one another about in cars. Woodrow waxed lyrical over the different varieties of flowers Edith resembled, said they lived apart but in the same home. They conspired to kiss in darkened doorways, sought omens in the meteorological moods of the day, grew mushily mystical watching each other in resplendent twilights, plotted spending a month together at Harlakenden. That would be the second chapter of their love story, they wrote, as this was the first chapter. In their letters at this time they were playwrights, painting various roles for themselves to fill. Some of these were:

WOODROW	EDITH
boy	girl
knight	lady
the intellect	the emotions
the seeker	the salver
the fencer	the target
the releaser	the prisoner
the humble servant	she who commands
the lonely man	the transfigurer
the light	she who needs the light
the custodian of the public trust	the custodian of the private trust

On the fourteenth of June, Woodrow wrote:

> I think I shall have to send a confidential personal message to the Kaiser telling him why I should like the German reply held back until about the tenth of July. If he is really human and has any heart in him he will understand and give me time to be with my love. Ah, Sweetheart, the colour and zest had gone out of my life when you came into it to restore them. I was trading on old capital and making shift to live and work without any real interest in my own life, just a tool of duty. And was not my dear, dear Sweetheart in very much the same condition (only used to it and fancying herself content with emptiness) and is it not infinitely sweet to find our lives full again, romantically full, of everything that stirs our hearts and justifies joy?

On the same day, another letter was being read at a conference in New York's Astor Hotel. The National Security League had gathered to discuss preparedness. Teddy Roosevelt, who could not attend, wrote in. There should be no peace feelers, he said,

> until as a preliminary we put ourselves in such shape that what we say will excite the respect and not the derision of

foreign powers. . . . It is wicked to be neutral between right and wrong, and this statement can be successfully refuted only by men who are prepared to hold up Pontius Pilate, the arch-typical neutral of all time, as worthy of our admiration.

Privately Roosevelt called the men of the Wilson administration, who had intervened in Mexico but wouldn't do so in Europe, "unlovely . . . probably the most undesirable citizens this country contains." Once he thought Wilson to be the worst president since Jefferson.

With his statements, Roosevelt put considerable distance between himself and other Republicans who were following more moderate lines of thought. Three days after the Astor Hotel conference, William Howard Taft spoke out in an address to the newly formed League to Enforce Peace. He articulated the primary and fundamental principle of that league to be

> that no war can take place between any two member [countries] of the league until they have resorted to the machinery that the league proposes to furnish to settle the controversy likely to lead to war. If any member refuses to use this machinery and attacks another member of the league in breach of his league obligation, all members of the league agree to defend the members attacked by force.

While Americans thought about peace, the summer offensives of the European war were in full swing. The Germans pushed east through Poland and on into Russia, and on the western front had begun to use new machines of war: poison gas and zeppelins. These produced initial results, but were soon countered. Casualties mounted daily, but there was little progress for either side. Meanwhile the British were preparing surprises for the Turks and had other plans to widen the war steadily beyond the European continent.

At home in the United States there was much talk and agitation for women's suffrage. The widow of a prominent industrialist told a predominantly male gathering, "You men ought to know by this time that everything we do is for you. We work for you and slave for you; now we want to vote for you." Women picketed the White House, tried on several occasions to hand Wilson petitions, and were generally more strident, taking their cue from their English counterparts who were increasingly militant now that they were working in factories as part of the war effort. The Congressional Union for Women's Suffrage hoped

that Wilson would modify his position that votes for women was a
question of states' rights. After all, he had once changed his mind on the
Panama tolls and again on Mexico. The union said that it was

> interesting to note that on both these questions it is rather the
> pressure of necessity than force of argument that changed
> Mr. Wilson. It is the business of Suffragists to show him that
> it will help other measures which he has deeply at heart, and
> not hurt them, if he assists the passage of the federal amend-
> ment in Congress.

Nonetheless, Wilson continued to resist their pressure.

It was mid-June. McAdoo met House when he returned from Europe
and, at Wilson's behest, offered him the State Department. He
declined, and suggested that Robert Lansing was the man for the job
because "It would be better to have a man with not too many ideas of
his own." House felt if the Germans had not sunk the *Lusitania* or used
poison gas and zeppelins, he would have been able to force peace
negotiations by this time; but now he could see us drifting into war with
Germany because that was what the German naval and military factions seemed to want.

Woodrow conveyed all this to Edith. She loved it:

> Much as I enjoy your delicious love letters, that would make
> any woman proud and happy, I believe I enjoy even more the
> ones in which you tell me (as you did this morning) of what
> you are working on—the things that fill your thoughts and
> demand your best effort, for then I feel I am *sharing* your
> work and being taken into partnership as it were.

She reminded him that she was not simply a housewife, but had plenty
of responsibility: "I wonder if you ever think of me as a business woman,
going over ledgers, notes, and interest due in Banks, safeguarding
credits, etc., etc." In response he confided in her more, and liked to do
his work when she was near.

At last the moment came when they could go to Cornish. Edith went
first, with Margaret and the other women. Harlakenden was beautiful
and the weather was perfect. Wilson and Grayson followed shortly,
stopping over first on Long Island to see House. What would he think,
Wilson asked House, if he were to get married again? The president
added that Ellen had talked to him about remarriage before she died.

Though Grayson and others had written House of Wilson's infatuation, House feigned surprise at the move, then suggested Wilson postpone any marriage until the following year.

At Cornish, Edith and Woodrow were truly alone. The house was far away from prying eyes, and there wasn't even a hotel for reporters to stay at within twenty miles. Wilson strictly limited visitors. He did his work on the porch, holding Edith's hand while he wrote out notes. Large packets of important papers would arrive daily from Washington, and he shared their contents with her. In the evenings, he or other members of the family group would read aloud from his *History of the American People*. Around nine the others would retire to bed and leave them alone before the fire.

On June 29, after ardent talk—and it seems likely, lovemaking—and while suffused with the happiness of being together, Edith consented to their becoming engaged, secretly. She sealed her intent with a pledge: "I promise with all my heart absolutely to trust and accept my loved Lord, and unite my life with his without doubts or misgivings."

They were lovers in every way, now. Wilson pocketed the slip of paper and carried it about with him for a very long time. The family approved and told them both so. There followed nearly three more weeks of happiness in the country together; Wilson was relaxed, despite the worrisome state of affairs in the world. With Edith's hand in his he could deal with many problems—Japanese ships inexplicably off the Mexican coast, Huerta poised in Texas for another takeover attempt, the German reply to his second *Lusitania* note, Cary Grayson's wishes for promotion. When he left for Washington in mid-July, Wilson took with him a note from Edith:

> Your visit has been the happiest one for me, and you have forgotten nothing that would add to my comfort or pleasure. Thank you again for all the tender little things that made me feel your love, and for the real confidence and sharing of the big ones that make up your busy life.

Woodrow replied that "the Second Chapter has been sweeter than the first," and yearned from Washington to discuss his reply to Germany's new note with her as he had done with others during their weeks together.

In a long and important cabinet meeting on July 20, Wilson discussed the outlines of his new note to Germany. It would acknowledge that German actions in the months since the *Lusitania* had been restrained, and that therefore restraint was possible. It would ask again for reparations and assurances that such an incident would never happen again. He wrote to Edith that the note "is so direct and emphatic and uncompromising (I did not see how, in the circumstances, to make it anything else) that it brings us to the final parting of the ways, unless Germany yields—which, I fear, is most unlikely." Next morning, he continued:

> These days of heart-breaking responsibility, in which each twenty-four hours seems to count more than a decade of ordinary life-time, are binding us so close together by every kind of tie that some day we shall be grateful for them and look back to them as to the days when we really read one another's souls and *knew* that love and sympathy and comprehension had grown perfect between us—the time when the real marriage of our hearts was consummated.

In daily letters of sometimes more than twenty handwritten pages, Wilson poured out his affection and his recital of the day's work. Edith responded with equal frequency and fervor, though less length. In her memoirs, Edith says she consented to marry Wilson at this time but only after he was out of the White House, which both thought would mean after 1916. She wanted him to know she loved the man, not the office. The fact of their secret engagement resounds through the letters continually, along with the heartache of not being able to be together. "Without you," Wilson wrote, "I am maimed and imperfect."

> You are my ideal companion, the close and delightful *chum of my mind*. You are my perfect *playmate*, with whom everything that is gay and mirthful and imaginative in me is at its best. You are the sweetest *lover* in the world, full of delicacy and charm and tenderness and all the wonder of intimate self-revelation. . . . Those wonderful mornings when our minds grew to be intimate friends; those conferences in which our affairs and interests seemed to draw together and become merged; those afternoons of mere irresponsible companionship in the simple pleasures of a drive or a game of pool; those never-to-be-forgotten evenings when our hearts were opened to one another without reserve and with the joy of young lovers. . . .

So what if the British were going to place cotton on their contraband list and devastate the South? Wilson hurried back to Cornish on the twenty-third, the German note having been sent off. He would deal with the British from his vacation idyll. He and Edith spent happy hours in a hammock, repledged their love daily.

On the same day on which Wilson arrived back in Cornish, Secret Service agents W. H. Houghton and Frank Burke were in New York shadowing one of the leading pro-German propagandists in the country, editor George Sylvester Viereck. They followed him to the headquarters of the Hamburg-American steamship line on lower Broadway. At three, Viereck came out of the building with an older man who had a dueling scar on his face and a heavy briefcase in his hand. They got on the Sixth Avenue El. At Twenty-third Street, Viereck got off, shadowed by Houghton, leaving the other man to be tailed by Burke. When they reached Fiftieth Street the older German, waking from a snooze, ran out of the train leaving his briefcase behind. Burke grabbed it and started running. The German realized what he had done and gave chase. Burke jumped on a trolley and told the motorman the guy chasing him was crazy; the motorman responded with a burst of speed and Burke got away. He took the briefcase to headquarters, where it was discovered to belong to Dr. Heinrich F. Albert, the head of a system of "intrigue, conspiracy, and propaganda" on which the German government had already spent $28 million and which had done some minor sabotage to factories and ships aiding the Allied war effort. "Albert's portfolio," Viereck later wrote, "was a veritable box of Pandora; it unloosed every half-hatched plan of the Germans; the inner workings of the propaganda machine were laid bare. . . . The loss of that portfolio was like the loss of the Marne."

The contents of the briefcase were taken directly to McAdoo, who was on vacation in Maine. Mac conferred with Wilson, who suggested he get together with House and decide how best to utilize the explosive information. They decided it ought to go to Frank Cobb of *The New York World* on the condition that he at no time divulge where the information came from. The matter was so secret that Wilson—in this instance—even kept it from Edith.

At the beginning of August, Edith left Cornish for a month-long vacation with her friends the Roses, traveling up and down the Eastern states. When she was gone Wilson hardly knew what to do with his time. He played pool for both of them; when she didn't arrive at a certain stopping place on her schedule he called up every hotel in the area trying to find her.

On the anniversary of Ellen's death, he woke with a pang in his heart in the middle of the night to find himself exclaiming "Edith, my darling, *where are you?*" The desolation and loneliness at not finding her, he wrote, were "unspeakable."

Vacationing, she took golf lessons so she could play along with him. He counseled her to golf in the Scottish manner: "Take a fir-r-m hold on your cloob, but ye must'na sput on your hands."

Every day, he sent her the most important papers of state, annotated with little comments of his own. She was to read them and then send them back. During this period Edith learned that Garrison and Daniels had been given the task of writing specifications for new armaments and military enrollment programs; that Mexico was still in turmoil; that the marines had landed and had taken over Haiti; that the cotton controversy was coming to a head in England; that German civilian and military factions were vying over what course of action to take with the United States. Wilson's comments to Edith show how he was educating her for the tasks ahead:

On a German note:
The note about the *Frye* case makes an interesting suggestion about arbitration, don't you think so?

On Mexico; several papers:
This is the Carranzista attitude, which seems rather hopeless.
It is noticeable that those who are getting the worst of it are willing, and that the rest are not.

On a letter from House, enclosing one from von Bernstorff:
All this is true—only too true! I wish he had not put in the sentence I have marked in the margin. It is not how I will stand that I am thinking, but of what it is right to do. You see he does not advise, he puts it up to me!

On Garrison's plans for the army:
I have written the Sec'y of War that this is not what I wanted. It was evidently prepared with a view to publication. . . . This is a most superficial paper . . . but . . . the idea is not bad.

On starvation in Russia:
From our consul. Surely panicky and generally exaggerated. 10 millions!

On Haiti:
These poor chaps are between the devil and the deep sea.
They dare not offend us and yet if they yielded to us their
enemies would make a great case against them in any subsequent elections. But we must insist. Control of the customs is
the essence of the whole matter.

On a Gerard cable (Ambassador to Germany):
Is this not characteristic? . . . Instead of giving full and
adequate report of conversation . . . goes off into his opinion—"I told you so," in effect. Does he not seem pleased to
make things as black as possible?

On a Lansing report:
Don't you think Lansing does these things well?

On a Page letter (Ambassador to England):
It is a little provoking to have Page do this kind of thing. *Of
course* that is the view over there; but we know how crazy
they are to have us follow them. This makes me wish to order
P. to visit his native land!

In her own letters of this period, Edith comments on various papers
he has sent her, showing how she has read and tried to digest the
material. Wilson wrote her that he didn't expect comments on everything, that the papers were to enable her to share his thought:

Don't you see how comparatively easy it is to keep the
threads of even a very complicated public matter in your
head when some despatch or memorandum about it turns up
almost every day? You used to wonder that I could remember so much of so many things. You no doubt think it easy to
do yourself by this time.

Edith had to confess that her day was not as bright when the "big
envelope" did not accompany the little one of his "mush notes."

While the letters flew back and forth between the lovers, a movement
was gathering strength across the country for military preparedness.
Twelve hundred men, mostly college graduates from the Northeast,
went to Plattsburg, New York, in August for officer's training. The
Plattsburg movement—strictly voluntary—was under the direction of
General Leonard Wood, a Republican and an outspoken advocate of

preparedness. Wilson declined an invitation to speak at the camp, but it was generally felt he did not officially disapprove, and Colonel House had seen Wood before the camp started. When Wilson would not go to Plattsburg, Teddy Roosevelt made the commencement address.

Roosevelt's address stressed patriotism, and intimated only those as interested as he in preparedness had such a virtue. Wilson, though, was no less a patriot. When a military band on the White House lawn played the "Star Spangled Banner," he stood up at attention in his study, though there was no one to see him, and, he wrote Edith,

> had unutterable thoughts about my custody of the traditions and the present honour of that banner. I could hardly hold the tears back! And *then* the loneliness! The loneliness of the responsibility because the loneliness of the power, which no one *can* share. But in the midst of it I knew there was one who *did* share—*everything*—a lovely lady who has given herself to me. . . .

Edith languished with the Roses, played "auction" in the afternoons and evenings, and waited impatiently for Woodrow's letters. They were communicating via Ike Hoover. The faithful Hoover would bring a letter to the president, usually just after breakfast, and take one to be mailed at the same time. He would even go down to the Washington post office on Sundays to pick up Edith's letters, though the post office was closed.

In addition to their own courtship, Edith and Woodrow were now in the midst of two personal affairs: that of Grayson and Altrude Gordon, and of Edith's niece and a handsome Panamanian. When the president and Grayson returned to Washington, Altrude was so busy that she could only see her suitor for a short time before whisking herself off to Wyoming, a sequence of events which Wilson labeled "inscrutable." Grayson seemed calm about it, but Wilson wished he were happier. At the same time Edith's niece, Annie Litchfield's daughter, was madly in love with a Panamanian. Her parents were tearing their hair out over it. Edith counseled patience to all parties, saying, in effect, that if the girl had her heart set on marrying the man, there was little the parents could do that would not rebound badly on them. The marriage went forward. Wilson, reading her advice to the girl, admiringly told Edith that she always "thought a thing straight."

His letters were alternately chatty and passionate, and always beautifully handwritten. (She may not have known that he wrote some of them out in shorthand and then transcribed them.) She laid one of her letters next to one of his, and got depressed:

> I am ashamed of these badly written sheets after reading your letters, where even the clear, legible writing bespeaks perfection. But on the other hand the two letters are characteristic of our personalities and there is no use my trying to impress you with even a pretence of law and order. I am what I am—and as you love me forgive the blots—and over look the faults—and make me happy by your tender comprehension.

That summer Edith also received letters from Margaret and Jessie and Nell—warm, welcoming letters—and felt good about them. She decided to write to her own family and tell them of happiness. Her mother and sister sent notes to Wilson, who replied courteously.

In mid-August, the liner *Arabic* was sunk without warning and with loss of American life. In the light of the third message Wilson had sent to Germany about the *Lusitania*, the sinking of the *Arabic* looked as if it might lead to war. Wilson was worried. On the twenty-first, he wrote to Edith that only a short time had elapsed since they had known one another, and yet

> What more could have been crowded into a long year? That is the time within which the sinister effects of the war on the United States have been disclosed and the questions—of life and honour—thrust upon us, which it is my grievous duty to decide. My Darling came to me as a gift from Heaven. I would have grown old in these few weeks without her.

He was shot through with dread. If the facts proved as they first seemed, he would recall Gerard and the Germans would do the same with von Bernstorff, and although that might not necessarily lead to war—he was convinced we would not unilaterally declare war—the Germans might take it upon themselves to declare hostilities open, and then

> . . . we are at last caught in the maelstrom and our independence of action is lost: I must call Congress together and we are in for the whole terrible business. . . . These are solemn thoughts, my precious One, my little partner, and they seem

somehow to draw me nearer to you than ever. As things
thicken about me I more and more realize what you mean to
me, and more and more feel my dependence upon you to keep
the *darkness* off, hold the lamp of love for me to walk by,
keep the loneliness at bay by your loving, intimate companionship. . . .

Edith quickly replied that she would stand by him no matter what.

While the resolution of the crisis with Germany was pending, Edith
felt bold enough for the first time, having read hundreds of state papers
in the past months, to comment on some of Wilson's close advisers.

She supposed Tumulty was all right, despite his lower-class background, because he was loyal to Wilson. Grayson she liked thoroughly.
House, however, rubbed her the wrong way, even though she hadn't yet
met him:

> I can't help feeling he is not a very *strong* character. I
> suppose it is in comparison to you, for really every other man
> seems like a dwarf when I put them by you in my thoughts. I
> know what a comfort and a staff Col. House is to you . . .
> but he does look like a weak vessel and I think he writes like
> one very often. This is perfectly unnecessary for me to tell
> you this but it is such fun to shock you and you are so sweet in
> your judgments of people and I am so radical.

Wilson was forced to reply:

> You are no doubt partly right. . . . House has a strong
> character—if to be disinterested and unafraid and incorrupt-
> ible is to be strong. He has a noble and lovely character, too,
> for he is capable of utter self-forgetfulness and loyalty and
> devotion. And he is wise. . . . But you are right in thinking
> that intellectually he is not a great man. His mind is not of
> the first class. He is a counsellor, not a statesman. And he has
> the faults of his qualities. . . . You must remember, dear
> little critic, that sweetness and *power* do not often happen
> together.

Grayson, Wilson thought, was a fine and devoted companion, who
won each day anew his affectionate regard, but he was not "intellectually stimulating." Nor was Tumulty, except occasionally in purely political matters, as he kept his nose to the ground and let Wilson know what

people were thinking. As a matter of fact, "there is no one here who really interests me in the sense that he gives the day vitality, gives me something fresh or of his own coinage to think about. . . . I must admit that I am often bored."

As Labor Day neared, Edith went to New York with the Roses, and Wilson waited impatiently for her return. She told him that she had never written words of love to anyone before, that she was coming out of not only a sheltered, but an essentially vapid existence. Soon they would be together again:

> My precious weary Pilot, I will come and hold those dear strong hands that steer the ship in both my own, and kiss the tired eyes that have strained so to see the right course through the blackness ahead, and try to shut out the tumult that is raging around you on every side by whispering in your listening ears these tender words: "I love you, my precious Woodrow, and I will stand by though the waters dash over the ship, and carry out your orders, knowing that, if devotion to duty, strong purpose, and intelligent guidance count for anything in such a storm, the good ship will ride the waves and stand in all her white splendor fixed and calm in the still waters that follow after storms, and send her life boats to rescue and succour those vessels that have gone on the rocks around her; and all because of the strong hand that guided her wheel and the brain that directed her course."

On the first of September 1915, Germany sent a message proving, in effect, that the course the Pilot had steered through the difficult weeks since the *Lusitania* had been sunk had, at last, paid off. The German government pledged unequivocally to halt submarine warfare against unarmed liners. This German pledge, wrested by Wilson despite opposition from both the jingoes (of Roosevelt's ilk) and the pacifists (of Bryan's ilk), kept the United States out of war for the time being.

In early September, the papers rang with praise for the president.

Though Wilson knew that it was far from a final reckoning with Germany, the kaiser's pledge did, however, give him a period of grace in which to enjoy Edith's return to Washington.

Something had occurred during this month of parting: the hundreds of pages of their letters had brought them closer together intellectually and emotionally. Absence had not only made the heart grow fonder, it had enforced a discipline of thought on each of them, a searching discipline to find and articulate—and embellish—what it was they felt about each other. In effect during this period they defined their roles and responsibilities toward each other and these definitions were to inform both of them for the rest of their lives.

At that moment, though, they just took joy in being together. They worried about too much publicity, made a pact not to write to each other on certain days—and both broke the pact within twenty-four hours. On September 6, Edith's mother and other relatives came to the White House for tea. After this, Wilson wished to announce their engagement publicly so they could spend time together in public.

This prospect was anathema to Wilson's closest political advisers. Over the summer both Tumulty and McAdoo had expressed doubts about the wisdom of early remarriage. White House staffers, though, were saying quite openly that the boss was "a goner." Edmund Starling of the Secret Service, detailed to keep Wilson in sight at all times, tried hard to look the other way when Woodrow and Edith interrupted their daily rides for long, amorous walks in Rock Creek Park, but could hardly do so, duty interfering with his Kentucky gentleman's sense of propriety. The chief would leap over rock barriers with the playfulness of a man half his years, and embrace Edith for long moments in the shade of the autumn trees.

In early September a group of cabinet members met unofficially to discuss the situation. All liked Mrs. Galt, and felt that Wilson should eventually remarry, but all were worried that remarriage close on the heels of Ellen's death would shock the electorate—perhaps especially those new voters, women—and end in Wilson's defeat at the polls in 1916 (and their own removal from office). A thankless job was awarded to Daniels, Wilson's oldest friend among the cabinet members: he should tell the president how they felt. But Daniels did not feel inclined to exchange his secretary's chair for

> the difficult and perhaps dangerous high and exalted position
> of Minister Plenipotentiary and Envoy Extraordinary to the
> Court of Cupid on a mission in which neither my heart nor
> my head was enlisted and in the performance of which my
> official head might suffer decapitation.

He declined, and no other cabinet member took it upon himself in official capacity to warn Wilson.

However, McAdoo had more than official status and more than ordinary interest in the matter. A Wilson defeat in 1916 would mean the crushing of Mac's own long-range political plans. Learning from Grayson that Wilson had sent Mrs. Hulbert money, and knowing that there were letters between the two, Mac concocted out of whole cloth a fake anonymous letter "sent" to him from California, about Wilson and Mrs. Hulbert. Exactly when this missive was written is not known, but there are hints of the desperateness of the situation in a coded letter of Grayson to Colonel House on September 10:

> Mr. Thomas [Wilson] is going to ask your opinion on an extremely delicate matter the next time he sees you, and he thinks that as soon as the weather permits you will be coming here. . . . He wants to know your opinion—from a political viewpoint—the effect it would have on the country, if it [the engagement] was announced this fall. He contemplates asking Hudson's [McAdoo's] opinion on this same subject. Hudson has expressed himself strongly—that it would be a fatal mistake; but Thomas has never in any manner whatever, alluded to the subject to Hudson. I am absolutely convinced that your judgment—not to talk to him about it, was wise advice. He has on his own initiative mentioned the matter to me in various ways. I know that he would resent anyone speaking to him about it. His whole mind and all is so absorbed on this subject that it seems a shame for anyone to have to give him an opinion contrary to his wishes. There are many angles to the question—That California situation [i.e., Mrs. Hulbert]—which I told you about . . . is embarrassing. It is important that I see you upon arrival.

The day this note was written, the United States learned of the sinking of still another ship. There was renewed pressure on Washington to break off diplomatic relations; von Bernstorff expressed his frustration in a private letter to the German chancellor, saying, "An evil star seems to hang over German-American negotiations on the submarine war. . . . Every time one seems to have reached the goal a new incident occurs to prevent further progress."

On September 12, in the clutch of the renewed foreign problems, Wilson wrote a pledge to Edith that was to be the mate of the one she gave him in Cornish. He begged her to keep it by her side as he did with hers. All that remained was to get House's permission, and they would announce the engagement. Meanwhile, it was so unbearably hot in Washington that Grayson thought the president might collapse. While they were waiting for the colonel—who could absolutely *not* come until the heat abated—McAdoo took the initiative and came to see Wilson with "grave news."

It was probably on Saturday, the eighteenth of September. We don't know precisely what Mac said to his father-in-law, but it is clear he either showed to Wilson, or told him about, an anonymous letter from California, which said that Mrs. Hulbert was showing Wilson's private letters around the state, and was bragging that he had given her money. The letter also evidently said that, should Wilson announce his engagement to Mrs. Galt, Mrs. Hulbert was prepared to make her whole involvement with Wilson public. There were enough half-truths and invented possibilities in this information Mac gave to the president to make him believe in its reality.

The outcome of the Wilson-McAdoo meeting was a note, in extremely agitated handwriting, to Edith.

> Dearest,
>   There is something, personal to myself, that I feel I must tell you about at once, and I am going to take the extraordinary liberty of asking you if I may come to your house this evening at 8, instead of your coming here to dinner. You will understand when I have a chance to explain, and will, I believe, think even this extraordinary request justified and yourself justifyed in granting it. I love you with the full, pure passion of my whole heart and *because* I love you beg this supreme favour.
>   With a heart too full for words,
>
>   Your own
>   Woodrow

Wilson arrived at eight, and was received inside, crossing that portico he had never before passed though both he and Edith had dreamed of the day on which he would. Great care had been taken to confuse any press vehicles which might have followed the president, and the whole visit was shrouded in secrecy.

Woodrow probably informed Edith that some Republicans who hated him and who wished to ruin him had gotten hold of his financial dealings with Mary Hulbert, and were preparing to drag him, Mrs. Hulbert, and herself through the muck in order to discredit him. The central fact in the supposed wrongdoing was that Wilson had given Mrs. Hulbert $15,000 to shut her mouth about certain alleged affairs in the past. Wilson told Edith that there was not a shred of truth in the allegations, and that he would have no cause to wince even if his entire correspondence with Mary Hulbert were to be published. He felt he could not, in conscience, allow Edith to be embarrassed along with him, and that he was therefore releasing her from her promise. That is, their engagement was broken.

7

THE ROAD WHERE LOVE LEADS

AS TO WHAT precisely happened next, there are two reports. The first is in Edith's book, *My Memoir*. In it she writes that Wilson was too upset to deliver the dire message himself, and instead sent the faithful Grayson to do so. Edith told Grayson that she would give Wilson her answer in the morning, and then sat up thinking all night. Finally she wrote a letter saying that she would stand by him, and sent it early in the morning. That day—Sunday—passed with no reply, as did Monday and Tuesday. On Wednesday afternoon Grayson arrived and asked her to come to the White House because the president was ill with a malady that seemed to have no somatic origin, and "you are the only person who can help." Grayson said Wilson had not asked to see her because such a plea would have been weak and unfair, but the doctor begged her to come because Wilson looked as he imagined martyrs did when they had been broken on the wheel. Edith agreed to go with him. On reaching the White House, she was ushered into a darkened room, where she saw on the bed a "white, drawn face with burning eyes dark with hidden pain." As Brooks the valet withdrew, a hand was held out to her in welcome. Taking it, she found it deathly cold, and warmed it in hers, and everything was all right between them. She asked if he had received the letter she had sent, and he said only yes. Months later he revealed to her that he had never opened it, fearful of what it might contain. They opened it together, and he made her promise that that beautiful letter would never be destroyed.

The touching bedside scene—alas!—is almost certainly poppycock, according to the evidence of the pair's letters.

What probably happened is that Wilson showed up that fateful night, and told her of his problem, and courteously offered to release her from the engagement. Agitated at the news, Edith perhaps momentarily agreed to be released, but then told Wilson that love would persevere somehow. This, basically, was what Wilson wanted to know; having done his duty as a gentleman, and having received the assurance he craved, he returned to the White House, more or less satisfied that they would remain together, even if there should be some mud slung at them.

But two letters were indeed written in the early morning hours of September 19. They follow in full:

1308 Twentieth Street   Sept 19, 1915

Dearest:

The dawn has come—and the hideous dark of the hour before the dawn has been lost in the gracious gift of light.

I have been in the big chair by the window, where I have fought out so many problems, and all the hurt, selfish feeling has gone with the darkness—and I now see straight—straight into the heart of things and am ready to follow the road "where love leads."

How many times I have told you I wanted to help—and now when the first test has come I faltered—But the faltering was *for* love—not lack of love. I am not afraid of any gossip or threat, with your love as my shield—and even now this room aches with your voice—as you plead, "Stand by me—don't desert me!"

This is my pledge, dearest one, I will stand by you—not for duty, not for pity, not for honour—but for love—trusting, protecting, comprehending love. And no matter whether the wine be bitter or sweet we will share it together and find happiness in the comradeship.

Forgive my unreasonableness tonight (I mean last night, for it is already Sunday morning), and be willing to trust me.

I have not thought out what course we will follow for the immediate present for I promised we would do that together.

I am so tired I could put my head down on the desk and go

to sleep—but nothing could bring me real rest until I had pledged you my love and my allegiance.

> Your own
> Edith

Wilson's reply—not to the letter, but to the events of the previous night—is written in a clear, firm hand, unlike the note of Saturday afternoon.

The White House   Sunday, 7.20 A.M.
19 Sept., 1915

My noble, incomparable Edith,

I do not know how to express or analyze the conflicting emotions that have surged like a storm through my heart all night long. I only know that first and foremost in all my thoughts has been the glorious confirmation you gave me last night—without effort, unconsciously, as of course—of all I have ever thought of your mind and heart. You have the greatest soul, the noblest nature, the sweetest, most loving heart I have ever known, and my love, my reverence, my admiration for you, you have increased in one evening as I should have thought only a life-time of intimate, loving association could have increased them. You are more wonderful and lovely in my eyes than you ever were before; and my pride and joy and gratitude that you should love me with such a perfect love are beyond all expression, except in some great poem which I cannot write. But I am equally conscious that it is anything but pride and joy and gratitude or happiness that the evening brought you; that it brought you, instead of a confirmation of your ideal of me, an utter contradiction of it, dismay rather than happiness, uneasiness in the place of confident hope—the love that is solicitude and pity, not admiration and happy trust—and that intolerable thought has robbed me of sleep. When it was the deepest, most passionate desire of my heart to bring you happiness and sweep away shadow from your path, I have brought you, instead, mortification and thrown a new shadow about you. Surely no man was ever more deeply punished for a folly long ago loathed and repented of—but the bitterness of it ought not to fall on you, in the prime of your glorious, radiant womanhood, when you embody in this perfection, for all who

know you, the beauty of purity and grace and sweet friendship and gracious, unselfish counsel. I am the most unde-
servedly honoured man in the world and your love, which I
have least deserved, is the crowning honour of my life. I have
tried, ah, *how* I have tried to expiate folly by disinterested
service and honourable, self-forgetful, devoted love, and it
has availed only to lead the loveliest, sweetest woman in all
the world, for whom I would joyfully give my life, to mortification and dismay. May God forgive me as freely as he has
punished me! You have forgiven me with a love that is divine,
and that redeems me from everything but the bitterness of
having disappointed you. For all but a little space I have tried
for a whole laborious life-time of duty to be worthy of such
love; but the little space defeats the life-time and brings me to
you stained and unworthy. I humbly sue for leave to love you,
as one who has no right to sue, and yet I know all the time
that I am offering you a love as pure, as deep, as void of
selfishness and full of utter devotion as any man ever offered
any woman, worthy even of your acceptance. I know I have
no rights, but I also know that it would break my heart and
my life if I could not call you my Darling and myself

Your own
Woodrow

There was no terrible, inexplicable illness in the next few days, nor
did Wilson pocket Edith's letter of the dawn and not open it, because his
own letters over the next several days refer to that one of hers. In fact,
they actually spent time together, and talked over a special telephone
line installed between their two residences. Earlier they had not trusted
to telephones because most at that time were party lines on which many
people might listen. Edith had, only a week or so previous to the
dramatic incident, suggested the special installation of the private
line.

If McAdoo had hoped to end or at least postpone the engagement, he
failed. Wilson felt that the incident had deepened the bonds between
him and Edith, forged them in common fire. He wrote her of love in
terms of redemption, pledged to repay her trust with "a life-time of
devotion." In her own letters of that week, Edith declared that "this
earthquake has left our love untouched," and that they must rebuild
their city on such a firm foundation that no other cataclysm could touch
it. Weathering the storm, they had both found new courage, deeper
commitment.

Before they announced the engagement, though, Wilson still wanted to speak to Colonel House, who was scheduled to arrive at the White House on September 22. On the eve of House's arrival, Wilson wrote Edith that he had only dreaded the public revelation because it would have given a "tragically false impression" of his own character, but concluded that it would be far worse to let

> the contemptible error and madness of a few months seem a stain upon my whole life. But now I know that to permit myself to live under the domination of such a fear and allow it to govern the whole course of my life in the matters of deepest concern to me—deprive me of my happiness and peace of mind—would be even more inconsistent with my true character than the offense itself.

Before coming to the White House, Colonel House had a talk with McAdoo, who was still terribly concerned over the impending engagement. After dinner with the family, House and Wilson retired to the study, where Wilson put all his cards on the table. He told him about the long-ago affair with Mrs. Peck, but added that his letters to her, though they may have been somewhat indiscreet, would probably not compromise him. He showed House a note he had written, for use should the letters be published. It began with his own summary: "Even while it lasted, I knew and made explicit what it *did not* mean. It did not last, but friendship and genuine admiration ensued." His statement said he was ashamed of the letters, that the purity of the lady in question was not in any way compromised, that the letters had been stolen from her. Nevertheless,

> These letters are genuine, and I am now ashamed of them— not because the lady to whom they are addressed was not worthy of the most sincere admiration and affection, but because I did not have the moral right to offer her the ardent affection which they express.

Wilson told House about the purchase of the Hulbert mortgages, and he also told him that, on learning of the affair, Edith had been splendidly supportive. What, he asked, should they do now?

First, House told Wilson that the letters written to Mary Hulbert were harmless, and that there would be no blackmail. Wilson was relieved, even though he had decided that he would not knuckle under to blackmail and would have let the letters be published if it came to that.

House did not tell Wilson his own conclusion, that McAdoo's letter was a phony.* He praised Wilson for his courage. He also gave high marks to Mrs. Galt for the way she had handled the situation, and gave his blessing for an announcement of the engagement in early October. There was, he concluded to his diary, no stopping the president on this matter, in any case.

In later years, Edith believed that House and McAdoo had been in on a plot to prevent the engagement, but the documentary evidence absolves the colonel of this particular intrigue. He seems to have understood, where other intimates did not, that to interfere with Wilson's wishes at this time would have been counterproductive.

On September 26 Wilson wrote to Ellen's relatives to tell them of his forthcoming engagement. In subsequent letters he told his own relatives and friends of his "great happiness and blessing." But before the public announcement the lovers still had to be secretive, a condition which prompted Wilson to write Edith a letter in the form of a dialogue between "W. W." and "The Imp Anxiety" which took place in "a dark bed-room" at four in the morning. The Imp squatted on W.W.'s solar plexus and needled him about the sadness he had seen on Edith's face, which they traced psychologically back to her reluctance to face the publicity that would follow the announcement of the engagement, and her simultaneous wish to be done with subterfuge. The Imp warned W.W. to let Edith alone when he was too tired to love her as she ought to be loved—and to deliver up the announcement, post-haste.

And, indeed, Edith was anxious to have everything made public, for she was tired of having to clear her visits to Wilson through third parties, tired of being unable to have her lover visit her openly. As she wrote him on September 30:

> I have never had to ask permission to do things in my whole life, I have always just done them, and that ended it. And I have seldom even discussed what I was going to do. Now, while I know it must be different, when things are all discussed and consulted over I get impatient, and restless. . . .

After dinner at the White House on October 6, Edith and Woodrow went into the president's study where Wilson typed out, from a first

---

*There is some evidence that House knew about McAdoo's letter before it was shown to Wilson, but that he concealed his knowledge.

draft by Stock Axson, an announcement of the engagement to be given to the press. It told a bit about Edith, then described how Wilson's daughters had brought her into the family circle. As this latter paragraph only opened the door to innumerable questions, reporters given the note by Tumulty were tactful enough to quote only the first paragraph. Tumulty gave out another release at the same time, announcing that Wilson would vote for women's suffrage in New Jersey. He somehow felt that these two announcements would balance one another, salve for wrath.

Next day the couple began to be seen in public together for the first time. In photographs taken just then, one can see the ecstatic happiness on Woodrow's face, the slight awe at the public nature of it all on Edith's. Wilson called on Edith's mother, then entertained the Bollings and McAdoos at dinner. Plans were made for a December wedding that would be private and at Edith's house rather than at the White House. Next morning Grayson, Tumulty, Edith, Wilson, Helen Bones, and Mrs. Bolling started for New York, with crowds of people gathered about to see what Edith looked like.

Public reaction seemed mostly favorable, but the "cave dwellers"—the Washington socialites—sniffed at this woman whose background was "trade." Bryan was outraged, feeling the sentiment he had expressed at the time of Ellen's death was wasted. Others whispered that perhaps Wilson had been involved with Edith before Ellen died. There were still further ugly rumors that the president had neglected Ellen's grave, though all a Hearst reporter could find was that the tombstone had not yet been erected. Other reporters assaulted the Galt's store to try to get employees to say bad things about Edith. They failed. In the West and Midwest it was reported that women had organized meetings to express their disapproval of the engagement.

Most people seemed merely curious about the new woman in the president's life, thrilled for her, and happy for their chief executive. Wilson's exuberance was so manifest in the period right after the announcement of the engagement that few could resist his charm.

The primary purpose of going to New York was to introduce Edith to House and his family. When they arrived, House had thirteen engagement rings waiting for the couple to view. A jeweler had sent them over, and House had liked twelve of them. But rather than send one back, he kept all thirteen, for that was the president's lucky number (and the amount of letters in the name Woodrow Wilson). Edith chose one. Then they all went to the theater to see a play called *Grumpy*. The evening passed pleasantly, and over the next few weeks Edith and House wrote to each other; House sent her a birthday present, flowers, and a book which he forgot to inscribe, and which had to be sent back for his signature.

The day after the theater party, the engaged couple and Mrs. Bolling went to Philadelphia to see the Red Sox and the Phillies in the second game of the World Series. Tumultuous crowds met them on arrival and nearly prevented their entrance to the stadium, where Wilson threw out the first ball. An avid fan, Wilson was the first president to attend a World Series game. The party all returned to Washington late in the afternoon, and next morning, accompanied by Woodrow's cousins, they all went to see the president's brother Joseph and his family in Baltimore. Starling and other Secret Servicemen were so exhausted by this whirlwind moving about that they hoped their weekend was over, but Wilson surprised them by motoring to Edith's home for dinner. Then he wanted to walk back to the White House at about midnight.

He went to Edith's for dinner regularly in the next weeks. Colonel Starling didn't mind, he later wrote; all the Secret Servicemen "were glad the boss had made good." After many hours of waiting outside Edith's door or in her lobby, Starling would welcome the walk back with Wilson:

> I remember those October and November nights—the air was clear, and just cold enough to make me conscious of my skin and the tip of my nose. The sky was spattered with stars, and sometimes there was a moon. We walked briskly, and the President danced off the curbs and up them as we crossed streets. If we had to wait for traffic—delivery trucks were all we found abroad at that hour—he jigged a few steps, whistling an accompaniment for himself. There was a tune he had heard in vaudeville which he liked, and almost unconsciously, it seemed, he would whistle it as he waited for something— for the caddy to hand him a club on the golf links, or a milk truck to pass us on the corner of N Street. He whistled softly, through his teeth, tapping out the rhythm with restless feet: "Oh, you beautiful doll! You great big beautiful doll! Let me put my arms around you, I can hardly live without you. . . ."

Starling had been ordered not to let newspaper photographers snap Wilson leaving Mrs. Galt's house—which, he reports, was for photographers like waving a red flag in front of a bull. Starling caught one man with a camera in Edith's shrubbery, lifted him up by the armpits, and scared him half witless.

After the notes to his relatives, Wilson had sent a letter announcing the engagement to Mary Hulbert. She was so outraged that he had said nothing of it at all during the long spring and summer of her negotiations with him that she wrote back angrily; their correspondence stopped and was never really resumed. Other friends were more joyful, for those who knew him well understood how important a woman like Edith was to Woodrow Wilson.

With each passing month the European war absorbed more of the president's time. As the mud began to get colder and freeze toward mid-October, there were last-minute maneuvers before the winter set in. On October 12, British nurse Edith Cavell was executed by a German firing squad in Brussels: her crime had been helping certain British prisoners of war escape to England. Young, beautiful, serene under sentence of death, Edith Cavell became a martyr, a rallying point for English-speaking people during the war. The conflict dragged on far longer than either side had initially expected.

German propaganda told the German people that the war was an essentially religious one for "trial, cleansing, simplification, introspection" and would lead to a Germany which would rise from the trenches repurified. The French painted it as a war against men who commit "unspeakable offenses against the innocent, the wounded, and the aged" and told the soldiers of France that even if they died, their glory would live on. A foot soldier in a muddy trench could not help but wonder why he was out in the no-man's-land or, for that matter,

> Why, indeed, this whole war? Is it not almost madness to murder each other? Why should just I have to give up my life? Couldn't we simply make an end of this mad war by mutual agreement? Has this entire conflict, indeed, any sense whatever?

Americans as a whole had the same thoughts and still wanted to stay out of the war, even as events moved inexorably toward our involvement. In New York on October 15, J. P. Morgan loaned a half-billion dollars to the British and French governments. In the opinion of von Bernstorff, it was only Wilson who was keeping America out of the war. He wrote to Berlin that:

* * *

One can think about the President as he likes; one may consider him neutral or not. But it cannot be denied that his whole heart is committed to the cause of peace. A Republican President could not have resisted the combined anti-German pressure of Wall Street, the press, and the so-called high society.

Von Bernstorff worked hard against the wishes of his own government to conciliate the United States. On the British side, there were more provocations: a British ship disguised as a tramp steamer flying the American flag sank a U-boat, then machine-gunned the submarine's crew in the water.

These international problems seemed insoluble, but one personal problem could be countered. Overflowing with his own happiness and prospective marriage to Edith, Wilson helped smooth Grayson's tempestuous affair with Altrude Gordon. The two youngsters agreed to marry, though the announcement would not be made public for some time: the junior lovers could not, of course, upstage the senior ones.

General Huerta, unable to return to his native land, lay dying in a hospital on the Texas-Mexican border. The Wilson administration finally let Venustiano Carranza know that the United States would recognize the legitimacy of his claims to the government of Mexico, because he seemed the only available answer to the riddle of Mexican stability.

On November 2, the New Jersey voters defeated women's suffrage by a large measure despite Wilson's appeal. Ex-President Taft, who had been outraged at the announcement of the president's engagement, especially coupled as it was with the New Jersey suffrage pledge, was happy that the New Jersey voters clapped Wilson "right on the nose where he ought to be hit." That election day was good for main-line Republicans such as Taft, for the Republican party regained control of legislatures in New York and New Jersey, showing that the party's voters were returning to the fold.

On November 4 and 5, Wilson came out swinging on two fronts. At a private dinner in New York he outlined plans which Garrison and Daniels had made for a strengthened army and navy, said he would put these to Congress for approval at the next session. This was embracing preparedness in a concrete way. Simultaneously he instructed Walter Page in London to give to Grey a lengthy memorandum expressing American displeasure at British abrogation of our maritime rights. This memo refused to recognize the British Order in Council of the previous March as legal, and also refused to recognize the British Prize Courts because they were working under that order. The British saw in the note evidence of the moral collapse of the United States government—the usual British response when Washington refused to go along with what London wanted.

Many applauded Wilson's first step in beefing up the military—but not all. Pacifists were alarmed and, on the other side, Teddy Roosevelt fumed at "half-preparedness" and called Wilson's program a milquetoast gesture. Yet Roosevelt's day seemed about over. The staid *New York Times* was bemused at Roosevelt as he lashed out in this latest controversy:

> Scanning the gall and vinegar of his adjectives, hearing the curious staccato of impetuous speech, the indulgent critic can only take refuge in the theory of the Everlasting Juvenile, the boy who has never grown up, as Dr. Eliot said of him. As Mrs. Berry in *The Ordeal of Richard Feverel* remarked delightedly of Dick's baby, "Ain't he got passion? Ain't he a splendid roarer?"

Roosevelt said much privately that was unprintable, including some things about Wilson and his bride-to-be. Newspaper reporters and photographers followed Wilson and Edith as if they were a royal couple. In New York, visiting with the Houses, Edith was forced to employ such ingenious devices as stalking-horse cars, back entrances, and rear elevators to escape the press. It was not to her liking. She stayed with Altrude on West Tenth Street in Greenwich Village, ventured out to get her wedding dress fitted properly. Once the president came to the door to see her there, and they wrote back and forth while the fittings went on.

Rumors about the president's supposed earlier amours heated up again. One paper had Mrs. Hulbert instituting breach-of-promise proceedings against Wilson. Others were dredging up stories about Edith's past. For some reason, no one informed the president about the rumors, though Edith (who read the papers whereas Wilson did not) heard them all, and they hurt her. Finally an old friend of the president's, Birmingham publisher Frank P. Glass, who had known Wilson since undergraduate days at Princeton, was persuaded by a number of political leaders to broach the subject of the rumors to the president. Glass at first talked in generalities, but Wilson questioned him closely until he got the full story, telling his friend he was rendering a great service by letting him in on the rumors. Glass told Ray Stannard Baker that "Before he got all of my story, tears came into his eyes, while his voice and demeanor showed that he was profoundly moved. He had not imagined that his enemies could be so unjust, so cruel." Wilson thanked Glass profusely for telling him the truth, a service which none of his usual intimates seemed willing to perform.

Wilson appeared so busy with his personal life that it seemed to House that he was neglecting state business (though Wilson comments on state papers were still being penned). House was miffed because the president had not written him in two weeks. On November 22, he told his diary:

> I would go to Washington, but I know I would not be very welcome at this time, if I attempted to stir him to action. . . . One peculiar phase of the President's character develops itself more fully from time to time, that is, he "dodges trouble." Let me put up something to him that is disagreeable and I have great difficulty in getting him to meet it. I have no doubt that some of the trouble he had at Princeton was caused by this delay in meeting vexatious problems.

> Another phase of his character is his intense prejudice against people. He likes a few and is very loyal to them, but his prejudices are many and often unjust. He finds great difficulty in conferring with men against whom, for some reason, he has a prejudice and in whom he can find nothing good.

The president eventually mollified the colonel with a phone call, saying he hadn't written because he'd been busy drafting his annual message to Congress—but from this time onward, House's diary reflects his increasing upset at Wilson, as if the colonel were a rejected lover. Wilson, however, continued to have good feelings toward House. In fact, about this time his hopes of mediating peace rose again, and House was to be his envoy. In answer to British and German feelers, Wilson asked House to make plans to return to Europe. Perhaps a year of killing and stalemate had induced the warring governments to consider sane alternatives to the seemingly endless war.

As House's plans firmed, Henry Ford began his own voyage for peace. In November, Ford had read a report of a battle in which 20,000 men had been killed in twenty-four hours without changing the position of either side one foot. Ford had strode into the hall outside his Detroit office and claimed he would be willing to spend half his fortune to shorten the war by just a single day. A reporter noted down every word. Pacifists led by Rosika Schwimmer and Louis Lochner of the Carnegie Peace Endowment got Ford to finance a gigantic "peace ship" which would go to Europe to persuade the belligerent governments by the power of oratory to "get the boys out of the trenches and home by Christmas." Said the *Boston Traveler*, "It is not Mr. Ford's purpose to make peace; he will assemble it." Other papers were not so kind, and neither was the Wilson administration. Though the president did see Ford before the auto man left on December 4. But the *Oscar II*, with fifty-four newspapermen, three newsreelers, a staff of twenty, and sixty-some delegates, sailed without official blessings.

The day of the peace ship's departure, the White House announced that the Wilson-Galt wedding would take place on the eighteenth of December. On the seventh, Wilson gave to the newly assembled Congress his annual message, which included preparedness plans and a report on foreign negotiations. After this his mind was on the plans for the wedding. The guest list was extremely small: the families, members of the cabinet, and members of the White House staff.

The state of California had sent a nugget of gold for Edith's wedding ring. There was enough left over to make a scarf pin for the president which was a miniature of the presidential seal, and a signature ring in which were engraved the shorthand characters he used to write "Woodrow Wilson." Preparations mounted, and ran into the usual last-minute tangles: the bishop who was scheduled to perform the ceremony canceled out, miffed that his wife would not be invited to the wedding; so Edith got two local clergymen, one from hers, and one from Woodrow's church, to officiate. Ike Hoover, who had served so well as the pair's go-between, was detailed to get the marriage license.

The day of the wedding, the president worked through the daylight hours, sending notes, doing his usual business. The wedding was to take place in the evening. Brooks the valet, who had long been trying to get the president to dress in a manner befitting his high station, had gotten a cutaway coat and striped trousers for the bridegroom. Edith wore a plain black velvet gown, a velvet hat trimmed with goura, and—of course—orchids. Secretly the pair spent a half-hour before the ceremony upstairs, then came down together to Edith's drawing room, which Hoover had filled with flowers.

The ceremony was brief. Edith's mother gave her away. Colonel House, whom many had expected to see as best man, had told Wilson only three days ago that he was too busy with the preparations for his forthcoming trip to attend (he left ten days later). Wilson had no best man. The wedding couple stayed for a brief period to receive the guests;

during this time, Altrude Gordon whispered to Stock Axson that she, too, would soon be wed.

Then came the difficult task of getting away for the honeymoon without benefit of press coverage. The Secret Service planted a "leak," saying the couple would leave from Union Station. It was a ruse. Not even the train's engineer knew where he was going when he was ordered to a siding in Alexandria. The bridal couple fled in an unmarked car in a zigzag pattern through dark streets. At the Alexandria yard Starling waved their car down by flashlight. A few signals got crossed and the newly married Wilsons had to wait for a half-hour until they could board the train, but no one seemed to mind very much. Heading for Hot Springs, Virginia, the pair had a wedding supper of chicken salad and retired for the evening. The train pulled into the resort city about seven the next morning. As Starling emerged into the sitting room of the private car he saw

> a figure in top hat, tailcoat, and gray morning trousers, standing with his back to me, hands in his pockets, happily dancing a jig. As I watched him he clicked his heels in the air, and from whistling the tune he changed to singing the words, "Oh, you beautiful doll! You great big beautiful doll. . . ."

The mountains were white with the snow that had fallen during the previous day and night. The Homestead Hotel was beautiful, and their suite was not only charming, but overlooked the golf course on which Wilson was determined they would soon play, despite the weather. Flowers filled the room. After a breakfast, the pair sat and held hands for a while, then decided to write a few notes. "The weather is cold but radiant," Edith wrote to her mother, "and so are we."

8

HE KEPT US OUT OF WAR

WOODROW AND EDITH Wilson had to cut short their honeymoon and return to the White House in early January of 1916. Another ship carrying Americans had been sunk, and the incident looked grave. Also, the president was eager to join battle with the opponents of his preparedness program: pacifists thought it unnecessary; militarists viewed it as inadequate.

While the couple was away, several changes had been made in the living quarters of the White House. Ellen and Woodrow had used separate bedrooms. Now Wilson's single bed was removed and the enormous, canopied Lincoln bed, eight feet by five-and-a-half feet, installed in its place. Edith and Woodrow would sleep together in it.

For years Wilson had taken breakfast with Ellen downstairs in a formal room at eight. He and Edith, on the other hand, awoke about six, ate a snack in their room, then played golf before returning to a more substantial breakfast again in their room at eight. After this they went to Woodrow's office, where Edith would often stay with him as he dictated. From ten to ten-thirty, the stenographer was dismissed and the president worked alone, or with Edith by his side. At ten-thirty he would see her to the door with a farewell kiss, and have appointments lasting three to five minutes each until one o'clock, when he and Edith had an hour's lunch together. Longer conferences began at two, and whenever possible the president and Edith went for a late afternoon drive. Dinner was at seven, often with more work after it—together—if there were no guests, and the Wilsons would retire for the night between ten and eleven.

Edith had no interests but her husband's and attended to these assiduously, trying to keep him relaxed and at his best, to make his job easier by providing occasional distraction. She accompanied him to golf, shepherded his dietary restrictions (no Charlotte Russe, his favorite dessert), and spruced up his appearance. Valet Brooks noted that under Edith's influence, Wilson took more interest in his own clothes. The couple began to dress in the evenings when they went out—often to see a vaudeville show. Wilson had always loved this amusement, and had not gone since Ellen died.

Edith made arrangements to sell her Twentieth Street house, but retained part ownership in Galt's. An accomplished businesswoman, she took over the household management of the White House and of Wilson's personal finances. She did not require or seek, as Ellen had done, the professional advice of Colonel House.

She also began to act as a shield against people Wilson did not want to see (hordes of tourists) and against letters with which he should not be bothered (pleas from Mary Hulbert for a conference about people "shadowing" her). From the very first she routinely took on the duties of a presidential assistant. Wilson received over three hundred letters a day, many of them marked "personal," and the White House staff routinely opened all but those known to be from such intimates as House, summarized many, answered even more. About twenty a day reached Wilson's desk. Many more went out over his signature. Through his years in office Wilson refused to use a machine to duplicate his signature and signed numerous form letters daily. In 1916, for instance, an average of four babies a day were saddled with the Woodrow or Wilson monikers; all parents who so notified the White House, often sending pictures to prove their claims, got hand-signed letters thanking them for the compliment. One set of triplets was named Wilson, McAdoo, and Bryan.

As 1916 began, three million women were wearing their hair in Mary Pickford style. Sixty blocks of a steeltown in Ohio were destroyed by a mob of thousands in the wake of a strike. Popular advertising had increased astronomically: a single magazine page carried ads for a pyorrhea preparation, a dictionary stand, a razor-blade sharpener, cough drops, and *The Secrets of Tangled Diplomacy in the Balkans* by "an anonymous high political personage."

Behind the scenes on the diplomatic front, Wilson was trying to mediate between the belligerents: in mid-January he was suggesting to the Allies that they disarm merchantmen, in return for a promise he was trying to extract from the Germans to surface and search vessels before attacking them. At the same time, the ban Bryan had long advocated— on Americans traveling on belligerent ships—was put on the congressional agenda. Wilson fought it. In January as well, Mexican bandits killed some American mineworkers, causing Senators Lodge and Albert Bacon Fall to immediately press for war. Wilson beat them back, admonishing Carranza to locate and punish the bandits.

Finding his programs misunderstood and blocked in Congress— especially his preparedness plan—Wilson decided to take to the hustings. This being an election year, the trip would help test the waters. Edith went with him, and at every stop audiences demanded to see the new First Lady and greeted her with enormous applause. Once again the political soothsayers had been wrong: controversy over the second marriage seemed dead as a doornail.

Wherever Wilson appeared in person he changed minds. Admitting he would be ashamed had he not learned something in almost three years on the job, he said his own stance on preparedness had changed. People listened. In Des Moines, he "won many to the side of preparedness and set others to thinking," the local paper said; in Topeka "the farmers did not cheer, but they thought," and in Cleveland he "presented no escape from the compelling logic of the case" and converted many to his position. Letters by the thousands started pouring in to balky congressmen. The trip showed Wilson once again he could counter congressional opposition by going over the heads of legislators directly to the electorate.

Wilson nominated Louis D. Brandeis to the Supreme Court. Six former presidents of the American Bar Association, including Taft and Root, said Brandeis was unqualified, though one of the justices then sitting on the Court said he was the most able man ever to have argued a case before that tribunal. Brandeis was vilified as a Jew, a radical, a theorist, and a "people's lawyer" in grueling Senate confirmation hearings which lasted through the spring of 1916. Wilson also nominated Newton D. Baker, the pacifist Cleveland mayor, to replace Garrison as secretary of war. Garrison, the only man in the cabinet faintly palatable to Republicans, had resigned over differences with Wilson on the speed and scale of the military buildup. It was all grist for the Republican mill. In mid-February Elihu Root sounded the keynote of the forthcoming campaign: he criticized Wilson's stand on Mexico, his refusal to go to the aid of violated Belgium, his notes without action on the *Lusitania*, and his dilatory attitude on preparedness.

Some Democrats feared Wilson might not win in November. At the annual Gridiron dinner, after a skit which defined preparedness as "drinking two cocktails before delivering a speech in Congress for Prohibition," Wilson answered the critics: "A man who seeks the Presidency of the United States for anything it will bring to him is an audacious fool. The responsibilities of the office ought to sober a man even before he approaches it." Principle, not expedience, he went on to say, was the watchword of our country, and the people we remembered were idealists and statesmen who had squared their conduct by their ideals of duty. He would do the same: "Valor is self-respecting. Valor is circumspect. Valor withholds from itself all small implications and entanglements and waits for the great opportunity when the sword will flash as if it carried the light of heaven upon its blade."

The possibility of war haunted him daily, he told Ida Tarbell, and it filled his nights with worry. House wrote him that it was more than tacitly assumed in Europe that the United States would come in eventually on the Allied side. Verdun absorbed the attention of the world. Strategists termed it the most decisive battle of the war: if the Germans could take the city, at whatever cost, they would overrun France; if the French could hold, at whatever cost, the juggernaut would be blunted and the Allies on their way to victory. All waited for the outcome; casualties pyramided daily.

The McLemore and Gore resolutions to keep Americans from booking passage on belligerent ships were heading toward congressional votes. Wilson warned Congress,

> I cannot consent to any abridgement of the rights of American citizens. . . . To forbid our people to exercise their rights for fear we might be called upon to vindicate them would be a deep humiliation indeed. . . . Once accept a single abatement of right, and many other humiliations would follow.

Even Lodge and Taft had to agree with that sentiment, and the resolutions were permanently tabled. This political victory freed Wilson to conduct foreign affairs as he alone saw fit.

House, whom the French had dubbed "the Sphinx in the soft felt hat," returned from Europe, eluded reporters at dockside, and hurried to Washington—where he got a bit of a shock. Instead of giving his report to the president alone, he had to render a summary in the touring car, sandwiched in between Edith and Woodrow. House soon realized that Edith took a lively interest in foreign affairs. She was privy to the correspondence of the Drawer, a receptacle in Wilson's desk in which all important papers were placed by his assistants. Sometimes she read the contents of papers in the Drawer to Woodrow, or decoded important missives—for instance, recent notes from House in Europe.

House described a memorandum prepared by himself and Grey for the British cabinet, which said Wilson was ready, on hearing from the Allies, to propose a peace conference. Should the Allies accept the idea and Germany refuse, this memo said,

> the United States would probably enter the war against Germany. Colonel House expressed the opinion that, if such a Conference met, it would secure peace on terms not unfavourable to the Allies; and if it failed to secure peace, the United States would (probably) leave the Conference as a belligerent on the side of the Allies if Germany were unreasonable. . . .

It was Wilson who inserted the "probably" before letting House cable Grey that he could use the memorandum. Without the "probably" it was a document of intervention, not an invitation to talk peace. Wilson believed the revised memo would not inextricably tie America to the Allies if they were losing, but it would ensure him the important peacemaker position which he desired.

No sooner was the cable sent off to Grey, than war threatened once again from Mexico. Supporters of Pancho Villa crossed the border and, in an orgy of looting and burning, killed seventeen Americans on American soil. Though Carranza was conciliatory, even Wilson's cabinet clamored for intervention. After writing Carranza, Wilson complained to Tumulty about the constant pressure toward war. It was easy, he said, for a president to declare war, and he knew it would be good for him politically in an election year, but "The thing that daunts me and holds me back is the aftermath of war, with all its tears and tragedies. I came from the South and I know what war is, for I have seen its wreckage and terrible ruin." He waited and watched and wouldn't be riled, and on March 15 Carranza agreed to let our troops enter Mexico and find the bandits, providing Mexico was allowed the reciprocal right of "hot pursuit." The Pershing punitive expedition was immediately readied to go into Mexico.

Unhappily this expedition bungled badly, and its mistakes graphically underlined the need for preparedness. Machine-guns jammed. It took a week to muster 8,000 men. Trucks to transport the men had to be bought. Of the eight planes sent south, three were lost—stranded in the desert—in two days. It turned out that Mexico actually had more guns and soldiers than we did. In response, the House of Representatives passed the army preparedness bill with alacrity.

Spring was in full bloom. Edith and Woodrow were able to golf nearly every morning. Laughing and joking together, they made a close pair. When Edith's shots went in the rough, Colonel Starling would cheat and put them back on the fairway. "There's not a bit of use denying it," he later wrote, "I was her slave." Edith's shoelaces loosened; she put her foot up on the running board and Starling tied the laces for her. He lingered over them a bit too long and the president didn't speak to him for two weeks.

By the end of March the battle of Verdun was over. Pétain had said "They shall not pass" and the French had held. The city was no longer deemed strategically important, but the symbolic gesture had cost the lives of 200,000 men on each side. In the United States, organized labor looked at Verdun and dreaded preparedness as a stalking-horse for militarism: in all wars, they contended, workers became cannon fodder. Labor tried to keep America out of the conflict by "waging war on war" with ten million dimes from ten million people to combat the "militarism of Wall Street."

And Wall Street did seem ready for war—war with Mexico. Financier Edward L. Doheny, whose multi-million-dollar oil interests in Mexico were imperiled by Carranza's new drilling restrictions, was yelling for war. Senator Fall, already in Doheny's pocket, was calling for an army of a half-million men to go into Mexico. Wilson blasted in the press the jingoistic fervor for war.

Then an unarmed French channel boat, the *Sussex*, was reported torpedoed with heavy loss of life. Lansing and House were both ready to declare war on Germany. House confided to his diary that he was afraid Wilson would write more notes "when action is what we need." The president believed notes were the only way, for if we went in there would be "no one to lead the way out." House wanted Wilson to threaten a break in relations if Germany wouldn't end submarine warfare completely. Wilson felt he couldn't go that far, but searched for a way to curb the underwater death machines. House arrived to help Wilson phrase a note. Both he and Edith thought Wilson's first draft needed strengthening.

From what we can conclude on the basis of skimpy evidence, Edith at this time was more belligerent than Woodrow, leaning to House's view that more action was now required. On this trip, in addition to agreeing on the tone of the note to Germany, House and Edith agreed on some other business. They made, so House wrote in his diary, a deal: House would endeavor to get rid of Tumulty, while Edith would work on jettisoning Josephus Daniels. The sins of Tumulty were his lower-class ways and supposed political ineptitude. Daniels's weaknesses were less obvious. He had not worked overhard for Cary Grayson's promotion and, perhaps more importantly, Daniels and his wife had been close to Ellen Wilson for many years. Also, Daniels seemed to be dragging his feet on preparedness. This deal made by House and Edith remains an unanswered question in the light of history; little is known about it beyond House's small diary entry. Although there was some agitation, not much came of the deal in the following months. It was enough, though, to keep House and Edith chummy for the time being.

While House was still visiting Washington, astounding news arrived from Mexico: American and Carranzista troops had clashed, and Pershing requested permission to seize control of an entire Mexican state in order to find the bandits without interference. Was everyone going war-mad? Wilson sent the more cautious General Scott to defuse the Mexican situation, then turned back to the final draft of his note to Germany, which now concluded:

> Unless the Imperial Government should now immediately declare and effect an abandonment of its present methods of submarine warfare against passengers and freight-carrying vessels, the Government of the United States can have no choice but to sever diplomatic relations with the German Empire altogether.

It was strong, but "present methods" gave Germany a way out if she would say her tactics would change.

The gist of the message (not the wording) was conveyed to Congress on April 19, which was the anniversary of the Battle of Lexington. Congressional reaction was positive: had Wilson wanted war at that moment, Congress seemed very likely to agree. But Wilson didn't want war.

While he waited for Germany to reply, trouble erupted in Ireland. The Easter Rebellion was over in seven days, but the brutality with which the British put down the Irish attempt at home rule shook the United States. Irish poet Sir Roger Casement was captured as he came off a German submarine to join the insurrection, and this was to cause more problems later for Wilson.

Elihu Root, Leonard Wood, Henry Cabot Lodge, and Theodore Roosevelt sat down to lunch in New York: all were Republican presidential possibilities. According to a current poll, Roosevelt was considered the greatest living American. Already he was recruiting men to his side to ride, Rough-Rider fashion, into Mexico. But as many people hated him as loved him. Would he run? He wouldn't say. The conferees agreed one of them should run, but which one?

The question was decided by the prominent Republican *not* at the lunch, William Howard Taft. He and TR had split the Republican party in 1912. Now Taft thought neither of them could win, but that a man who was "above" the 1912 split might win—and his nominee was Supreme Court Justice Charles Evans Hughes. Think, Taft wrote Hughes, of the vacancies on the Court which Wilson could fill if reelected—alluding to Brandeis, whom they both disliked, and whose nomination to the Court was still hanging fire. Wilson, Taft wrote, would destroy the Court, and was "the greatest opportunist and hypocrite ever in the White House. . . . the exigency presented to you is whether you will save the Party from Roosevelt and the country from Wilson." It was a siren call. Hughes didn't rise to the bait yet, but enthusiasm for him mounted steadily.

In Germany, Wilson's note threw the government into crisis. The kaiser had to choose between civilian authorities who advocated giving in to Wilson's demands, and military commanders who argued that doing so would mean the end of the submarine as Germany's most powerful weapon. The civilians won. The sleeping colossus of America must not be waked. Conciliatory notes began to come into Washington: submarine warfare against merchantmen would cease. It was a complete and smashing victory for Wilson's diplomacy. The notes that Roosevelt, Lansing, House, and virtually everyone else had derided, produced the desired effect without bloodshed, just one year after the sinking of the *Lusitania*.

The afternoon the German response was publicized, Wilson and Edith went to a circus. When the president made a joking gesture of throwing his hat into a ring, the crowd went wild. Leaving for a weekend on the *Mayflower*, the Wilsons were on top of the world. In letters to friends, Wilson wrote that he and his new wife were inseparable and happy. He discussed everything with her, often clarifying his thought as he spelled out the options before him. The friendship which he used to lavish on House, Tumulty, Grayson, and his daughters, was now largely given to Edith. Their intimacy was foreclosing all others. Edith was reading her way through Wilson's library so they could talk of books and of "permanent things that the present unrest could not disturb." The vacuousness of Edith's life prior to meeting Wilson was gone; her self-assurance mounted daily. If the president of the United States held her in such high regard, she must perforce be worthy of respect. Altrude wrote her that she was "helping such a wonderful man—and so helping his work and the whole country. Those latent powers, abilities, and charms of yours have found their opportunity— and are being used to such wonderful advantage and good purpose."

In late May, Altrude finally married Cary Grayson, in New York City; Edith gave her away, and the president beamed through the ceremony. The foursome was now complete.

A few days later, the first national assembly of the League to Enforce Peace gathered in Washington to hear Senator Lodge and President Wilson. Lodge encouraged the idea of an alliance to diminish war and foster peace. For now, both he and Wilson seemed to be on the same side of the question.

War had come suddenly, the president said in his own speech, out of secrecy and with no opportunity for prior conference among the belligerents to try and head it off. Had the countries been forced to talk before shooting, war might have been avoided:

> Only when the great nations of the world have reached some sort of agreement as to what they hold to be fundamental to their common interest, and as to some feasible method of acting in concert when any nation or group of nations seeks to disturb those fundamental things, can we feel that civilization is at last in a way of justifying its existence and claiming to be finally established.

Wilson said that he believed the United States would join such an association of nations guaranteeing to all the right of self-determination, and national sovereignty free from the domination of aggression.

Behind the scenes, unknown to the public, Wilson was pressing England to begin peace talks. The English refused, saying the time was not ripe. It was a slap in Wilson's face. The British, he commented, just wanted America's arms and money.

Money was the problem all over Europe. Inflation. Governments paying bills with newly minted money with not enough tax revenues behind the bills had sent prices skyrocketing in Germany and in England. In America, prices were up, too, but not yet far enough to distract people from the political circus, the quadrennial summer entertainment.

Both Republican and Progressive conventions opened in Chicago—

separately—on June 7. The Progressives wanted Roosevelt, who was unacceptable to the Republicans, who in turn wanted Hughes, a man who did not sit well with TR or with the Progressives. Roosevelt had made his nomination conditional on getting the nod from both parties. He got only one, so he accepted neither. Then he suggested Lodge as a compromise, actually woke the senator up in the middle of the night to see if he'd agree to a draft—but nobody wanted Lodge. And so the candidate who emerged from Chicago was Charles Evans Hughes.

The most incredible thing about Hughes was his resemblance to Wilson: both sons of clergymen, university professors, reform governors who had fought party bosses and united divided party factions. Both believed in world organization. They were so close that TR labeled the justice as "Wilson in whiskers." The Hughes and Wilson families had even been on familiar terms: Frank Sayre stayed at Hughes's home the night before he married Jessie Wilson. On hearing of his nomination, Hughes resigned with a curt note to Wilson. Wilson replied in kind— and may have gotten a chuckle out of the fact that Brandeis was sworn in to the Supreme Court the very next day.

The Democratic convention was scheduled to start on June 14, the newly designated Flag Day. Wilson prepared a platform of firm progressive policy, internationalism in foreign affairs, and increased federal government intervention in economic and social progress. Martin H. Glynn, the cocksure former governor of New York, made a keynote speech which became famous. Reciting a litany of what other presidents had done when faced with crises escalating toward war, he formed a recitative duet with his audience. He gave the particulars of each case, and then said that peace had come by negotiation, just as President Wilson was trying to do today. He ended each example by shouting, "What did we do?" The assembled delegates roared in answer, "We didn't go to war!" As a magazine put it:

> It was one of the most notable events that ever happened in a political convention . . . not because of the emotion, not because of the eloquence, but because the response seemed to be from out of the very depths of the aspirations of human souls.

William Jennings Bryan was so moved that he wept, believing the speech a tribute to his moral teachings.

At the very moment Glynn was speaking, the president who had kept us out of war was marching in Washington in an enormous parade promoting military preparedness. If it was curious that preparedness and pacifism should be so linked, it was certain that Wilson was one of the few men in history who could link the ideas, for it was his very pacifism which made his advocacy of preparedness ring true. Edith watched him march with a lump in her throat: the Secret Service had learned of a threat to kill him if he marched. Fortunately, nothing happened.

When he heard of the success of Glynn's refrain, Wilson said sadly to Josephus Daniels, "I can't keep this country out of war. They talk of me as though I was a god. Any little German lieutenant can put us into the war at any time by some calculated outrage."* So could a Mexican president at the end of his tether. As the Democratic convention was denouncing intervention south of the Rio Grande as something to be done "only as a last resort," Carranza threatened to make war if Pershing didn't go home forthwith. Again Wilson let Carranza know that he was Mexico's best friend, because everyone else seemed to want a war which could only end in the smaller country's defeat and possible annexation—and Carranza backed off.

At the beginning of July the British began an offensive on the Somme. After Verdun, the French army's morale had broken down and many soldiers no longer wished to fight, but the British politicians and generals wanted an offensive. So on the first of July the British charged the Germans anticipating hand-to-hand combat with bayonets. Entrenched behind well-dug lines, the Germans mowed them down with machine-guns. The result was 20,000 dead and 40,000 wounded in the single bloodiest day in mankind's entire history of war.

On the Eastern front, the Russian General Brusilov attacked Austria-Hungary and took 250,000 prisoners in three weeks. For a time it seemed the tide of war had turned, but the tsar refused to support Brusilov, and by the summer's end Russian casualties numbered a million, encouraging revolutionary propaganda.

Stories of the bloodshed encouraged American resistance to the war. Staying out remained an election issue. The troubled position of "hyphenates"—Irish-Americans, Anglo-Americans, German-Americans—was another problem for both parties. Catholics were upset because Wilson wouldn't intervene in Mexico, where a number of priests were being held against their will. They were also angered because of a supposed slight of a cardinal by Wilson, and by the

*This famous story is possibly apocryphal.

administration's failure to properly appeal for clemency for Sir Roger
Casement. At the summer's close it looked as if the president were
losing many traditionally Democratic votes.

Hughes was out in front, and was expected to win by a large margin,
the candidate of a united majority party, but his stiff style was making
him appear unimpassioned. He had no causes to espouse, just seemed to
be weakly echoing Wilson, and the Democrats called him "Charles
E-Vasion Hughes." Wilson noted to Bernard Baruch, "If you will give
that gentleman rope enough he will hang himself. . . . His speeches are
nothing more or less than blank cartridges and the country, unless I
mistake the people very much, will place a true assessment upon
them."

Every Monday, Democratic chairman Vance McCormick came to
the White House, and often spent the night talking strategy with Wilson
and Edith, and eating popovers made from Edith's family recipe. The
theme "He kept us out of war," and Wilson's solid domestic achieve-
ments were to be stressed.

The campaign suffered from many ugly slanders and slurs. It was
reported that Wilson had bought off Mrs. Peck with $75,000 from
Baruch. The socialist candidate was given an affidavit by a man who
claimed he had seen Wilson and Mrs. Peck *flagrante delicto*; the
candidate sent it to Tumulty saying he'd never use it, but word of it still
got out. Mrs. Peck insisted she had been offered thousands to talk about
Wilson, but wouldn't do so. Newspapers wrote that a pregnant lady had
visited Wilson and left with a check, but it was not reported that she was
an indigent relative. In Chicago a salacious phone campaign was
mounted. Women told one another that Wilson had been seeing Edith
before Ellen died, and relayed stories such as the following: *Question:*
"What did Mrs. Galt do when Wilson proposed?" *Answer:* "She fell out
of bed." It was the dirtiest campaign in anyone's memory.

Happily for Wilson, whatever Hughes did seemed to backfire.
Republican society women in his entourage visited a small town to rally
the women's vote; this tactic worked well until an enterprising reporter
wrote a story headlined "Rings In, Rings Out," which detailed how the
volunteers, upon entering the poorer sections of town, turned their
diamonds in on their hands so they wouldn't be filched by the lower
classes.

The war issue pressed home when four barges loaded with munitions
for the Allies exploded in New York harbor, killing forty and causing
$20 million in property damages. One newspaper called the bombs
bursting into yellow blossom a thousand feet high "the manifestation of
an American Verdun." Wilson's people believed the event to be, very

possibly, German sabotage. There were also problems with the British, who were opening American mail, denying American ships the right to buy coal in British ports, blacklisting American firms suspected of trading with the Central Powers. All of these acts produced headlines unfavorable to the administration. A magazine reported that a young Harvard man invented a device to write out dramatic scenarios by printing six words, each picked out of a set at random, that formed a plot, such as "Brilliant Atheist Corrupts Clergyman Change Outcast" or "Indulgent Warden Entertains Prisoner Opportunity Escape" or "Beautiful Widow Marries President Inspiration Election." This last scenario seemed near to improbable as September approached. It became clear the president would have to make some startling moves to get himself back into the White House.

A nationwide railroad strike was threatened by 400,000 workers. In dramatic personal interviews with both sides, Wilson challenged railroad executives to institute the eight-hour day, and told them he'd hold them personally responsible if the economy were derailed by a strike. Then he called in the labor leaders and told them they'd better compromise. At the same time he urged Congress to pass the Adamson Act legislating the settlement. It worked. The strike was averted. When Hughes blasted Wilson for overreaching actions, Progressives jumped Hughes's ship because they had backed the actions. This episode also brought important labor and Irish-American support back toward Wilson's side. Wilson increased his following among Progressives who didn't like Hughes, with bills for an eight-hour day for government employees, workmen's compensation, rural credits to aid farmers, and new legislation against child labor.

Edith and Woodrow had taken to getting up at five instead of six, to steal up on the days. They were alone at this hour, and he could talk openly about the pressures on him. His sister Annie Howe lay dying; the girls were out living lives of their own. On a visit to Lincoln's birthplace, the president made some of his feelings public. He had, he said, read everything he could about Lincoln, but never found that any of the man's friends had penetrated Lincoln's heart, and perhaps no one could, for

> That brooding spirit had no familiars. I get the impression that it never spoke out in complete self-revelation, and that it could not reveal itself completely to anyone. It was a very lonely spirit that looked out from underneath those shaggy brows and comprehended men without fully communing with

them, as if, in spite of all its genial efforts at comradeship, it dwelt apart, saw its visions of duty where no man looked on.

It was, Edith believed, as if Wilson were opening his own heart to fathom Lincoln's. His speech continued:

> There is a very holy and very terrible isolation for the conscience of every man who seeks to read the destiny in affairs for others as well as for himself, for a nation as well as for individuals. That privacy no man can intrude upon. That lonely search of the spirit for the right perhaps no man can assist. This strange child of the cabin kept company with invisible things, was born into no intimacy but that of its own silently assembling and deploying thought.

In early September, after his sister Annie's death, the Wilsons moved to Shadow Lawn in New Jersey: the president thought it unseemly to run a campaign from the White House. The estate looked like a "gambling hell," and they pushed some furniture around to spruce it up. Edith maintained strict privacy about them, wouldn't even let the Democratic National Committee take pictures of them at home.

In the opposing camp, a motion picture of Hughes showed him to be so wooden that the candidate himself declared it would make him vote for Wilson. It was never shown. Magazines which had earlier favored Hughes were now reassessing Wilson. Hughes was hurt further by his supporter Roosevelt, who was increasingly warlike on the campaign trail. Senator Fall, never one to mince words, made things worse by suggesting "a Hughes war would be preferable to a Wilson peace." In California the Hughes steamroller ran into serious trouble. California's Senator Hiram Johnson, who had been TR's running mate in 1912, spent a night in the same hotel as Hughes in one city, but the candidate didn't even make an effort to speak to him. Later Johnson's friends in the state clobbered the Hughes campaign. So did nominal Progressives elsewhere: a large percentage of the men who had written that party's 1912 platform declared publicly that the Wilson administration had legislatively fulfilled about two-thirds of their goals, and pledged to support Wilson for reelection.

In late September, Wilson delivered a master political stroke. A violently anti-British Irish-American named Jeremiah O'Leary wrote to Wilson, saying he wouldn't vote for him. In answer, Wilson sent O'Leary a telegram which Tumulty gleefully released to the press on September 30: "I would feel deeply mortified to have you or anybody like you vote for me. Since you have access to many disloyal Americans and I have none, I will ask you to convey this message to them." Far from offending Irish-Americans, this telegram made many of them repudiate radical extremists such as O'Leary, and brought them into the president's camp.

The following day Wilson posed a problem in logic to a visiting group: if the Republicans wanted to change policies, the only antithesis to his own policy of pursuing peace was—to be logical—pursuing war. And no one could reasonably want that. The speech was a success and, with it, Wilson returned to the "He kept us out of war" theme at last. He yielded to the label of the apostle of peace. Democrats in the Midwest, where pacifist sentiment was the greatest, began to echo this theme.

Ambassador Gerard came to Shadow Lawn, talked to Wilson and Edith, told them that the Germans, restive under the submarine restrictions, might soon renew undersea warfare. Gerard was impressed with Edith's knowledge. So, too, was Ambassador Page, when he visited. The international situation entered into the campaign even more when Senator Lodge made headlines, charging that Wilson had originally intended to send a postscript to the first *Lusitania* note which would have made a mockery of our protest. Wilson denied this with a carefully worded statement that, his friend House wrote, "grazed the truth." The incident snuffed out what little cordiality remained between Wilson and Lodge: now they hated one another.

As election day drew closer, the Democrats found themselves short of campaign funds. Josephus Daniels met with two well-heeled pacifists, Thomas Alva Edison and Henry Ford. At lunch in a New York hotel, Daniels had trouble getting down to business. Edison pointed to a large chandelier with many globes and bet Ford that he, Edison, could kick higher than the younger man. Edison got up a running start and kicked a crystal to smithereens. Ford tried, but missed by a fraction of an inch. A flustered Daniels tried to get the loser to pledge the needed dollars, but Ford objected, saying campaign spending was "the bunk." In response Daniels asked both men to sponsor advertisements telling why they were for the president. They did. The secretary of the navy thus proved himself to be the highest kicker of all three.

As the campaign climaxed, Edith proved a good trouper, on a stumping trip shaking innumerable hands, using her vast capacity for small talk to bind the lower-rank politicians closer to the president. Party stalwarts noted how much she had learned since the president's January tour.

Still, in November, many of Wilson's political intimates believed defeat imminent. In order to spare the country a period of interregnum should Hughes be elected, Wilson approved a dramatic plan to turn the government over to his rival ahead of inauguration. Lansing would resign and be replaced by Hughes; then Wilson and Marshall would resign, and Hughes would succeed to the presidency. Lansing, Marshall, and Attorney General Gregory agreed to the plan's legality and said they would go along.

On election eve Wilson, Edith, Margaret, Altrude, Cary Grayson, and the visiting Frank Sayre played "twenty questions," waiting for the returns. At nine o'clock, Margaret got a call of condolence: though the polls were still open in the West, the *New York Times* was announcing in an early edition that Hughes had won. At Shadow Lawn the news produced some consternation, but not chaos. Margaret went upstairs to sniffle. Even Edith was convinced Wilson might lose, but found consolation in the idea that at last they would really be alone together. "Delightful pessimist," Wilson chided her, saying one must never court defeat by anticipating it because that destroys the fighting spirit. His sentiments ran to Kipling's poem "If," a copy of which his friend Cleveland Dodge had recently presented to him: "If you can keep your head when all about you/ Are losing theirs and blaming it on you . . ." He and Edith had wept when they had read that.

Now Wilson told the family there was no hope that Hughes would be able to keep the country out of war, since he would have to repudiate Wilson's policies. Cary Grayson suggested Wilson might run again in 1920, but Wilson retorted that he felt like the Confederate soldier returning to his burned-out farm who said, "I'm glad I fought. I'm proud of the part I played. I have no regrets—but I'll be darned if I ever love another country."

He went up to bed at ten and fell promptly asleep. Grayson couldn't do the same; he put his coat on, and went over to the Democratic party's headquarters in Asbury Park. Insomniac Edith stayed awake most of the night.

The news was bad. Hughes carried New York by 100,000; he was sweeping New England, he was breaking the solid South. But at four in the morning, Margaret—who also couldn't sleep—got new information, probably from Grayson at the Asbury Park headquarters, that early returns from Ohio and the West were more favorable. She went to Edith, who forbade her to awaken Woodrow.

At breakfast, the family glanced at newspapers whose headlines proclaimed a victorious Hughes. The Republican candidate, however, was refusing to claim victory himself. Out on the golf course, Wilson played with his usual intensity. Reporter David Lawrence yelled,

"How's your game, Mr. President?" "Grayson's got me three down, but I've picked up four states!"

By the end of the day, the results were still inconclusive. Some of the votes in the West had to come in on dogsled from the High Sierras, and had not yet been counted. California's vote would decide the election. At 8:30 in the evening, with the outcome still unsettled but looking better—the West was strongly pacifist, and had many new women voters who didn't want their men going to war—the presidential family embarked on the *Mayflower* for a trip up the Hudson. They were going to visit the Sayres, where a new grandchild, Ellen Axson Sayre, was to be christened. Though the big question was still unsettled, Wilson's private life—so important to him—would go on.

The boat was traveling quietly up the Hudson, and the family was all sleeping, when at 5:30 the next morning, valet Brooks waved a wireless message at Secret Serviceman Starling. "Safe at last," Brooks said, pointing to California returns showing Wilson had won over Hughes by more than 3,000 votes. "Does he know?" Starling asked. Brooks shook his head, and said he wouldn't be the one to wake Wilson and tell him either, because if he did he'd be fired for sure.

9

THE RIGHT IS MORE PRECIOUS
THAN PEACE

By A SLIM margin of just over a half-million votes, Wilson was reelected, the first incumbent Democrat to be so chosen since Andrew Jackson. A group of Democrats who had supported Hughes sent to Roosevelt a telegram saying that he, more than any other American, had contributed the most to Wilson's victory.

In the inevitable letdown after the campaign, both Wilsons were unwell. It was one more bit of evidence of how their lives had meshed. Psychologists point out that second marriages are usually more stable than first ones because the partners have more realistic expectations. The Wilsons' extended courtship had served to define what each could expect from the other. Romance, students of marriage suggest, is a quality not so much of juvenile pairings as it is of a mature relationship, and has much to do with the regard in which the participants hold one another. Marital compatibility, a recent researcher found, is associated with a tendency to rate oneself above average on most personality traits, but to rate one's spouse even higher—which the Wilsons did continually in their letters to each other and to friends. It has been found that older, childless couples who have a healthy sexual relationship, adequate income, social activities, no in-law problems, and a sharing of religious convictions, are generally the happiest of all married pairs. The Wilsons fit that bill of particulars perfectly.

With the election safely over, though, Edith seems to have decided to flex her muscles. She and House jointly demanded that Tumulty be put out to pasture. To ensure his financial future, the president asked the secretary to take an appointment to the Board of General Appraisers, and asked him to resign. Shocked, Tumulty wandered the White House halls in a daze, but refused to resign, and—curiously—Wilson refused to compel him to do so. At heart he could not fire a man who had been so loyal. Historians have concluded that Wilson was quite softhearted when it came to personal matters such as this one. After a deeply felt letter from Tumulty, saying he would resign but would never accept any other position, the president backed down, and Tumulty stayed on—but the old trust between them was compromised.

Shortly after the election, while still in bed, Wilson wrote out an appeal to the European belligerents asking them to set forth their war aims, an exercise which he believed would hasten the war's end. Edith listened to it when she came to minister to him. The German government had been asking Wilson to intervene for some time, and the president believed, now that the Allies were seriously dependent on the United States financially, that they would listen as well. In addition, von Bernstorff had privately assured Wilson that Germany would evacuate Belgium and France if a treaty could be hammered out.

By Thanksgiving, Wilson's message was ready, but House counseled delay, saying that governmental changes in both Great Britain and Germany would make new officials even more responsive. While waiting for the opportune moment, Wilson and Edith sailed to New York and stood on the *Mayflower*'s deck for the lighting-up ceremonies of the Statue of Liberty. There Ambassador Gerard whispered to him that Bryan was trying to get to the kaiser with a peace plan. Still, House counseled patience. Then Germany had some success in the field, and on December 11 surprised the world by floating its own peace proposal. Chagrined, Wilson had to rewrite his and notes finally went out on December 18, which was his and Edith's first wedding anniversary.

Early that morning, with snow falling outside, Woodrow gave Edith a pendant of diamonds surrounding a black opal (her birthstone). They went out to golf, but it was too cold, so they came back and motored to the Corcoran Gallery for an exhibit of American paintings, none of which they liked well enough to buy. At a press conference later in the day, Wilson told assembled reporters his notes had pointed out that all belligerents desired the same goals—equal rights for large and small states, security against aggression, an international body to safeguard the future peace—and he had simply asked the governments to state their war aims so they could be compared, worked out, and the war ended.

Two days later, Lansing told the press there was a possibility of our being forced into war if the notes miscarried. This made Germany and

Great Britain read the notes in a warlike, rather than a pacific, light. Was Lansing's error intentional? Almost certainly: he had been privately advocating a break with Germany and had long used his position to tip the balance toward the Allies. Wilson got Lansing to clear up the matter, but the damage had been done.

The Wilsons nevertheless tried to have a pleasant Christmas season. All three daughters came for a family dinner. They played charades, using the upstairs White House hall for a stage. Nell played one character with the train of her velvet gown over her arm, a kerchief tied round her head, a knife in her teeth. Three days later, the family quietly celebrated Woodrow's sixtieth birthday.

In early 1916 Edith had initiated a series of morning meetings with the wives of cabinet members to establish closer ties among them and to discuss issues of "precedent and precedence." In January of 1917 Edith suggested these meetings be abandoned, their purposes achieved. She was tired of the old-fashioned attitudes of official Washington, anyhow. The January round of parties which had seemed fabulous to her last year this time were merely exhausting. A year in the limelight had proved there were drawbacks to being First Lady. Edith and her family were hurt at this time by a report that accused her brother Randolph, in conjunction with Tumulty, McAdoo, and Bernard Baruch—an odd crew, to be sure—of having profited on stock transactions by virtue of inside information about government plans regarding the note to Germany in late 1916. Randolph, a member of a brokerage firm, was supposed to have sold steel short on the knowledge that the American note would stop the war and thus undercut the boom in war-related industries. The rumor was eventually traced to a man out for publicity for himself—the insiders had known nothing at all—and Randolph Bolling, as well as the others, was cleared, However, the affair left a bad taste in everyone's mouth.

On January 9, in an action unknown to the Allies and to the United States, the kaiser ordered unrestricted submarine warfare to begin again on February 1. In vain Chancellor Bethmann Hollweg argued that this would lead to American intervention and the end of Germany forever. The military commanders insisted U-boats would win the war in five months, before an American soldier could even set foot on the continent's soil. They didn't care if the United States came in. The kaiser believed them. This mistake was based on misinformation as well as miscalculation, for the Germans believed the Allies were not serious about negotiating at this time. In turn this misinformation was based on misdirection: Lansing had given the Allies private assurances that the

United States would support their negotiating position over the German one.

Filing essentially false balloons for peace then, the Germans hoped to end the war with their submarines. After the kaiser's order went out, Germany's new foreign secretary, Arthur Zimmermann, sent a telegram to Mexico, saying that if America entered the war Germany would ally herself with Mexico on the following basis:

> Make war together, make peace together, generous financial support, and an understanding on our part that Mexico is to reconquer the lost territory in Texas, New Mexico, and Arizona.

Carranza was told to invite Japan to join with Germany and Mexico. The British intercepted and decoded this telegram, but could not yet figure out how to use it without revealing to Germany that they had broken her codes. And they kept it—for the nonce—from the United States.

On January 22, Wilson appealed for "peace without victory." In the modern era, he argued, no one really wins a war; therefore the peace that follows must redress fundamental grievances or be doomed to failure; further, it must incorporate the same principles that underlie American democracy—equality of rights for nations and peoples, with governments deriving their just powers from the consent of the governed. Speaking for the silent mass of mankind, he said all peoples must be left free to determine their own policy and develop "unhindered, unthreatened, unafraid." These were not only American principles but "the principles of mankind, and must prevail."

Though the belligerents scoffed that the speech was naïve, liberals everywhere found in "peace without victory" an ideal to favorably echo Lincoln's "with malice toward none."

Near the end of January, von Bernstorff was put in the untenable position of telling Wilson that, while Germany wished the president to continue his efforts toward peace, unrestricted submarine warfare would resume on February 1.

Wilson was shocked. In cabinet he wondered who, if we went to war, would survive to help nations ravaged by the conflict. Nevertheless he bade Lansing draft a note severing relations with Germany. As he waited for Lansing's draft, he nervously rearranged his library books, talked distractedly to House and Edith. She suggested golf, which House thought unseemly. Wilson did not go out. On February 2, he met again with the cabinet; a majority wanted war or armed neutrality, but Wilson insisted he must wait for an overt act. On February 3, von Bernstorff was handed his passports as, simultaneously, Wilson told Congress relations were severed, but that if no American ships were sunk, he would still try to avoid war. Even so, the grounds of the White House, and the Departments of State, War, and Navy were closed, security measures put into effect, passenger ships told to stay in port. Major companies telegrammed, putting their resources at the government's disposal; Republicans suggested a coalition cabinet should war come. Wilson commented bitterly to House, "You notice the suggestion is being actively renewed that I call their crowd into consultation and have a coalition cabinet at my elbow. It is the *junkerthum* trying to creep in under cover of the patriotic feeling of the moment. They will not get in."

Meanwhile he battled Congress over whether merchant ships now setting to sea should or should not be armed. Pacifists said it would lead to war; Wilson, that it was necessary. At a stormy cabinet meeting on February 23 Houston and McAdoo argued so vociferously for war that Wilson reproached them for their spirit of *code duello*. Privately both secretaries talked of resigning. Next day in London, Arthur Balfour handed Page a copy of the Zimmermann telegram to Mexico and told him it could be verified because it had actually been transmitted across the ocean by U.S. State Department cable that had been loaned to the Germans to facilitate peace negotiations.

This report, released in Washington, was a bombshell. The House responded by passing the Armed Ship Bill; but La Follette filibustered it to death in the Senate, and Congress adjourned. On March 3, though, Zimmermann admitted to having sent the telegram and, as Lodge wrote jubilantly to Roosevelt, "Wilson does not mean to go to war but I think he is in the grip of events."

On March 4, Wilson took the oath of office privately, and then was urged by House to vent his anger at the filibusterers. He did so, giving the press a statement about "a little group of willful men" who had tied this great government up in knots. The next day the president received a warning that an attempt would be made on his life. He and Edith went to the Capitol in a horse-drawn carriage, escorted by guards who formed a hollow square around them. Nothing happened on the way there, but going home there was a sudden halt in the procession, and then—plump!—something fell onto Edith's lap. *The bomb,* she thought, and had a terrible moment until she saw it was a bouquet of flowers.

War or peace now waited on what Germany would do. With Woodrow in bed again with a cold, Edith was designated to tell Josephus

Daniels how he could arm the merchantmen under the authority of an old anti-piracy statute, in spite of the congressional impasse. Edith carried out this assignment in perfect secrecy, and Daniels was able to arm the merchantmen without the public knowing about it.

Edith offered or suggested to House that he might take the ambassadorship to London, since Woodrow's friend Cleveland Dodge felt he was unable to take it himself. This was probably Edith's idea of a wonderful way to get House out of the country, but the Texan politely declined.

To help amuse Woodrow while he was still in bed, Edith and her brother Randolph played with him at the Ouija board. Admiral Nelson announced his presence and proceeded to discuss submarine warfare—was there no escape from the onrushing steamroller of war? News came that the tsar had been overthrown in Russia—which meant to Wilson that all the Allies were now democratically based governments, as everyone believed the revolution would lead to a democratic Russia in the near future.

The German overt acts, for which Wilson had been waiting with dread, began to appear. After several American ships had been sunk, on March 16 the *Vigilancia* went down with the loss of over a dozen American lives. Then on the seventeenth, a relief ship for Belgium was struck, and on the eighteenth, three more American ships were torpedoed. There was no longer the possibility of peace.

On the afternoon of the nineteenth, Frank Cobb, the editor of the *New York World*, visited the president and found "the old man" worn down and afraid that war was inevitable. Wilson painted for Cobb a dark panorama: war would destroy Germany and mean a dictated peace rather than a just one. At home it would mean "illiberalism" because one couldn't fight with strength and at the same time maintain true democracy:

> Once lead this people into war, and they'll forget there ever was such a thing as tolerance. To fight you must be brutal and ruthless, and the spirit of ruthless brutality will enter into the very fibre of our national life, infecting Congress, the courts, the policeman on the beat, the man in the street.

Free speech and the right of assembly would go, even the Constitution might not survive the assaults of war; neither, Wilson prophesied, would he himself. At the cabinet meeting on the twentieth, Josephus Daniels, the last holdout, agreed to war with tears in his eyes, and the decision was taken. Congress was called to assemble.

On April 1, the president was up all night, working on a war message. Edith found him at four on the south portico, brought him an overcoat for the early morning's chill, some milk and biscuits, and stayed to talk. House was right, Wilson thought, for saying he, Wilson, was "too refined, too civilized, too intellectual, too cultivated" for war. "Mine should have been a constructive, not a destructive administration," the president told Edith. He told her that he was determined to profit from the ideas and mistakes of Madison, Lincoln, and all those who had lived in this great house before him—but he wasn't sure how he would do at making war.

In New York men marched, carrying broomsticks because they had no rifles. A hundred thousand spectators lined the Wilsons' route to the Capitol, just after dusk on April 2, waving flags, carrying candles. The president went into a small chamber to ready himself, while Edith went into the hall where the congressmen waited, nearly all of them carrying small flags.

Believing himself alone, the president looked into a large mirror. His face, a hidden observer thought, showed the sufferings of the damned: drawn, chin awry, flushed, seeming as if he had had a stroke. He lifted one hand to smooth away the wrinkles in his brow, the other to set his chin into a firm pose. Only when the features reflected a mask of grim determination did the president enter the main chamber.

We would not choose the path of submission, the president said. We were the enemy of the military autocracy that had wrought evil on the world, and we would war against Germany to make the world safe for democracy:

> We desire no conquest, no dominion. We seek no indemnities for ourselves, no material compensation for the sacrifices we shall freely make. We are but one of the champions of the rights of mankind. . . . The right is more precious than peace, and we shall fight for the things we have always carried nearest our hearts. . . . To such a task we can dedicate our lives and our fortunes, everything that we are and everything that we have, with the pride of those who know that the day has come when America is privileged to spend her blood and her might for the principles that gave her birth and happiness and the peace which she has treasured. God helping her, she can do no other.

10

THE WAR YEARS

On Good Friday, April 6, 1917, Jeannette Rankin, newly seated congresswoman from Montana, the first woman ever elected to the House, faced a moral dilemma. When she made no reply to the roll-call vote, Uncle Joe Cannon, dean of the House, told her, "Little woman, you cannot afford not to vote. You represent the womanhood of the country in the American Congress." At the second call she stood up and, against the rules and with tears in her eyes, she pleaded that she wanted "to stand by my country, but I cannot vote for war." She fell back into the arms of Fiorello LaGuardia. Her vote was recorded and overwhelmed. America was going to war.

The completed war resolution reached the White House while the Wilsons were having lunch. Edith loaned Woodrow a gold pen and he signed the document. Moments later, a navy signalman was semaphoring the war decree from a window in the executive offices; within minutes it was on the wireless to ships at sea. From that moment a shroud seemed to fall over the White House. Security became tighter; never again would the president sneak out for an unattended walk.

Wilson had gone to war to play a leading part in the peace, but first the conflict must be won. As with most Americans, the president envisioned our participation as massive in finance and supply, minimal in manpower. A token force under Pershing was sent over to show the flag. One man, however, was ready to immediately lead a division of volunteers to France if Wilson would but let him.

The most significant hour of his life, Theodore Roosevelt had written, was when he led the Rough Riders up San Juan Hill in 1898. Afterward he had lobbied for the Medal of Honor and, failing to obtain it, had longed for the opportunity to try again. In 1911, and again in 1914 and 1916, he wanted to go to Mexico, but each crisis fizzled. By 1917 he had a proposed division's administration all worked out, a permanent application on file with the War Department. On February 9, Newton Baker told TR he couldn't give permission to raise the division "without express sanction from Congress," which would only come with a declaration of war. Now war had been declared. Roosevelt believed he could do his own country the most good "by dying in a reasonably honorable fashion" on a European battlefield. "If you can convince Wilson of that, Theodore," Elihu Root told him, "I am sure he will give you a commission."

Roosevelt went to see the president on April 10. Wilson received his old nemesis in the Red Room, traditionally reserved for visiting royalty. TR said boldly that, faced with the present emergency, all he had written or said in the past was "as dust in a windy street." He was a patriot, wanted to serve, pleaded for permission to raise his division. If Wilson would now press the war forward with vigor, he, TR, would behave toward Wilson as Light Horse Harry Lee might have acted toward Jefferson should war with England have come during Jefferson's presidency. (It was well known that Roosevelt thought Jefferson one of our worst presidents.) Wilson tried to show the Rough Rider that his scheme might seriously hinder the government's regular draft efforts, as he might well attract the cream of the crop and leave the regular army without adequate middle-rank leadership. Roosevelt said he would await the president's decision; then together with Tumulty they framed a statement to the press. TR slapped Joe on the back, complimented him on having six sons (as opposed to Wilson's three daughters?), and promised Joe a soft berth if he came with him. When he had gone, Wilson told Tumulty that the ex-president had tremendous charm, and was almost irresistible.

Almost. The army's commanders said it would be bad for Roosevelt to have a division, and Wilson agreed. On hearing their decision, Roosevelt wrote that Wilson was "an utterly selfish, utterly treacherous, utterly insincere hypocrite" surrounded by "YMCA *banditti*."

There had never been a draft in America—Lincoln had tried and failed—but when it seemed there would not be enough volunteers, the Wilson administration decided to try again. Wilson, Baker, and top generals worked out an ingenious plan. Instead of sending uniformed officers to people's homes to pluck out able-bodied young men, as had been done in the past in all countries throughout history, they initiated a system which allowed eligible draftees to sign themselves up as if they were voting. Men would register at their regular polling places. Civilians would decide who was fit and who was not. There wouldn't be a uniformed man around—but eventually the draftees would be passed on to the military just as surely as if a press-gang had shanghaied them. It worked like a charm. June 5, 1917, the day of registration, was made a festive and patriotic occasion. Ten million eligible young men registered for war in twelve hours.

The women mobilized a bit differently. Edith got cabinet wives to pledge with her to

> reduce living to its simplest form and to deny ourselves
> luxuries in order to free those who produce them for the
> cultivation of necessities. . . . In the management of our
> domestic economy we pledge ourselves to buy simple clothing
> and food and not demand out-of-season delicacies. We make
> an appeal to all women of America to do everything in our
> power along these lines . . . to hasten the end of the strug-
> gle and to win the war.

Accordingly, when the president determined to save $2,000 a month personally, Edith put the White House on an even tighter budget. As for herself, she bought in the next few months only one new piece of wearing apparel, a riding habit. Grayson, who had once said "the outside of a horse is good for the insides of a man," thought the president should ride to supplement his golf exercise, and worked out with Edith a scheme to get Woodrow to agree. Edith would say *she* wished to take up the sport, and as the president could deny her nothing, he would then agree to accompany her. Within hours of the proposal the horses were ready to go, and Edith had to rush about borrowing Marga's breeches, Nell's coat, and Altrude's boots. Next day she bought a habit of her own, and from then the three rode almost daily in the warm weather—the doctor, Edith, and the president.

Edith's other new activity was to set up a Red Cross unit at the White House. With Helen Bones and several Bolling relatives, Edith began sewing pajamas for the boys overseas. The sewing machine which Helen had said Edith would never have time to use was busy several hours a day.

In the late spring the survival of the Allies was in question. Petain in France had fifty-four divisions refusing to fight. He court-martialed over 100,000 soldiers, while simultaneously giving his men better food and general conditions—but he did not dare ask them to make any more advances. In Russia, Lenin had arrived in his sealed train, Trotsky had come back from being a film extra in New York, and they were fomenting a second Russian revolution. In the meantime, Germany was rapidly winning the war at sea: German U-boats were incredibly effective, sinking over a million tons in April—far more than the capacity of the world's shipyards to replace in a similar span of time. One out of every four vessels leaving an Allied or neutral port never completed a round trip. Great Britain was down to a one-month's supply of wheat.

While waiting for the United States Army to come to the rescue and break the stalemate, the Allies might go under. To prevent that, America must provide enormous quantities of money and war materiel. To raise that money, Wilson turned to McAdoo, who initiated the first Liberty Loan from the American public to help its government fight the war. Under Mac's energetic direction, it was quickly oversubscribed. Mac's personal power was great, but his relationship with Wilson was somewhat strained. Prior to America's entry into the war, he had been too hawkish for the chief's comfort. Then he had wanted to resign and volunteer—which Wilson persuaded him not to do. Mac hadn't been inside the White House except on official business or to large social functions in six months. Being son-in-law seemed to have brought him no luck, and his cabinet colleagues saw him as grasping power and lusting after a post-position for the 1920 nomination.

Besides his problems with McAdoo Wilson had also to contend with a balky Congress. The draft had had difficult sledding; a fiscal package for war-related expenses had been blocked because it was not itemized; an omnibus censorship bill was passed only in emasculated fashion. Wilson had to go around Congress and use executive discretionary funds to allow Burleson, Lansing, and Gregory to set up essential security units in their departments. It was the second bad year in a row for farmers, and increased European demands for wheat pushed up prices; when farmers started to hoard, prices also went skyrocketing on eggs, poultry, and meat, and Wilson asked for controls. Pressed by many lobbies, Congress dallied. Tired of waiting, Wilson appointed Herbert Hoover temporary food administrator. Congress screamed that Wilson was a dictator, and tacked onto the price control bill a resolution for a joint committee on the conduct of the war.

Such a committee had crippled Lincoln's efficiency in the Civil War. Wilson would have none of it. By August, public pressure and adroit maneuvering got the price control bill passed and the joint committee scotched, but not without making the president several new enemies. With each legislative victory, the anti-Wilson ranks grew. Senators were quoted as disliking Wilson for the tariff, the Federal Reserve, the income tax on the wealthy, the omnibus censorship bill, the rejection of Roosevelt—and for such petty things as not putting an army camp in a man's home state.

On the other hand, Wilson was proving himself a capable wartime manager not afraid to reach out for new blood. Hoover was a find; so was Harry A. Garfield as fuel administrator, and newspaperman George Creel to head the Committee on Public Information. Wilson also relied heavily on Bernard Baruch, who had endeared himself by bringing his parents to see the Wilsons during the campaign: the market wizard was deeply involved in the effort to get American industry united behind the war drive. "When it comes to doing new things and doing them well," Wilson told a bunch of midshipmen one summer's day,

> I will back the amateur against the professional every time because the professional does it out of the book and the amateur does it with his eyes upon a new world and with a new set of circumstances. . . . Do the thing that is audacious to the utmost point of risk and daring, because that is exactly the thing that the other side does not understand, and you will win by the audacity of method when you cannot win by circumspection and prudence.

The first summer of the war, Edith and Woodrow carefully observed meatless, sweetless, wheatless days, put Mr. Hoover's stickers to this effect on the White House windows. Out for a ride, when Woodrow saw similar stickers on other people's houses, he told Edith he wished to know the people in those homes because "it is from them that I draw inspiration and strength."

Mac took to the hustings to sell a second Liberty Loan. Grayson accompanied him and wrote back to Colonel House:

> The McAdoo trip was a success from start to finish. He made 87 speeches, every one good—hit the bull's eye every time. . . . Every place he went, I heard him mentioned as the next president. . . . We have all got to be very careful about mentioning McAdoo's name around the White House for future honors—especially with the female members.

Edith was, they all knew, a good hater, and would never forgive Mac his indiscretions of 1915. Grayson's letter was catty and chatty, apprising House as well that Tumulty was being more cooperative to the House-

Grayson faction, and mentioning some other gossip. House noted dryly in his diary that the president's house was full of intrigue.

Late in the summer Edith was ill. Woodrow read to her daily, postponed a visit from House to spend time with her. In the Oval Room after dinner he wound up a Victrola to show her how to do a jig step, imitating Primrose, the minstrel dancer at Keith's. He liked people who "took no more at their hearts than they could kick off at their heels," and wished he could change jobs with Primrose. They talked wistfully of 1921 and what they would do when Woodrow was no longer in office. Perhaps they'd bicycle together, but Edith said she didn't know how. A few days later a brand new Columbia bicycle arrived at the White House, and the couple went down to the basement where Woodrow tried to teach her. Edith did more pratfalls than the vaudevilleans and never was able to learn, but they laughed a lot and felt young.

During the war's first year, the chairman of the shipping board asked Edith to rename interned German ships. Consulting many registers, she found all the easy names taken and turned in despair to Indian ones, looking them up in dictionaries loaned by the Library of Congress. She also spent hours every night helping Wilson with his foreign cables, and even acquired his habits of writing, such as "okeh" rather than "okay." The former, a Choctaw word, was more correct, the schoolmaster said.

Honoring a pledge made to one of Pershing's men, Wilson read a chapter of a small soldier's Bible every night. Often Edith joined him. Woodrow said his prayers on his knees every night, and called on his faith to sustain him in the great moral crusade he supposed the fight in Europe to be. Lloyd George recognized this quality when he wrote to the president:

> I believe that your statements have been not the least impor-
> tant of the contributions which America is making to the
> cause of human freedom. . . . They have given to the
> bruised and battered peoples of Europe fresh courage to
> endure and fresh hope that with all their sufferings they are
> helping to bring into being a world in which freedom and
> democracy will be secure.

It was Woodrow's voice, crying peace in the midst of chaos, together with his personal kindnesses, that was moving Edith's love for him into ever-deeper channels. As she listened to him, as she watched his actions in a soiled and soiling world, her admiration mounted. They were both religious, but she would miss a night of her prayers now and then, and did not go to her knees in devotion—but he did, and she envied him the depth of feeling necessary to do this. He was more softhearted, more forgiving, and she was more inclined to hate and to harbor grudges for a lifetime. She venerated the way his eyes and mind reached continually further than those of other, ordinary men. Only he, she felt, understood to the greatest depth how terrible this war was, and how necessary it was for it to end in a magnanimous peace.

Wilson had long been working toward this goal, and now, with the initial push of organizing the country for war about over, he could devote more time to it. He asked House to set up "the Inquiry" to gather information and opinions on which to base a peace settlement when the time should arrive. House's brother-in-law Sidney E. Mezes, president of New York City College, became head of the organization and Walter Lippmann became its secretary.

The time for peace seemed to be nearing. In the autumn the British went into the mud of Flanders Field. In Italy the Germans and Austrians took 250,000 prisoners in a week. House, sent to England to coordinate America's efforts with those of the Allies, learned on his arrival of the second revolution in Russia. Lenin and the Bolsheviks had overthrown the Kerensky government and had then declared the new Russia's intention of seeking an armistice with Germany—immediately.

"Take the whip hand," Wilson cabled House about his meetings with the Allied war council; insist on a plan for unified conduct of the war. America was beginning to take the lead.

In an off-the-record conversation with a retiring journalist, Wilson said his main job this first year of the war had been to unify America behind the war effort. He observed that the primary task of a president was psychological: to gauge public sentiment accurately enough so that actions taken could receive the support of the great majority of the people. He considered himself the master, not of the right action, but of the possible action.

The president's tremendous absorption in public work was cutting him off from those who didn't work for him, so he was glad to see Stock Axson and Colonel Brown when each came and stayed for a week in November. Edith thought Woodrow was working longer hours than any of the boys in the training camps—and so was she. They both got a laugh when, on November 29, the papers announced that a millionaire had left $12,000 a year "pin money" to the wives of presidents. The money was never used for that purpose.

Portions of the White House were sealed off to save fuel, and heatless days were decreed to save coal for Europe. The railroads transporting this coal ran into delays and McAdoo agitated for a government take-over with himself in charge. Wilson thought it a good idea though possibly unconstitutional, and believed Mac to be the best person to run the rails; yet, he told Stock Axson, he didn't want to be accused of nepotism. Ask Brandeis, Stock suggested. One snowy evening Wilson walked unannounced into the justice's house and did just that. Brandeis said a takeover was legal, but suggested Mac give up the treasury to take the job.

In his annual December message to Congress, Wilson asked for a declaration of war against Austria, a request met with war whoops and rebel yells, but he also held out an olive branch to the German peoples, whom, he suggested, were being deceived by their leaders.

However, Colonel House pointed out on his return to the United States, unless things changed, Germany might well win the war. The Allies were mistrustful of one another, and the Supreme War Council had neither power nor efficiency. The worst thing, House believed, was that no one had formulated Allied war aims. Wilson determined to do so, and to put them in such a way that his very statement of them would be the moral turning point of the war.

One day during his visit, House spent nearly an hour with Edith, criticizing Wilson's position on the railroads and his proposed speech on the matter. Edith defended Woodrow's stand, said she'd tell him of House's comments, but suggested House talk directly with him after dinner. Later, when Wilson asked House about his objections, which Edith had summarized, House said he'd now been convinced by Edith's arguments (and a rereading of the speech) and would henceforth agree with Wilson's position: translated, that meant House had changed his mind. Edith didn't like the way he did so, and never forgave him.

At Christmas the Wilsons gave 125 turkeys to various members of the White House staff, and distributed presents to the children who lined the auto route on the way to the golf course. The *Washington Post* reported that it was difficult to say who had more fun, the kids or the presidential couple.

In the trenches, for the first time since the war had begun, there was no fraternizing between Allied and German troops. The poet Robert Graves dates the end of the old world from this incident. There was, he suggests, no longer a wish to see each other as reasonable enemies; it was a sign that the sort of warfare that had existed since the time of

Christ was gone, and in its place had come merely a dishonorable and mechanized hell.

Wilson believed that peace and a new direction for the world was what all humanity wanted and needed. With help from House, and using the preliminary researches of the Inquiry, and drawing from files he had been carefully building for years, Wilson prepared his January 8, 1918 address to Congress which became known as the Fourteen Points. On hearing the speech in advance, Edith was enthralled. Wilson stated with empathy and precision the case for an organized and peaceful world. No one who heard the speech, she believed, could differ with its aims.

In the speech, Wilson insisted that the time had come for peace-loving nations to state what they were fighting for. America's goals were self-determination for all nations and peoples, and the establishment of an organization in the post-war world that would ensure peace. These aims translated into fourteen specific points which included open diplomacy, freedom of the seas, post-war world disarmament, the smashing of tariff barriers, impartial settlement of claims to colonies, and the establishment of an international league to assure territorial integrity and political independence to all states. After the war, lands were to be restored to those people whose language and culture were indigenous to them.

To Woodrow Wilson, these principles were the "moral climax of this the culminating and final war for human liberty," and a cause toward which the American people were willing to put "their own strength, their own highest purpose, their own integrity and devotion to the test."

Woodrow Wilson himself would spend the rest of his life doing precisely that.

In January of 1918, during a record-breaking cold spell, Edith Wilson tried to help Washington's poor by putting a White House truck at the disposal of an agency distributing free coal to the needy. It was the home problems that still concerned Americans, even though immersed in a war. *Life* printed a satire of a polite thank-you note to a hostess:

> I cannot thank you for your bread,
> Because there wasn't any,
> Nor any butter, either, though
> Its substitutes were many.
> But your pecan and fig croquettes;

> Your muffins, flour- and eggless;
> Your beefsteak, raised in window-box;
> Your mock duck, wing- and legless . . .
> Composed a menu so conserved
> That Mr. Hoover'd better
> Commend my cheer in sending you
> This meatless, wheatless letter!

Edith joined with the chairwoman of the Women's Committee of the Council of National Defense to write an open letter to women of the Allied countries, with the purpose (never stated openly) of preventing soldiers from contracting venereal disease from camp followers:

> In all our countries, mothers are willing and proud to give their sons to defend the ideas which underlie the supreme sacrifice which their government demands of them, and to accept with fortitude and calmness their death. But they shrink from the greater sorrow which comes from the loss of moral fiber that robs them of health and manly vigor.
>
> It is no wonder that their hearts fail them when they realize the temptations which beset their sons, removed from homes and family ties, living the unnatural life of the camp. . . . These abnormal conditions place upon all women tremendous responsibilities and urge the closest union in an effort to conserve the moral forces of our society, to protect our young men . . . that they may be kept pure and chivalrous, so that after the conflict is ended, we may look with hope to the future life of our people. . . .

Despite the popular response to Wilson's Fourteen Points address—it was being hailed all over the world; even Lenin applauded it as a step toward peace—the president's relations with his own legislature were increasingly troubled. The short honeymoon he had enjoyed at the start of the war was already over. Republicans were attacking the "diseased" conditions in U.S. training camps, supposed incompetence in the War Department, the failure to supply adequate weapons to troops in France, and supposedly inadequate regulation of food, fuel, and the railroads. Bills were in the hopper that would take virtually all power away from Secretaries Daniels and Baker; a Senate committee grilled Baker for three days abut the competence of the War Department.

While people were still debating whether Baker or his accusers were right, a new shock hit.

Garfield's fuel administration took radical measures to ensure adequate coal supplies to the Allies. He ordered the closing of all factories east of the Mississippi for a week, after which nonessential industry was to go on a five-day-a-week schedule until late March. There was a public outcry, but the measure enabled nearly a million tons of ocean shipping to have fuel enough to get underweigh within a week. Two days after the Garfield order took effect, the bill to provide a "supercabinet" to oversee the war effort came out of a Senate committee. Its sponsor, Senator Chamberlain, charged that the war effort had broken down completely, that administration officials were blunderers, that we faced defeat by Germany if the bill were not implemented. The president lashed out, accusing Chamberlain of "an astonishing and absolutely unjustified distortion of the truth," and "absurd charges" based on "total ignorance."

To counter the opposition, Wilson had Senator Overman introduce a bill into Congress which would give him great emergency powers for the duration of the war. His position was difficult to refute. When ten Republican senators assembled for a dinner at Alice Longworth's to meet with Theodore Roosevelt, the consensus was that Wilson could not be successfully attacked until the war was over. Then the gloves could come off; but until that day the best that could be done was to win the 1918 congressional elections and gain control of Congress.

On March 3, the Germans imposed the harsh terms of Brest-Litovsk on Russia and peace hopes dimmed, because the settlement showed Germany was bent on conquest. On March 21, under cover of dense fog, German General von Ludendorff launched an enormous offensive, overrunning Allied positions at the Somme which had held for four years. In fierce fighting, Haig and the British were split from Petain and the French. Realizing that the long-awaited crisis had come, Lloyd George sent everything he could muster to France, and appealed for immediate and massive American aid. Wilson understood that unless we responded there was danger of Germany winning the war and making the United States pay *all* the costs. He increased the numbers of troops and supplies making the Atlantic crossing. On the battlefields, finally, the Germans were finding out what the Allies had already realized after the years of fighting: that an advancing army, without the cover of its trenches, could win territory and at the same time lose strength rapidly. The tide of the war began to shift.

In Washington the Overman bill was passed, but Wilson chose not to use the virtual dictatorial powers it gave. Also signed into law was daylight saving time, a concept in use in Allied countries. Wilson told his cabinet a joke. Negroes, he reported, were saying that Lincoln had freed the slaves, but Wilson was the greater man because there was now Jesus's time and Wilson's time—and Wilson had taken the railroads from the rich and given them to his son-in-law.

Mac now held two of the biggest jobs in the country, yet he had daily problems with his chief. Once, when invited to lunch and asked by Wilson to give the blessing, Mac had stood up, said "Jesus," and sat down. Upon learning from his wife that this was inadequate to the occasion, Mac went home and studied. Next time Wilson asked him to say the blessing, he read it off the inside of his cuff, where Nell had lettered it.

At April's end, a flock of Shropshire Downs sheep arrived at the White House, to keep the lawn clipped and save labor needed elsewhere. Cartoonists had a field day, and even the Secret Service now referred to Edith as "the shepherdess." The wool gathered from the sheep was eventually sold to benefit the Red Cross.

Inspecting a British tank one afternoon, the president burned the inside of his right hand. The insurance company which covered him refused to pay because, they said, the burn did not incapacitate him, as he could write with his left hand. He could also play golf that way, but it wasn't easy. Four days later, Edith went in Wilson's stead to Philadelphia to review a Liberty Loan parade, the first time she had ever stood in his place. Wilson saw her off and was waiting at the station for her train in the evening.

One night at Poli's Theater a man announced he would buy a $5,000 Liberty Loan bond if ten other people would take $500 each. Wilson told an usher he'd take one, and on the strength of that a wave of buying erupted that brought the night's total over $100,000. The Wilsons put most of their money in these bonds, and their leadership helped others follow.

As the war effort reached mammoth proportions, and as the war itself neared crisis, Wilson became impatient with the usual mechanisms of government, and instituted a Wednesday meeting of himself, McAdoo, Garfield, Baruch, and others concerned with domestic production for the war. This became known as the war cabinet, and the regular cabinet was much exercised by the new team. Interior Secretary Lane confided to his brother that he was frustrated by attending cabinet meetings during which not one word was said about the war.

During this period, Edith wrote, Wilson was

* * *

buoyant and happy, no matter how hard the problem, and goodness knows how many and how hard they were! He met them with ease, and was never sad. To me that was the wonder of it. Every one else would have long faces, for particularly during the war the problems were insuperable. But he—never! The fact that he was the final arbiter of grave decisions—often concerning the lives of all our men—naturally weighed upon him; but he was *never* sad.

As to her own influence on him, Edith wrote that Wilson loved diversions of all kinds, and yet "he had never had time to play much, and he needed someone to show him how. When he had it, the latent boyish love of fun bubbled up and kept him going." When the cares of the world deepened, Edith and Woodrow held fast to one another and sought every opportunity to shut out the problems and relax together. In White House usher Ike Hoover's diary at this time, there are many references to Saturday afternoons and Sundays with "no breakfast, no church, no guests" because the Wilsons wanted to be alone with each other. Edith also had a billiard table installed in the White House, and they began to play together.

In May the Wilsons went to New York to see Colonel House. Notes between the Houses and Wilsons were still friendly around this time, but House had already begun to note in his diary the president's occasional lapses of memory, his tiredness, his unwillingness to do precisely what it was the colonel wanted.

House did one particular favor for Wilson on this trip. McAdoo was thinking of resigning because of a disagreement over a railroad issue. Wilson didn't want to lose Mac, and didn't want the public to think he was purging a possible rival for a third term, but he was adamant on the railroad matter. House counseled Wilson to be more receptive to McAdoo, and told Mac by letter that his views had been aired and overruled, and now he should obey like a good subordinate. It seemed to work. Back in Washington, Wilson and McAdoo met three times in two days and ironed out their difficulties, at least for the moment.

At the end of May, with the Germans still on the offensive, Wilson addressed a Congress which had done little but harry him during an entire session, and exhorted the legislators to pass a needed tax bill before they recessed. He told them that for the duration of the war "politics is adjourned." The next day politics and war came calling in the person of General Leonard Wood. Wood wanted a European command. Wilson told him that Pershing and army superiors did not want

Wood in France because of his history of disobeying orders, and his well-known inclination to being divisive and outspokenly political, and that as president he was backing up his commanders. Much to the dismay of Republicans, Wood was relegated to training soldiers in the United States. A cartoon showed Wood and Theodore Roosevelt commiserating, "Well, at least he kept *us* out of war!"

That same day the Germans broke through at Amiens, and by June 3 had reached the Marne, fifty-six miles from Paris. Big Bertha, the longest-range cannon ever made, shelled the city from there, causing death and destruction among civilians from a weapon so far away it was unseen. But even as the Germans advanced, there were peace feelers from her largest ally, Austria. The war was nearing its climax. The question was, how could its conclusion be reached?

That Wilson had an answer—an arbitrated peace—was obvious from an article by journalist L. P. Jacks:

> The germinating idea of Mr. Wilson's policy is that America, because of her greatness, of her power, of her vast potentialities, is a *servant* among nations, and not a *master*. It is a noble conception, and particularly fitted to inspire a young and mighty people with a vision of its destiny. . . . Though the idea of greatness in service has long been familiar in other connections . . . President Wilson is the first statesman to make it a guiding principle of international politics; and this alone, whether he succeeds or not, assures him a distinct place in history and in the grateful remembrance of mankind.

Wilson wrote Jacks that the article mirrored his thoughts very well.

At home, however, he had to face increased political snipings. Roosevelt had broken bread with Taft, apparently healing the breach between them. The two Republicans united were formidable opposition. Roosevelt was now in the vanguard of a crusade for "100 percent Americanism." This movement called for dismissal of teachers who wouldn't sign loyalty oaths, a prohibition on teaching German in schools, and the forced repatriation of immigrants who didn't learn English within five years. TR coupled this crusade with attacks on the administration, thereby linking a supposedly incompetent war effort with those whom he considered less than 100 percent Americans.

Wilson quietly intervened to save several teachers from this virulence, and Vice-President Thomas Marshall was sent out to make a round of speeches. TR, Marshall said, had held in 1900 that a refusal to support McKinley during the Spanish-American War would be taken as a refutation of the president's efforts to win the war; Marshall said the need to back up Wilson was far greater than the need to back McKinley twenty years ago.

On the other side, Taft's strivings for peace threatened to upstage Wilson's efforts.

By June 1918 the president knew he needed to accomplish peace as soon as possible and on the best terms because, as Dr. Arthur S. Link suggests, the Roosevelt line was more persuasive than the Taft line, and

> There was the danger that he and his people would succumb to the fascination of total war, become intoxicated with hatred of the enemy and love of fighting, and forget the great political objectives which they had taken up the sword to vindicate.

When George Creel had first suggested he speak at Mount Vernon on July Fourth, Wilson said the conjunction of site and date was presumptuous, but he later agreed. A few days before the speech, American troops won a great victory at Belleau Wood, preventing the Germans from breaking through to Paris.

On a torrid July Fourth, Wilson spoke magnificently, outlining the four ends for which the associated powers were fighting: the destruction of "arbitrary" powers that could disturb peace, the settlement of economic and political questions on the basis of "free acceptance" by the people "immediately concerned," the consent of nations to be governed by the same moral laws which governed the behavior of individuals, and the establishment of "an organization of peace" to enforce these provisions.

Within days, Wilson asked House to draft a charter for such an organization and, on obtaining the draft, the president reworked it himself. He was concerned about the league as an integral part of the peace. A returning official told the president that Lloyd George had laughed at Wilson's concept of a league of nations, and that Clemenceau had been quoted as saying that though God had needed only Ten Commandments, Wilson needed Fourteen Points. Wilson replied that he knew Europe was still governed by forces as reactionary as the ones that had controlled the United States until he took office, but that when the time was ripe he would reach over the heads of the rulers to the people of Europe for support. In fact, he was doing so already. Along with the Fourteen Points address, his Mount Vernon speech was being distributed throughout the world—translated into a dozen languages, dropped behind enemy lines. These speeches provided to hundreds of thousands plagued by endless war a standard to which they could rally. Harold Lasswell points out in his study of propaganda techniques that Wilson's

> monumental rhetoric epitomizing the aspirations of all humanity in periods at once lucid and persuasive . . . declared war upon autocracies everywhere, and solemnly adhered to the distinction between the German people and the German rulers. His speeches were one prolonged instigation to revolt. . . . Such matchless skill as Wilson showed in propaganda has never been equalled in the world's history. He spoke to the hearts of the people as no statesman has ever done.

On a blistering afternoon that summer, Stock Axson sat out on the south portico with Edith and Woodrow. Wilson asked whom he would name as the next president. McAdoo, said Stock. Wilson disagreed, said he loved Mac as much as anyone, but his son-in-law was a man of action who never reflected upon anything, and that wouldn't do because the next president would have to make decisions affecting the character of the world for generations to come: "The next president must be a man who will be able not only to *do* things, but, after having taken counsel and made a full survey, he must be able to retire alone, behind his own closed door, and think through the processes, step by step." Edith agreed Mac was not the man, but that was because she harbored her grudge against him for what he had done in 1915.

That spring Edith had joined a Red Cross unit. Every day she donned a striped and starched blue-and-white uniform and helped feed soldiers going through Washington to embark for Europe. Many recognized her, and she bantered with them. At this time rumors surfaced in the papers that she was pro-German, which she found particularly galling since she had always been strongly pro-Ally. Hurt, she had Woodrow turn down many requests for her time, saying she wanted to keep out of the papers, but she continued her Red Cross work. Often the president would come by in the late afternoons to pick her up from work, and would shake hands or wave to the platoons as they got on the trains. Wilson viewed each one of the boys going over as a son. When the draft was later widened to include all men between eighteen and forty-five, the number Wilson drew from a bowl was held by the son of a White House guard, who said, "I give the best I have to help you, Mr. President." Wilson grasped the guard's hand, and replied in a muffled voice, "God grant that he may come back to you."

On July 17, Theodore Roosevelt learned that his youngest son Quentin, not yet twenty-one, would not come back from France. Although TR had not expected to see all of his four sons alive at the end of the war, he was nevertheless crushed by Quentin's death. From this moment on, the ex-president believed the future held little for him.

Meanwhile the "100 percent Americanism" movement which Roosevelt had championed was bearing vicious fruit. Witch-hunts for draft evaders and subversives began. Eugene Debs, formerly the Socialist candidate for the presidency, was arrested for an anti-government speech. As he awaited trial, Debs had the pleasure of seeing many of his own goals inch toward reality. A solid working class of thirty million was consolidating rapidly into unions. A fact-finding board appointed by Wilson and headed by ex-President Taft made unanimous recommendations which were to change the face of American society: Taft's board held that labor unions had the right to organize and bargain collectively, that there should be a universal eight-hour day and a minimum wage, and that the government should gather employment statistics. Meanwhile the cost of living was up 40 percent from pre-war levels, and was continuing to climb.

Once such measures as the Taft board suggested were considered overly socialistic. Now the majority considered them reasonable, because the menace seen by the democracies at the moment was rampant communism. For months, Wilson had resisted a half-dozen direct appeals to join with the British, French, Czechs, and Japanese to intervene in Russia and overthrow the Bolsheviks. Wilson wrote to House that he had been "sweating blood over the question of what it is right and feasible to do in Russia." The Czechs wanted to rescue their army there, the Japanese wanted easy conquest in Siberia, the French and British wanted to keep the two-front war going. A Madame Botchkarova, of the Russian Women's Battalion of Death, entered Wilson's office, and during the course of an interview threw herself on the floor, clasped the presidential legs, and begged Wilson for food, aid, and troops to solace her own anti-Bolshevik faction. After talking with the cabinet, getting advice from Pershing and Foch, and being heavily pressured by the Allies and Japanese, Wilson finally acquiesced in assisting their intervention, and in midsummer sent some troops to Russia.

French resistance to the German offensive had halted von Ludendorff's troops on the Marne. Now the Allies for the first time were able to launch a real counterstroke. On August 8, British and French troops in Picardy started a new drive that had surprising effectiveness. Tanks were used in large numbers. The Germans started to retreat. New blows kept them on the run. The cumulating Allied victories began to shatter the kaiser's soldiers. No longer believing they were going to win, the soldiers started pressing for the war's end. It seemed possible for the first time that the Allies and the Americans were going to emerge the victors because the Germans had finally run out of steam, their own effectiveness shattered by Ludendorff's ill-advised push against heavily fortified positions.

The Wilsons' excitement and hope grew. In mid-August they went to Magnolia, Massachusetts, for a vacation, renting a place next to Colonel House. Hydroplanes, submarine chasers, torpedo boats, and a detail of marines guarded them; the protection was so thorough that once the president was nearly arrested by an overzealous local policeman. One afternoon Wilson read his own draft of the Covenant for the League of Nations, and told House something like it must be incorporated into the peace. The two men sat out on the lawn in front of House's cottage, maps of Europe on their laps. Sir William Wiseman, the only other guest, observed they were "discussing ways and means of organizing Liberal opinion to break down the German military machine, and how the nations which had suffered from oppression might be safeguarded in the future." The Allied embassies in Washington were so disturbed by the thought of these two men deciding the fate of Europe, that they tried many ruses to get to see Wilson or House at this time. No one was allowed in.

Edith, too, was excluded from these discussions. House would draw the president out onto the lawn and not invite her. As the Wilsons were basically guests of the Houses, perhaps the president did not think it polite to invite Edith on his own to join them, as he regularly did when they were all in the White House. Then, too, Edith was detailed to entertain Mrs. House, and couldn't be in two places at once. Not being in on the discussions galled Edith.

House and Wilson were themselves experiencing a fundamental clash in viewpoints. Wilson wanted a strong League with economic and military clout, House preferred an international court. Wilson wanted small nations to have equal voice with large ones, House voiced the practical objections to this of the major powers. Most importantly, House wanted to get Great Britain and France to secretly commit in advance to Wilson's draft of the League's constitution, while Wilson insisted a League could only have proper moral standing if it were evolved jointly with others at a peace conference, because there must be

no hint of balance-of-power politics in it. House deferred to Wilson—
but only for the moment.

Republicans were publicly stating their own objections to Wilson's
positions. Root wondered at the wisdom of agreeing to put American
troops under international command in the future. Lodge told Congress,
"No peace that satisfies Germany in any degree can ever satisfy us."
Roosevelt wrote that in the post-war world the issue would be "100
percent Americanism" versus the holier-than-thou Wilsonian internationalism.

There was a rash of "slacker raids" which attempted to imprison
those who would neither work nor fight. A. Mitchell Palmer, alien
property custodian, and Attorney General Gregory were in the forefront
of those pressing the fight on aliens, slackers, and those not in agreement with the war effort. In September, Eugene Debs came to trial and
was convicted and sent to prison; in time he became a martyr to the
cause of freedom in a country obsessed with patriotism. Wilson was
accused of being unable to see that Debs should be freed but, when Debs
was first imprisoned, Wilson had to back the men who arrested him.
Later in the summer those men got out of hand, and Wilson tried to
curb them. Thinking of Palmer and Gregory and other governmental
zealots, Fuel Administrator Garfield wrote to Wilson, "Should your
hand be taken from the helm there is the greatest danger that reactionary forces . . . will turn us back and the cause of democracy be
indefinitely postponed."

Cries for a harsh peace were aided by daily reports of barbarities and
random destruction by retreating German troops. Acting alone for the
first time, the American army overran positions at Saint-Mihiel which
the Germans had held for four years. On the twenty-sixth, Americans
drove into the Argonne to break German transportation lines. The
difficult terrain and stiffened resistance resulted in high American
casualties for the first time.

On the Macedonian front, events were also escalating. After a long
period of inaction, the Allies broke through the southern end of the
Teutonic fortress, and in days Bulgaria cabled Wilson that she wished
him to "mediate to terminate bloodshed in southern theatre of war by
an armistice." Bulgaria approached Wilson, rather than the Allies,
believing the president would be more lenient with them. Wilson
replied—as he had earlier to the Austrians—that he would mediate
only if the terms were left up to him. He was in New York to speak at
the Metropolitan Opera House on behalf of the fourth Liberty Loan. In
this speech the president again declared his great principle: that all

must keep peace together, or all would suffer together in the prolonged
fire of another war. His speech was so clear and moving that even his
long-standing critics seconded his sentiments and reasoning.

The next day crowds gathered at the railroad station and caught a
glimpse of the president on his way back to Washington, sitting in his
compartment with outstretched hands, holding a skein for Edith to
unwind.

Wilson's speech, translated, was dropped behind German lines.
Within days, Hindenburg and Ludendorff decided that Germany must
give in and end the war. As Wilson had long said he would not deal with
Germany's present autocratic rulers, the kaiser changed governments.
On October 6, Germany told Wilson the new government would accept
Wilson's Fourteen Points, July Fourth, and Metropolitan Opera
speeches as a basis for peace. Financial panic hit Germany, though
fighting continued on the front lines. Wilson at first thought to accept
the offer but, under considerable private and public pressure, made a
tough reply. He demanded the removal of German armies from foreign
soil and the formation of a truly democratic government before talks
could begin. Frantically, Clemenceau, Lloyd George, and Sonnino
cabled Wilson that a cease fire must include reference to Allied and
American superiority in the field so Germany couldn't use the lull to
rebuild her armies. Wilson again agreed and sent a note to that effect.
On October 12, while the Wilsons were again in New York, the
president learned that Germany had accepted his terms. The couple
were about to go in to a formal dinner, and knowing he would be seated
apart from Edith, Wilson wrote a note to House telling him to give her
the news. It was something the Wilsons had to share together.

Reading over the new German note when the text arrived, Wilson
found it unacceptable because it had not used the word "surrender" and
did not include specifics about changing the government. Seeing the
note in print, Roosevelt trumpeted that he hoped the offer would be
rejected and that the Senate and the people should "emphatically
repudiate the so-called fourteen points and various similar utterances of
the President." The press castigated TR for having let Wilson's points
lie unanswered for nine months and only now, when they were actually
being used for negotiation, speaking out against them.

Wilson's next note further demanded that atrocities cease, that submarine warfare stop, that our military superiority be acknowledged,
and that democracy be allowed in Germany. At the same time he
announced that 250,000 Americans and supplies would be sent to
Europe each month until the cease fire went into effect. Lodge pronounced himself "genuinely pleased" now.

While waiting for total capitulation, and concerned about the November elections, Wilson drafted an appeal for a Democratic Congress which Burleson and Tumulty had long been after him to write. Edith objected to the note and its partisan words. "I would not send it out," she said, "it is not a dignified thing to do." Wilson agreed, but having promised it, said he had to send it out. His appeal called for a Democratic Congress, and criticized Republicans who "At almost every turn, since we entered the war . . . have sought to take the choice of policy and the conduct of the war out of my hands and to put it under the control of instrumentalities of their own choosing." Anything other than a Democratic Congress, he said, would be taken in Europe as a repudiation of his leadership. When printed the next day, this appeal enraged moderate and conservative Republicans, and lit a fire under them for the closing ten days of the campaign.

But the president could pay the campaign little heed, because cables from Colonel House in Paris were keeping him and Edith up late almost every night. House was asking for a free hand, and though Wilson had confidence in him, it was awkward to communicate this way in the midst of delicate negotiations. The sticking point now was that, while Germany was ready to accept the Fourteen Points, the Allies were not. Lloyd George had serious objections. In a dramatic confrontation, House refused to shelve Wilson's peace terms, and made what he later said was the longest speech of his life:

> If the Allies are unwilling to accept the Fourteen Points upon which Germany has based her request for an armistice, there can be, as far as I can see, only one course for the President to pursue. He would have to tell the Germans that the conditions which they had accepted are not acceptable to the powers with which America has been associated.

It was a clear threat to have the United States conclude a separate peace treaty with Germany. Faced with this, the Allies gave in and agreed to the Fourteen Pounts with certain stated objections to freedom of the seas and reparations. House and Wilson then believed—though it was not so stated in writing—that, having objected to only two points, the Allies accepted the other twelve as a basis for the peace.

On the day House's compromise was officially sealed, November 4, there was open revolt in the former Austrian empire and near-chaos in Germany. Foch and Pershing imposed harsh military terms into the settlement—French occupation of the Rhineland and internment of the German navy—adding to the chaos.

On November 5, the voters of the United States returned a Republican Congress. Dissatisfaction over controls on wheat and lack of controls on cotton, and other regional issues, tipped the scales. Organizational ineptitude and the Spanish flu contributed to a poor turnout of Democratic votes. Republicans regained the majorities they had held prior to 1912. Seward Livermore's analysis of the votes suggests "The result was not so much a repudiation of the President as a want of confidence in the 65th Congress, whose obstructionism, irresponsibility, and quarrelsomeness in a time of great crisis had made a very poor impression on the electorate."

When the results of the election became known, Edith and Woodrow were so tired they paid them little heed. It seemed a small setback in comparison to the triumphs for Wilson taking place in Europe. The president's moral force had joined with the volcanoes of revolt to topple autocratic governments in Austria, Hungary, Romania, Serbia, the Czech and Slovak lands, Poland, Germany, and in other small states. Democratic-based governments were struggling to take over. This was revolution on a scale grander than even Lenin had accomplished.

On November 8, the Germans asked for a cease fire. On November 9, Kaiser Wilhelm abdicated, and a democratic German republic was proclaimed. On November 11, an armistice was signed. It was the eleventh hour of the eleventh day of the eleventh month, and the war to make the world safe for democracy had been won. That night, for the first time in months, the Wilsons went out of the White House to a party. Happy, triumphant, victorious, they danced and toasted with the crowd.

11

AT RISK IN THE TOWER OF BABEL

THE PRESIDENT'S ADVISERS, including House, thought he should not go to the peace conference in Paris, their main objection being that his influence would lessen in daily, face-to-face combat with leaders of other countries. Virtually alone, Edith argued that he must go. She knew from working on the complicated cables that it would be cumbersome and unsatisfying for Woodrow to work from Washington while the world sat in Paris. Also, having entered the war to obtain a seat at the peace table, it was inconceivable for Wilson not to attend. On November 18, he announced he would go to Paris.

Then he had to make up the rest of the team. A logical choice was House, who would have his first official position in Wilson's government. Secretary Lansing must go because of his rank. General Tasker H. Bliss, who had proved astute during the closing phases of the war, was selected to be military representative. Wilson knew he had to take a Republican. This posed a problem. If he took a senator it would have to be Lodge, who was slated to become the chairman of the Foreign Relations Committee. Wilson refused. Of the other leading Republicans, Root was too much in favor of a world court, Hughes too recent an opponent, and Taft was needed at home as head of the League to Enforce Peace. Wilson chose Henry White, a career diplomat and a long-time friend of Henry Cabot Lodge.

On the eve of the president's departure, Lodge handed White a secret memo for Clemenceau and Lloyd George, to strengthen their hands against Wilson. It said that the League of Nations must *not* be included in the treaty because, if it were, the Senate would reject the treaty as a whole. White was thunderstruck. He took the memo, slipped it into his briefcase, and resolved privately never to show it. He did, however, agree to keep Lodge informed about events at the conference on a weekly basis.

Wilson's ship, the *George Washington*, steamed from New York on December 4, passing a returning transport packed with American doughboys. First day out, Wilson spent his time alone with Edith. They took long naps, strolled the deck, had meals in their cabin. Edith Benham, daughter of an admiral and engaged to another admiral, accompanied them as the First Lady's social secretary. Grayson, now an admiral, also came along, as did Ike Hoover and a small staff. In addition the ship carried ambassadors, other government officials, newsmen, and the entire library put together by the Inquiry. In the evenings the president went to Fairbanks and Chaplin movies with the crew, and sat through a lively performance of *Uncle Tom's Stateroom*, with sailors cavorting in women's clothes. As there was still real danger from floating mines, the ship had an unannounced lifeboat drill. The president immediately found Edith, hurried with her to their appointed station, and gallantly refused to don his life jacket until he had helped her into one.

At home, the government Wilson left behind was undergoing rapid change. Dollar-a-year men were returning to civilian life. Prices and unemployment were both rising. McAdoo had announced his resignation from all posts, effective January 1, even though there were still major problems with the railroads. His personal health and fortune were depleted. This act might cost him his political future, but, he wrote to House, he didn't care, for there were some actions

> about which no man can be expedient, and those are the things which indicate unmistakeably the path of duty and honor. . . . I wish I could have stayed on until [the president] returned, and yet I think that there were obvious embarassments to him and to me if I had, as the ranking Cabinet officer, in his and Lansing's absence, to take charge of the general run of things, even though subject to his directions by cable from Europe. Republicans would have raised the cry of "hereditary government," "the Crown Prince," etc., and while I attach very little importance to that, I think it might have an unfavourable impression upon some elements of our people.

* * *

The *Literary Digest* suggested the following image: if all the men killed in the war on all sides were to march down Fifth Avenue twenty abreast, from sunup to sundown every day, it would take *four months* for them to pass in review. It was to prevent such carnage from ever happening again that Wilson was going to the peace conference. The Wilsons arrived in Brest on Friday, December 13, which he considered a lucky day. There was a great and grand welcome, with people in colorful local costumes, quite a bit of military panoply. The Wilsons were met by Margaret, who had been in France entertaining the troops and who was a bit ill; they all boarded the president of France's drafty railroad car and proceeded to Paris.

Thus began a month of virtually uninterrupted triumphant receptions all over Europe, welcomes grander than any other living human being had ever received. For the first time in a half-century the Arc de Triomphe was opened; hundreds of thousands jammed the Champs-Élysées to see *Wilson le Juste*. Riding in a second carriage, Edith noted that the Place de la Concorde was filled with hundreds of German tanks, big guns, and other machines of war. It was an unforgettable reminder of why they were here.

The Wilsons found themselves installed in a grand palace of another age, the Murat, a fortress of Napoleonic excess with heavy velvet carpets, carved furniture, the emperor's eagles and insignia everywhere. When the king of Italy visited the Wilsons there, he said the surroundings were too grand even for him. The Wilsons were uncomfortable at the Murat. Nightly celebrations were another strain. On being escorted into a formal dinner by French president Poincaré, Edith wrote:

> The lady finds a vise-like hold fastened upon her, which apparently nothing but death can relax. . . . I was towed along . . . and being a head taller than he I felt like a big liner with a tiny tug pushing her out from her moorings. . . . The approach was through a narrow aisle lined with liveried attendants. Single file there was ample space but two abreast made it an adventure. However, mowing down waiters as we went, we arrived breathless and panting. This was my first experience, but as time went on I got so expert that I felt I could qualify for a football rush.

After four days of such festivities, Wilson wanted to know why there was no progress toward the opening of the conference. He learned it was because Lloyd George was still at home campaigning vigorously for reelection. The prime minister's position was tenuous, and he sought a mandate on how to handle the peace settlement. "Hang the Kaiser" was the message delivered by the electorate; Germany was to be squeezed "until the pips squeak." Lloyd George actually promised to make Germany pay the costs of the war—which was directly counter to the agreement he had signed before the cease fire.

Back in New York, Senator Lodge spent hours visiting a very ill Theodore Roosevelt, hospitalized with rheumatic arthritis. TR was an impossible patient, and enjoyed the distraction of plotting with Lodge how to defeat a Wilson peace treaty and the League of Nations. As Roosevelt's sister later wrote, the men agreed that no matter what form the League would take, they would try to strike out its most vital provisions, and if they couldn't do that directly then they would do so by alteration. As Lodge described the game plan to a friend,

> It would be a mistake to admit that the League would be a good thing, but I think we should make a mistake if we met the proposition with a flat denial. . . . Any practical League that involves control of our legislation, or our armies and navies or the Monroe Doctrine, or an international police, and that sort of thing, then our issue is made up and we shall win.

Unaware of these machinations, the Wilsons in Paris visited American and French hospitals. Edith felt her heart aching, was sure she would disgrace herself by bursting into tears among the dying and disfigured men, but was heartened by their faith in her husband. The president gripped the hand of a sightless man so hard and for so long that the others in his party worried that the emotion was too great for him to bear. Then a ward full of wounded Frenchmen burst into the "Marseillaise," and everybody cried. The Wilsons spent their wedding anniversary alone, but on Christmas day visited American troops in barns, haylofts, and temporary shacks. The following day they started for London.

Lining their route to Buckingham Palace was a sea of humanity, wildly cheering. Edith, used to the crowds now, was more impressed by the personal kindnesses she received from King George and Queen Mary. She felt, she wrote home, like Cinderella playing out a role not only for herself but for all the women in America. Actually, the treatment she received made Madame Poincaré and wives of other heads of democratic governments jealous. Edith, worldly but at the same time naïve, was shocked when Margot Asquith gave her the lowdown on all the important women gathered at the court.

For Wilson the emotional highlight of the trip was not in London, but in a visit to the church where his maternal grandfather Thomas Woodrow had preached, and where his mother had lived with him until the age of seven. Unexpectedly requested to speak, Wilson recalled the grandfather who had often queried him, "Tommy, what is the chief end of man?" Now he had an answer:

> I believe that as this war has drawn the nations temporarily together in a combination of physical force we shall now be drawn together in a combination of moral force that will be irresistible. . . . It is from quiet places like this all over the world that the forces accumulate which presently will overbear any attempt to accomplish evil on a large scale.

Winding up his tour in Manchester, Wilson let the world know why there must be a League of Nations:

> Heretofore the world has been governed or at any rate an attempt has been made to govern it, by partnerships of interest, and they have broken down. Interest does not bind men together. Interest separates men, for the moment there is the slightest departure from the nice adjustment of interests, jealousies begin to spring up. There is only one thing that can bind people together, and that is a common devotion to right.

France's Premier Clemenceau answered Wilson by saying flatly that only a balance-of-power alliance would keep Germany from future aggression. Aware of the contrast between the barren, wasted cities of France and Belgium, and the sleek, untouched cities of Germany, the French Chamber of Deputies backed Clemenceau's strategies for the peace conference overwhelmingly.

In Italy, Wilson's receptions were even more idolatrous than they had been in France and England. People displayed his picture next to that of Christ. The whole country seemed enamored of "the best friend of humanity" who had ended the war and who held out hope for all. At one point during the trip, musicians at the famous La Scala opera house drowned out a Wilson speech. Woodrow responded by conducting the orchestra. Several observers saw this as *hubris*, and said Wilson's head was turned by adulation, that he now believed himself nearer to angels than to men. It was not so. Wilson merely hoped he could live up to the enormous responsibility placed on him by the adulation he received. The praise, he knew, was not for him, but for what he espoused; he was an imperfect vessel, but the wine he bore might aspire to grace.

Evidence of his all-too-human disposition came at Modena when a messenger handed him a telegram that Roosevelt was dead. His first reaction was relief: the implacable enemy was gone, while he himself lived and was on the verge of triumph. Then he saddened and, mindful of the necessities, wrote out a condolence note and ordered all U.S. flags at half-mast for thirty days. When Dostoyevsky died, Tolstoy had felt the same relief, then had cried for a day because, he said, he knew that for all their antagonism he and his rival had been closer under the skin than any two men alive. Both Roosevelt and Wilson, William Allen White wrote, were great spirits and moral teachers, towering over the pygmies of their time.

"The war will last a hundred years; five for the fighting, ninety-five for rolling up the barbed wire." Preliminaries for the peace conference seemed to prove the old soldiers' maxim. The structure of the conference was unwieldy. Detail work had to be divided among sixty commissions, while important questions were to be decided by the Council of Ten. When Wilson returned to Paris on January 12, no substantive work had been accomplished. There were conferences, yes, but they all seemed to result in delay. The French asked Wilson to visit the battlefields in the interim before the formal opening ceremonies, but he refused, knowing the devastation would affect him too deeply.

Paris was a Babel, an Olympic village of victors. Five hundred reporters alone had descended on the city, among them Americans Ray Stannard Baker, William Allen White, Herbert Bayard Swope, Mark Sullivan, S. S. McClure, David Lawrence, and Lincoln Steffens.

Reporters and delegates alike watched the great panoply—Lawrence of Arabia and various eastern potentates in unfamiliar costumes; cabarets which featured Mistinguet and Chevalier; uniforms of what seemed like fifty armies. Elsa Maxwell, after a party one night, was awakened by harsh metallic sounds in the garden below her room. Looking out she saw a British and an Italian officer hacking away at each other with sabers. In the spirit of Wilson she rushed down, separated the two men, and offered them cups of coffee.

Wilson asked Ray Stannard Baker to act as liaison to his former news colleagues; he would arrive at Wilson's room at seven each evening for a half-hour talk. Edith would often sit in as Baker probed for what had gone on that day, then went and translated it for the journalists. Those who didn't like this arrangement went after the more accessible Colonel House, who consequently received a great deal of personal publicity. This angered Edith, and also irked other American officials who pointed out that House had brought to Paris a large number of relatives. There was Sidney Mezes, his brother-in-law; Gordon Auchincloss, his son-in-law; and David Hunter Miller, Gordon's law partner. And all had brought their wives. Innuendoes about House's family were particularly galling as they compared badly to Wilson's well-known strict adherence to rules against any of his family gaining governmental position or favor. The president had, for instance, initially opposed Margaret coming and singing for the troops, and had talked Frank Sayre out of accepting a government post which would have taken him to France.

It was because of his principles that among the younger members of the international delegations, Wilson's star was still untarnished. He was their hope for the conference. Young Harold Nicolson wrote:

> I believed, with him, that the standard of political and international conduct should be as high, as sensitive, as the standard of personal conduct. I believed . . . that the only true patriotism is an active desire that one's own tribe or country should in every particular minister to that ideal. I shared with him a hatred of violence in any form. I conceived, as he conceived, that this hatred was common to the great mass of humanity, and that in the new world this dumb force of popular sentiment could be rendered the controlling power in human destiny.

The peace conference finally, formally opened on January 18, 1919. Forty-eight years earlier on that date, a victorious Germany had proclaimed the Second Reich. Now those who had vanquished Germany were to decide the fate of that country and all of Europe. The decisions of the victors were largely in the hands of four men.

Clemenceau, France's premier, had seen his country through two German invasions, and was determined there should never be another. Of peasant stock, a newspaperman who had once practiced medicine in Brooklyn and had been married to an American woman, he had one goal, the protection of France. With his black skullcap and gray gloves (to cover his eczema), he was a distinctive figure. *Lloyd George*, British prime minister, consummate Welsh politician, was debonair, mercurial, able to forget in a moment what was not expedient. He had led the British to victory and had some fixed goals, including the protection of British mercantile interests, the gaining of colonies, and the repayment of Britain's enormous war costs. *Orlando*, the Italian premier, was a decent man but out of his depth at the conference; he wanted to secure the material gains promised by the Allies in secret treaties to persuade Italy to join the war on the Allied side. *Wilson*, as ranged against these three, had a basically moral position: America was the only nation that had come with no wish for territory, money, or aggrandizement. Wilson's great cause was the League.

Since the other nations had accepted the Fourteen Points as a basis for peace, Wilson thought they would now adhere to them. But once the conference opened, the major powers sought to negotiate everything anew. In the opening weeks Wilson struggled to implement the concepts he believed had already been agreed to, in particular working to get a commission set up to write a constitution for a League of Nations. Clemenceau and Lloyd George wanted to settle military terms and repayment first and work out a League later. In the president's view that was putting the cart before the horse, because he felt that if settlements were made first the League might never be realized or that it would end up merely implementing the old balance of power. Through January he took a hard line while House conversed in a soft voice in unofficial settings. This "bad cop, good cop" approach got them within ten days the go-ahead for the commission.

On a second matter, Wilson wanted to allow for some form of self-determination for the former German colonies, and advocated the ideas of South Africa's Jan Smuts for mandates over these colonies to be distributed by the League. Secret Allied treaties had already promised France certain territory, and she objected. So did Australia, which wanted New Guinea immediately, and when Wilson disagreed with Australia's Prime Minister Hughes, the man gave a nasty interview to the press about the president. Outraged, Wilson told the conference that if this kind of publicity was continued he would air all of their greedy motives to the press. Hughes was squelched, and that evening Wilson told Edith he was sure there would be no leaks from *that* meeting. The outcome of the colonies issue was compromise: Wilson agreed to mandate the colonies on the basis of occupation, but did not yield on the principle of self-determination.

Edith's main function in Paris was, as William Allen White put it, the care and feeding of an American president. Miss Benham described the relationship of the Wilsons in a letter to her fiancée:

> I am struck by their unrivalled home life. I have never dreamed such sweetness and love could be. One never hears anything between them but just love and understanding, and it is very beautiful to see his face light up and brighten at the very sight of her and to see her turn to him for everything.

* * *

Edith walked with him mornings to the Quai d'Orsay, knowing if she didn't he would get no exercise, for he found no time to golf. She dined with him, taught him solitaire to relax, kept his spirits up. Miss Benham described Edith as

> unusually self-contained, admits scarcely anyone to her friendship, though always wonderfully gracious. Her smile and her charm are proverbial. I do not believe there has been any other woman who has occupied the position she has who has her beauty and charm and is so good. . . . She is very quiet about her dislikes, but is a very intense and very loyal friend. There never was anyone with a keener sense of humor. He has the same, but she is a born mimic. I have never seen anyone enjoy anything more than he does one of her stories or experiences after she has been somewhere without him, for she always sees something funny.

On a quiet Sunday, Henry White, erudite old diplomat, took Edith Wilson for a walk around Paris. He had observed some things at the conference he didn't like. "Intrigue" in the upstairs rooms of Colonel House, for instance; House was actually beginning to negotiate with the other delegations which felt more comfortable with him than with the seemingly unapproachable president. Wilson, White had noted, was wonderful when you were alone with him, but with a group he was reserved and remote. White had also noted that the president was often not as well briefed as he might have been because House was keeping expert information from Wilson when it differed with his own opinions. Another matter that bothered White was the bypassing of Lansing by Wilson. Could Edith intercede with Woodrow so that the secretary of state would not continue to be slighted? She did, and soon the president began some measures to include Lansing, but these lapsed as the two men were not personally compatible.

On another weekend, the Wilsons, Baruch, Herbert Hoover, and Grayson finally went to see the battlefields near Château-Thierry. An ashen, muddied, and inhuman landscape assaulted them: uncountable millions of shell holes, twisted trees, fragments of buildings. Starling was so shocked he never got over the sight. In Rheims, the Wilsons discovered a few thousand people living in cellars in a city which had once housed tens of thousands; there was snow falling through the roof of the beautiful cathedral. Soissons was deserted when the party first drove through the city, but when the Wilsons unexpectedly went through it again on their way back to Paris, it teemed with French soldiers who cheered the president. Inquiring, Wilson was told that the soldiers had been initially ordered to stay indoors while the president's car passed. "I am surrounded by intrigue here," Wilson told Hoover. To Edith he said spies were all around, even in their own quarters, so much so that he was deliberately omitting to write things down when at all possible.

During the days Wilson met with the high commissioners, and in the early February evenings he sat with a smaller group that was drafting a constitution for a League. The two sets of meetings left him exhausted. There was pressure to separate the Covenant of the League from the peace treaty because their intertwining fostered delays, but Wilson held out for a peace treaty which would incorporate the League and its Covenant, or constitution. As his interpreter Stephen Bonsal noted in his diary,

> Even a blind man could see the disadvantages of further delay, which the President's plan entails, and truly the danger of the present state of uncertainty is very great, but I am still convinced the President is right. He is dealing with men who are not entirely trustworthy, and from what he has learned by bitter experience in the last six weeks he knows that any treaty they sign will be in great need of copious libations of holy water, such as will flow, it is hoped, from the font of the Covenant.

Through his own enormous efforts, Wilson had the draft of the Covenant ready by February 13. House and Clemenceau helped shepherd it through shoals of amendments, and the constitution for the League of Nations was adopted that same day. Wilson viewed it as one of the most signal accomplishments of his life. On the fourteenth, Edith connived with Grayson to share Woodrow's moment of triumph. Clemenceau condoned their hiding behind a curtain at the Quai d'Orsay so they could hear the president present the Covenant to the plenary session for formal approval. "A living thing is born," Wilson said; he hoped that whatever mistakes were made at the peace conference, the League would help to right them.

Before returning to Washington for the close of the congressional session, Wilson put House in charge and told him, "I do not wish the questions of territorial adjustment or those of reparations to be held up." House told friends he understood the limitations on his powers and was glad of them: he knew he wasn't to make any final decisions, but was rather to get things in shape so that Wilson could act decisively on his return. House pleaded with the president to be patient and try to reason with recalcitrant senators who were already talking of not ratifying the treaty—Hoke Smith, for example. Wilson lost his temper, calling Smith an "ambulance chaser." He and Smith had been rival lawyers in Atlanta years before, and Smith had gotten more business than Wilson. House gently quoted Burke—"to govern is to compromise"—and Wilson promised to entertain the senators at a dinner to get their views.

When Wilson went home the other leaders did so as well. On February 19, while Wilson was still in mid-Atlantic, Clemenceau was shot by a would-be assassin. None of the bullets proved fatal, but the French premier was laid up for several weeks, making him, he joked, more than merely an irascible old man—now he was a martyr and everyone would have to give him what he wanted.

The *George Washington* pulled into Boston harbor in a driving snowstorm that nearly ran the vessel aground. Lodge's home state gave Wilson an impressive reception. The press universally urged support of the president and the Covenant. Lodge said privately he was flabbergasted by this, and believed it merely demonstrated how misled the public was. Meanwhile ex-President Taft and the League to Enforce Peace were mounting an enthusiastic groundswell for the treaty. The night after they returned to Washington, the Wilsons hosted a dinner for thirty-four congressmen, including Lodge and many others opposed to the League. Two major opponents, Borah and Fall, refused to attend at all. Edith sat next to Lodge, and proceeded to needle him in a seemingly innocent way by talking of their wonderful reception in Massachusetts. After dinner the president told what had been accomplished in Paris, and was grilled for more than two hours by Senators Knox and Brandegee while Lodge listened in silence. Afterward, Lodge and Brandegee went home complaining to each other about Edith's behavior, the absence of cigars, and the weakness of the host's liquor.

Two days later Lodge opened fire in the Senate, warning of "supranational government" and "international socialism and anarchy," and suggesting amendments to safeguard the Monroe Doctrine and to prevent American soldiers from marching under foreign or international flags. He and Brandegee put together a resolution stating that a League such as the one currently proposed would not pass the Senate. Within a few short hours they had thirty-seven signatures—enough to reject a treaty—and this "Round Robin" gave Wilson notice he would be fighting an uphill battle. Republicans also filibustered to kill eight bills of appropriation, hoping that by preventing passage they would force

Wilson to call a special session of Congress allowing them to debate the League endlessly.

Ex-President Taft read the senatorial speeches and the headlines his Republican brethren made, and wrote to a friend,

> When I think of the viciousness of Reed, the explosive igno-rance of Poindexter, the ponderous Websterian language and lack of stamina of Borah, the vanity of Lodge . . . the selfishness, laziness, and narrow lawyer-like acuteness of Knox, the emptiness and sly partisanship of Hale, and the utter nothingness of Fall, in the face of this great world's crisis, I confess I don't see where we have any advantage over the women—at least at this juncture.

After two weeks the Wilsons left Washington to begin their trip back to Paris. On March 4, they stopped in Philadelphia to see newborn Woodrow Wilson Sayre and his mother Jessie. The baby's eyes were closed but his mouth gaped wide; Wilson observed "I think from appearances that he will make a United States Senator."

The evening before Wilson was to embark again for Paris, he and Taft were principal speakers at a peace rally at the Metropolitan Opera House. The two men clasped hands on stage and the crowd went wild. Taft had actually been forbidden to come to this rally by his doctor, but believed the cause of peace more vital than his health. He spoke first and refuted all the arguments made against the Covenant. (Similarly, Henry White wrote Lodge about this time that no member of the peace conference from any nation agreed that the League would do the "startling things" which Lodge feared it would.) The band played "Over There" and Wilson sang along, his voice choked with emotion. Indeed, he told the crowd, he would not come back until it was over, over there—and when he did come back, "gentlemen on this side will find the Covenant not only in [the peace treaty], but so many threads of the Treaty tied to the Covenant that you cannot dissect the Covenant from the Treaty without destroying the whole vital structure."

Colonel House thought otherwise. While the president was home, he had been negotiating with Clemenceau and with British Foreign Secre-tary Lord Balfour. House viewed his job as disposing, by "horse trad-ing," of the remaining problems of the conference, and boasted that he was making great progress now that Wilson was away. Months had gone by and there was no treaty and no guarantee that Germany might not get fed up with the delay and renew hostilities. Brushfires of revolution already burning in Bavaria and Hungary might torch all of Europe. The cost of delay was enormous, both financially and psychologically. So House was proud that, within ten days of Wilson's departure, resolutions were adopted by the Council of Ten which would crowd the entire peace settlement into a preliminary treaty that would fix Germany's frontiers and her war guilt, settle reparations, and prevent Allied armies from demobilizing until the Germans were forced to accept the terms. About the only thing this "preliminary" document failed to touch on was the League of Nations.

House told himself in his diary he had done a wonderful job. Later George Creel would point out that having a diary by House was as addictive as drugs or alcohol, and led House into self-befuddlement and purposeful self-delusion. House knew that he had to some extent betrayed his friend's trust when he went to meet Wilson at the boat. Wilson was engaged in singing an inspirational "Auld Lang Syne" with the crew when the colonel's presence was announced. While Edith greeted the French officials, House and Wilson retired and talked alone for some time. Later, in the special train to Paris, Wilson opened the door to Edith's compartment and, looking terribly changed, told her

> House has given away everything I had won before we left Paris. He has compromised on every side, and so I have to start all over again and this time it will be harder as he has given the impression that my delegates are not in sympathy with me. His own explanation of his compromises is that, with a hostile press in the United States expressing disapproval of the League of Nations as part of the Treaty, he thought it best to yield some other points lest the Conference withdraw its approval altogether. So he has yielded until there is nothing left.

Woodrow and Edith stayed up all night on the train, talking about what could be done.

It was after this that Edith started systematically to come between Wilson and House, showing the president articles overlaudatory of the adviser, and using other tactics. Basically, she believed Wilson had been betrayed, and did not want him hurt further. This accorded, on the whole, with Wilson's attitude toward House after he returned to Paris.

Wilson's position had been weakened on two counts. He would now have to compromise to get the League of Nations back to where he wanted it. Second, he would have to compromise to get needed modifications of the treaty and Covenant to satisfy the senators who had signed the Round Robin.

Meetings to iron out these knotty problems started informally at the new Wilson residence. The house on the Place des États-Unis was smaller than the palace but had plenty of room for entertaining. The Wilsons' bedrooms were on the ground floor and opened together onto a beautiful garden. Woodrow laughed when he found a bathtub with a gallery over it where musicians could play while he performed his ablutions. He decided Brooks could press his pants there.

During the war, Wilson had on his side the Allies' fear of German military might balancing the scales against the Allied demands; but now the war was over this was no longer the case. Now he had only one weapon, the threat of going home and signing a separate peace with Germany—and it must be used carefully.

Clemenceau was insisting on annexation of the Rhineland and Saar valleys in repayment for the damage Germany had done to France's industrial regions. He also wanted an Anglo-American pledge of military assistance if France were attacked in the future. Lloyd George wanted enormous sums in reparations from Germany and an American pledge guaranteeing British naval superiority.

Wilson had to contend with these demands and at the same time insert a clause in the treaty upholding the Monroe Doctrine. Although the president considered such an insertion redundant under the League, he knew it was necessary to mollify the Senate. Henry White asked Lodge by letter for a proposed wording, but Lodge refused, saying that Wilson hadn't considered suggestions while the Senate was in session, so he wouldn't send any now while the Senate was in recess. Taft sent a proposed clause, and Wilson fought for his wording. Knowing how much it meant to the American president, the other leaders traded hard. When Wilson claimed French annexation of the Saar would put too many Germans under French domination, violating self-determination, Clemenceau erupted, saying "You're pro-German!" Infuriated, Wilson said icily, "Then if France does not get what she wishes, she will refuse to act with us? In that event do you wish me to return home?" "I do not wish you to go home," Clemenceau said, "but I intend to do so myself!" And he did, throwing the conference into acute crisis.

During that crisis, in the weeks following March 28, House overreached his authority in pressing hard for compromise, swayed by notions of his own importance and his natural sympathy with the French and British. In many instances he sided with them against Wilson, ostensibly to keep the dialogue flowing. Then Wilson was suddenly taken violently ill, with a fever of 103°, heavy coughing spasms, and diarrhea. Dr. Grayson feared for his patient's life.

For a time Grayson thought the president had been poisoned, but changed his diagnosis to influenza and hoped it would not become pneumonia. Edith, he wrote home, was an angel through it all. They had one terrible night; then the fever seemed to break, but the president continued ill for some time.

Ike Hoover and others at Paris believed Wilson had had a stroke. Examining the medical evidence in the light of modern practice, Edwin A. Weinstein, M.D., concludes the president had a form of encephalitis, a viral inflammation of the brain and spinal cord. This, Dr. Weinstein believes, left the president's health permanently impaired. After his illness the president was obsessed with unimportant details involving the use of cars and furniture, and was convinced some employees at the mansion were French spies: Dr. Weinstein ascribes this behavior to the state of befuddled euphoria that comes in getting over encephalitis.

Despite his serious illness, after one day in bed the president continued to drive himself and all around him hard. He convinced Lloyd George, Clemenceau, and Orlando to meet at his residence and had House take in messages from his sickbed. Edith worried for his health, but he was adamant the world's business must not go on without him when things were at a critical stage. Still, there was a deadlock, and on April 7, Wilson asked Grayson to send word home for the *George Washington*. He had had it with European statesmen.

This threat broke the logjam, and in the following weeks the president was able to get the Allies to modify their positions on almost all the issues except for reparations, which Wilson felt might not work as planned anyhow. The Monroe Doctrine clause went into the Covenant. The compromises which House had been urging—which would have led to a harsher peace more in line with what the Allies had originally desired—were toned down. As a consequence, perhaps, these weeks brought the House-Wilson relationship to its ultimate phase.

When Orlando wanted to claim the Adriatic port of Fiume (which had been promised to the new nation of Yugo-Slavia), some of the American experts wanted to reach Wilson and provide evidence to back up the president's gut feeling that Fiume should not go to Italy. Colonel House blocked them from seeing Wilson. He went so far as to tell the president that the experts agreed with his (House's) position that Italy was right and should have Fiume. When asked which experts, House pointed to David Hunter Miller. Henry White later wrote that the Italians were misled by House's dealings, and

* * *

> there is no doubt in my mind that Fiume and other questions
> would have been settled . . . if they . . . had not been
> hampered by a feeling upstairs [House's quarters] that no
> decision should be attempted, much less reached, which
> would in any way be likely to cause jeopardy to the adoption
> of the League of Nations Covenant.

In other words, House was withholding evidence from Wilson in
order to keep the Italians in the bargain for the League, and feared that
if we didn't give them what they wanted, they would drop out of the
deal. It was a classic instance of the disciple deciding that the gospel,
rather than the prophet, must be followed when the prophet was "mis-
taken." This was the final blow in the break between Wilson and House.
As Paul Birdsall notes, House's actions were "a climax of appeasement
philosophy" which "revealed a rift . . . cutting deep to roots of philosophy and method." Edith's view was similar. She felt vindicated in her
animosity to House when Wilson recognized how deep the chasm was
between him and his old friend.

When Wilson did deny Italy Fiume, Orlando went home in a huff.
Wilson had been told that the British and French would publicly
support him, but when Orlando left, Clemenceau and Lloyd George
maintained their silence and Wilson had to take the heat on the Fiume
issue alone. In a few days, faced with the possibility that the Allies
would adopt the treaty without them, the Italians came back. In late
April the League and the treaty were formally adopted.

The initial reaction in the United States was overwhelmingly positive.
The *Literary Digest* found 718 papers for unconditional acceptance,
and 478 for conditional acceptance—and most came over to the unconditional side when it was learned that the Monroe Doctrine clause was
in the document. Taft cabled that his League to Enforce Peace counted
sixty-four senators to ratify, twenty doubtful, and only twelve definitely
opposed. One of those twelve was Lodge, who issued a dour statement:
"It is obvious that [the Covenant] will require further amendments if it
is to promote peace and not endanger certain rights of the United States
which should never be placed in jeopardy."

Wilson disregarded this warning and on May 7, 1919, four years to
the day after the sinking of the *Lusitania*, the terms agreed upon by the
victors were presented to Germany's representatives.

Would the Germans sign? Edith wrote to her mother that she and
Woodrow were not at all certain that they would. The Germans took the
214-page treaty home under advisement and returned on May 29 to say
that it violated the armistice agreement and the Fourteen Points—and

that they could not sign it as it was. This bombshell shocked Lloyd George. The British prime minister, also under pressure at home from his Liberal party, which agreed the treaty was too harsh, decided to seek concessions toward leniency. At a breakfast with Bernard Baruch he confided he wasn't sure the British army or fleet could or would force Germany's acceptance. The two men went immediately to Wilson, who listened to the Welshman's pleas, then erupted, "Mr. Prime Minister, you make me sick! For months we have been struggling to make the terms of the Treaty exactly along the lines you speak of, and never got the support of the English. Now, after we have finally come to agreement you want to rewrite the Treaty!" Despite his anger, Wilson agreed to modifications, and he and Lloyd George planned out how to persuade the immovable Clemenceau.

On Memorial Day Wilson went to speak at Suresnes cemetery. One part was an American graveyard with rows on rows of white crosses and freshly dug mounds of earth; ranged up the hillside like a vast jury were many of the conference leaders, members of the American delegation, wounded American soldiers, quite a few French people, and Edith, on crutches from an infected foot. Many people were reminded of Gettysburg. It was an emotional moment for Wilson, through the rest of his life. The great gift that those buried here had left behind, he began, was the League of Nations, to maintain security so there would never be another war. Such a gift demanded much from the living:

> If we do not know courage, we cannot accomplish our purpose and this age is an age that looks forward, not backward; which rejects the standard of national selfishness that once governed the counsels of nations and demands that they shall give way to a new order of things in which the only questions will be, "Is it right?" "Is it just?" "Is it in the interest of mankind?" . . . The spirits of these men are not buried with their bones. Their spirits live. I hope—I believe—that their spirits are present with us at this hour.

He hoped he felt the compulsion of their presence, and asked rhetorically what the dead men would say if they were alive. All about him people were crying. The dead, he contended, would remind us why America was born. It was for liberty. Therefore:

> Make yourselves soldiers once for all in this common cause, where we need wear no uniform except the uniform of the heart, clothing ourselves with the principles of right, and

saying to men everywhere: "You are our brothers and we invite you into the comradeship of liberty and peace." . . . I sent these lads over here to die. Shall I—can I—ever speak a word of counsel which is inconsistent with the assurance I gave them when they came over? It is inconceivable. There is something better, if possible, that a man can give than his life, and this is his living spirit to a service that is not easy, to resist counsels that are hard to resist, to stand against purposes that are difficult to stand against, and to say, "Here I stand, consecrated in the spirit of the men who were once my comrades, and who are now gone, and who left me under eternal bonds of fidelity."

At the speech's end he laid a wreath sent by the Boy Scouts on a grave. A Frenchwoman whose sons had been killed in battle added flowers of her own. Driving back to Paris, the president and Edith did not trust themselves to speak, their hearts were too full.

In the following days there were negotiations with Clemenceau to modify the treaty toward leniency, and Wilson won some concessions, though not many. Riots in the Paris streets, with crowds yelling for his downfall, made Clemenceau reluctant to yield now. Colonel House was now desperate to get Wilson alone as he had in the past, but could only manage to see him in the daily meetings among a crowd of people. He complained that he could change everything if he could only convince Wilson to push toward leniency. But House's positions, later observers conclude, were ably advocated at the time, and he had not the stance any longer to plead with the author of the Fourteen Points that those points were being violated. Edith, acting as usual on the president's wishes and preference for avoiding unpleasantness, found ways to keep House from Wilson. The colonel repeated to his diary the canard going around Paris that "Wilson talks like Jesus Christ and acts like Lloyd George."

How had the Fourteen Points fared? On the whole, not too badly. Less than 3 percent of Europe's people would be living under government of foreigners. Colonial spoils had been blunted, if not avoided. The president had prevented French occupation of the Rhineland on a permanent basis. There was a League of Nations with a reasonable constitution. So much for Wilson's victories. The failures? Open covenants, at least in the view of journalists. But Wilson had never meant for all deliberations to be open, merely their results. There were to be no secret treaties, and there were none. As for freedom of the seas, which had not explicitly been recognized, Wilson thought that since in the next war there would be no neutrals, that point was moot. The issue of reparations was his real failure, with a settlement that economists such as John Maynard Keynes believed would bankrupt Germany and throw Europe into chaos (though later economists have demonstrated that Germany had the economic capacity to pay the reparations if that capacity had been rightly used). The other major failure was the treatment of Russia. The peace conference did not follow Wilson's wish for the Russians to be allowed self-determination. The president did manage, however, to prevent Marshal Foch from sending a large-scale Allied "Grand Crusade" to try and crush the Communists in their own homeland. The shadow of Lenin was like a ghost haunting the Conference though never accepted or present. The failure to recognize the USSR would have large ramifications in the coming years.

In early June the president gathered the American delegation for a short valedictory. He had tried to fight for what was right: "Though we did not keep them from putting irrational things in the Treaty, we got very serious modifications out of them. If we had written the Treaty the way they wanted it, the Germans would have gone home the minute they read it. Well, the Lord be with us."

For weeks they waited impatiently in Paris for the Germans to sign. Grayson snuck away to the race track, shared bottles of fine wine with Baruch. The Wilsons toured Belgium. Queen Elizabeth relegated daughter Margaret to a rumble seat, and Herbert Hoover was tricked into sitting in an open car until covered with dust. The reality of the war was brought home to them when they entered Louvain, the town whose name had become synonymous with destruction wreaked by the Germans. Edith Benham wrote home that before the president got away he would be forced to see every devastated corner of Belgium.

Finally Germany, threatened with starvation and blockade, agreed to sign the treaty. The ceremony took place on June 28, in the Hall of Mirrors at Versailles, with the delegates in frock coats and top hats. Wilson throughtfully ordered a red rose to go with Edith's blue gown. She watched the signings with a lump in her throat.

That night, as their train moved away from Paris, the Wilsons stood at an open window looking at the vanishing lights. "Well, little girl," Woodrow said, "it is finished, and, as no one is satisfied, it makes me hope we have made a just peace; but it is all in the lap of the gods."

12

WEARING THE UNIFORM OF THE HEART

On the long voyage home the president stayed in his cabin, walking the deck only when Grayson or Edith insisted. He had not completely recovered from his illness; his face twitched occasionally, and he was exhausted. On Grayson's advice, the captain slowed the ship down and took two extra days in the crossing.

Wilson lunched with Baruch and McCormick, and found in these two men good company and sincere advice without flattery, but neither was yet able, as Colonel House once had been, to be intimate with him. A great many people had failed Wilson in Paris—the whole concert of statesmen and advisers, perhaps even he himself had failed—and understanding this set Wilson apart from nearly everyone else. He had always seemed isolated in a crowd of humanity; now he was virtually alone.

On board, thanks to the Wilsons' special intervention, were twenty Frenchwomen, war brides of American soldiers who would otherwise have been unable to join their husbands in the United States, for transport places were at a premium. Seeing them, fresh and young and recently married, made Edith recall the summer of 1915, only four years ago; now it seemed inordinately far in the past.

Vice-President Marshall, Governor Al Smith, and a host of other dignitaries met the ship. New York's reception was generous, and if it did not rival the throngs of Paris and Rome, it was clear the president was regarded as a hero returning from a great victory. Margaret gushed about how wonderful the reception was, and "all for you." There never

190

was such a triumph, she told him. He looked at her and with deep conviction said, "Wait until they turn."

Next day as the Wilsons returned to Washington, Alice Longworth, daughter of Roosevelt, was near the White House and she cast an evil eye upon the president, made a sign, shouted an old curse: "A murrain on him, a murrain on him, a murrain on him!" Alice noted bitchily that the sound of the crowd gathered to welcome Wilson was high-pitched— evidence, she concluded, of a preponderance of women, the only sort of misguided creatures who would still support Wilson and his peace treaty.

It was a greatly changed America to which the Wilsons returned. A backlash of conservatism had begun as a reaction to the war's end, and had gathered steam from such events as a series of labor upheavals in the spring and the bombing attempts on the lives of Attorney General A. Mitchell Palmer and other high officials. The vast majority of Americans wanted to get back to the old ways, to take up the threads of lives which had been interrupted by the war. In Congress, the dominant Republicans were determined to do away with many of the innovations of the war period, to return railroads to the private sector, to dismantle government control of shipping, and to roll back the advances labor had made.

The problems of reconversion of industry from guns to butter and the demobilization of four million men collided with inflation and racial hatred—and these factors made the summer of 1919 one of the most nightmarish in American history. The purchasing power of the dollar had dropped dramatically: from 1913 to 1919 food costs increased 84 percent, clothing 114.5 percent, furniture 125 percent, while most salaries and wages had gone up only 10 percent. Organized labor was on a tear to recover lost ground. The year 1919 saw 3600 strikes involving more than four million workers, and strikers gained very little as industrialists continued to take a hard line. Even the least militant of the strikers got tarred with the brush of Bolshevism, as the big capitalists stressed "Communist danger" in order to refuse money to the strikers.

Returning servicemen, Liberty Loan workers, and others infused with the spirit of "100 percent Americanism" attacked everyone faintly tinged with Red. Worse than the economic riots were the racial riots. In July, a young black swimming in Lake Michigan crossed an imaginary boundary between black and white areas and was stoned to death. In the ensuing melee, thirty-eight Chicagoans were killed and thousands left homeless. Similar blood was spilled in Washington, Charleston,

Knoxville, and Omaha. "In 1919," Robert K. Murray writes, "America's soul was in danger."

Abroad Romanian, Hungarian, Armenian, Soviet, Turkish, Polish, and Ukrainian armies were fighting each other, and many whole nations were starving. It was with the backdrop of these actions, as well as the turmoil at home, that, the day after returning to Washington, Wilson presented the Versailles Treaty to the Senate. He asked for immediate ratification, because the League of Nations was the best hope for mankind. "Dare we reject it and break the heart of the world?" he asked.

> The stage is set, the destiny disclosed. It has come about by no plan of our conceiving, but by the hand of God who led us into this way. We cannot turn back. We can only go forward, with lifted eyes and freshened spirit, to follow the vision. It was of this we dreamed at our birth. America shall in truth show the way. The light streams upon the path ahead, and nowhere else.

Meeting reporters later, Wilson exuded confidence. The treaty was the best that could be gotten; reservations would necessitate renegotiation of the treaty with foreign governments, which would be impossible; it should be ratified as it stood, and he believed the Senate was ready to ratify. Thirty-two state legislatures, thirty-three governors, a thousand out of twelve hundred newspaper editorials backed Wilson's stance.

Senator Lodge had a different fate in mind for the treaty. Earlier he had packed Republicans onto the Foreign Relations Committee which he chaired, in a move which Taft called "rank political partisanship." Lodge knew the treaty must not be voted on immediately, for it very well might pass, given the public support and Wilson's returning-hero popularity. Faced with an either-or choice, enough senators might very well vote yes. What Lodge wanted was a "yes-but" vote. So he proceeded to read the treaty's 87,000 words to an often empty Senate chamber, buying two weeks maneuvering time. As Lodge droned on, Wilson met with small groups of senators, explaining the treaty's provisions, where he had had to compromise, and why it must be ratified. He didn't like these meetings, but went ahead with them dutifully.

Wilson had spent many months treating with the giants of the world; the men at home seemed like pygmies. His counselors Lansing and House had proved wanting in the balance and had been eclipsed, and now he had to convince individual senators to vote for the treaty whose goodness and rightness he found overwhelmingly self-evident. It was a difficult task to bear after the atmosphere of Paris.

For Edith, too, homecoming was difficult. The capital was in its chronic summer doldrums, the heat thick and stultifying. Paris had been continually exciting with its theater and parties, its great and exotic people. There she had been treated very nearly as a queen in her own right. During the days she had done many things without Woodrow, but in Washington there were no hospitals to visit, no army divisions from which to receive honorary memberships, no grand boulevards in which to shop, no exquisite cuisine to tempt her palate and assault her waistline.

She had suffered with Woodrow through the strains of the negotiations in Paris; they now spoke the same language about that subject, and when he discussed it with her he did not have to fill in any of the background or convince her of the reasoning. She made his goal hers. It was idealistic and rather simple—to take the United States into the League so that body could prevent future wars—and she understood it. This was not as complicated as, say, the Federal Reserve System. It was a task of Woodrow's with which Edith felt comfortable and, to a certain extent, knowledgeable. She had been there when he had hammered out the compromises that made up the treaty, and believed as he did that it was important to have it passed without a comma changed.

Over the summer she began to judge their friends on how they stood on the treaty. Those like Baruch, who had been at Paris and who had worked for and with Woodrow and who supported his position absolutely and completely, were taken in more to the White House inner circle. Those with misgivings, or who had no appreciation of the difficulties that had been experienced, began to be shut out. Loyalty became more important a criterion for Edith than ever.

The loyalty of William Howard Taft began to waver in July and caused great problems. Earlier, in June, Elihu Root had published some suggested modifications of the treaty—the gist was that we enter the League only after we reserved to ourselves the power of decision concerning our degree of participation—and Taft had opposed these. But then the president had come home and had not invited Taft to the White House, and Taft came under pressure from the Republican party. On July 23 Taft declared publicly for the Root modifications and simultaneously tendered his resignation as head of the League to Enforce Peace. The resignation was not accepted, but the LEP lost force in assisting ratification and Wilson lost a valuable ally.

Wilson told moderate Republicans he would have fought for such modifications if he'd had them in Paris—as he had fought for the

Monroe Doctrine clause—but now that was impractical. In any event, he said, the machinery of the League would solve their objections.

The question of the treaty absorbed the energies not only of the president and the senators, but of a great number of Americans during the coming months. In the cold light of 1980 it is a bit difficult to understand the virulence with which Americans debated whether they were to have a treaty without reservations or an amended one, but in 1919 everyone had an opinion. Here are some groups which disliked the treaty, and some of their reasons:

1. Idealists, because it did not absolutely adhere to the Fourteen Points.
2. Irish-Americans, because the League was "pro-British" and did not mean home rule for Ireland.
3. German-Americans, because it was too harsh on Germany.
4. Jingoes, because it was too soft on Germany.
5. Italian-Americans, because of Fiume.
6. Chinese-Americans, because of Shantung.
7. Californians, because too many Orientals would be allowed to emigrate here.
8. Anti-Catholics, because "the Pope would run the league" since many member countries were Catholic.
9. Anti-blacks, because the majority of countries in the League were nonwhite and would outvote the white ones.

These groups commanded the headlines and made a lot of noise, but as Arthur Link points out, most thinking people had serious questions about the limits to which the United States should involve itself in international affairs. They were neither extreme isolationists nor extreme internationalists. America's problem was just exactly how, and to what degree, we should be involved with the rest of the world.

On July 27, Republican Senator James Watson, a crafty politician, asked Lodge what would happen if Wilson accepted the treaty with Lodge's reservations (which codified the Root scheme). Lodge replied, "My dear James, you do not take into consideration the hatred that Woodrow Wilson has for me personally. Never under any set of circumstances could he be induced to accept a Treaty with Lodge reservations appended to it."

A few days later, a troubled Wilson called Watson into conference at the White House, and forthrightly asked, "Where am I in the Senate on this fight?" Having the figures for each reservation and permutation of the treaty in his pocket, Watson produced them. "Mr. President," Watson said, "you are licked." He gave the details and concluded, "There is only one way you can take the United States into the League under the Treaty."

"Which way is that?"

"Accept it with the Lodge reservations."

"Never," said Wilson, and told Watson he'd appeal to the country. He planned a speaking tour. Grayson and Edith at first dissuaded him, saying it was too hot, that he was not well enough for such a grueling trip, that he must try harder with the senators. He agreed. On August 19, the entire Foreign Relations Committee, replete with stenographers to later give the record to the public, questioned Wilson at the White House. The session lasted three hours, plus a strained lunch, but failed to change any minds. As Professor Link suggests,

> What Wilson did not know, and never did seem to know, was that virtually all of the so-called mild reservationists had already coalesced into the central hard-core Republican pro-League group in the Senate. . . . Thus, confer as much as he could, Wilson made no headway in winning the support that would be vital when the Senate voted on the Treaty.

After Republicans made motions to introduce nearly *fifty* objections to the treaty, Wilson finally decided to go to the people. This tactic had worked for him before—on preparedness, on the McLemore and Gore resolutions, in his various election campaigns. Further, the tactic of appealing to the people over the heads of Congress had worked for others on prohibition and on women's suffrage. Wilson, a formidable speaker, believed he could change enough minds to get the treaty ratified.

Momentous problems were threatening in several areas of American life, but for Wilson the terrible thought that the treaty and League might fail for lack of American support meant he had but one task—to raise support for American entry into the League. Before he left, Wilson met with his cabinet, set up an industrial conference to head off some coming strikes, dealt with food problems and the railroads, tried to clear the decks. He called into conference Senator Gilbert Hitchcock, the Democrat who was leading the floor fight for the treaty, and gave him four interpretive reservations to the treaty. Hitchcock was to accept these, if he had to, to save the treaty, but he must never reveal the source of them, for if Lodge got wind of this small concession he would demand endless revisions of the treaty.

Edith worried about the trip. There was no provision for a vacation in it; each time she or Tumulty put one in, Woodrow would take it out. When Sir William Wiseman came to call shortly before they were to leave, the president was tired and drawn, and Edith hovered over them, telling Wiseman by a nod of the head when to steer away from subjects that would unduly tire Woodrow. When journalist H. H. Kohlsaat visited and pleaded with Wilson not to travel in the intense heat, Wilson told him, "I don't care if I die the next minute after the Treaty is ratified."

Opponents to the treaty, led by Senators Knox, Borah, and Hiram Johnson, were planning a speaking tour in the wake of the president's own, acknowledging their fear of Wilson's effectiveness on the stump. Organizations such as the League for Preservation of American Independence, and the Friends of Irish Freedom, had war chests of over a million dollars each to defeat the League. George Harvey, who once had championed Wilson for president but who now was his enemy, got Frick and Mellon to finance the speaking tour of the anti-League senators.

The evening before the western trip, Grayson tried to dissuade Wilson one last time, but the president reminded Grayson that in the crucial test of the trenches American soldiers had not turned back, and that he, as the commander-in-chief who had sent them there, could not turn back now. "I cannot put my personal safety, my health, in the balance against my duty," he said. "I must go."

On Wednesday evening, September 3, the Presidential Special left with Woodrow, Edith, Grayson, Tumulty, the Secret Service, and over a hundred reporters for a ten-thousand-mile trip across the country. Edith and Woodrow traveled in the last car of a train, a car they dubbed the Mayflower, after the presidential yacht. There were just a few compartments. Valet Brooks had to sleep on a bench to be closer to the president. In comparison to the luxurious state trains of Europe, the Presidential Special was modest.

Wilson told Tumulty he was in a nice fix because, with about a hundred speeches scheduled, he had not had a moment at the White House to prepare even one of them. He added that during the past few weeks he had been suffering from daily headaches, but hoped that a good night's sleep would make him fit for the morrow. Despite his headaches the president was, as usual, kind to those about him, and grateful to well-wishers who met the train in Baltimore. To relax the chief, Tumulty planned a little joke. When the foursome—Wilson,

Edith, Tumulty, and Grayson—ordered cool drinks, a black messenger from the White House brought them in, wearing an enormous white mushroom of a hat. His appearance made the president laugh.

There were only modest crowds in Columbus, Ohio—opposition country, represented in the Senate by Warren G. Harding, who voted regularly with Lodge. The train continued on through Indiana, stopping several times for Wilson to make rear-platform speeches before reaching Indianapolis. Just before the train would pull into a city, a welcoming committee of local politicians would get aboard. It was Edith's job to greet them and talk with them, and only let a few in to see Woodrow. Then the president would get off and speak, and in an hour or two would get back on the train and they would pull toward another stop. At many places, the crowds demanded to see Edith and gave her a big hand when she appeared. People wanted to see more of her but, as the president had often to explain, she was shy and did not like public appearances.

Children were everywhere; when Wilson saw crowds of them, he told Tumulty that the journey and the cause were for the children, that he was their attorney, the advocate for the future of mankind. Exhausted from dozens of halls filled with cigar smoke, and thousands of people who wanted to shake his hands, he would nevertheless—on the train in the intervals between stops—dictate notes for future speeches to stenographer Charles Swem. By Kansas City the intense heat made the steel cars feel like ovens. Wilson had to shout to make himself heard, and was soon hoarse. His major theme was that the public had been misled about what the League would or would not do. The strength of the League was mostly economic. If an aggressor made a move the rest of the world didn't like,

> We absolutely boycott them. . . . There shall be no communication between them and the rest of the world. They shall receive no goods; they shall ship no goods. They shall receive no telegraphic messages; they shall send none. . . . The citizens of the member states will never enter their territory until the matter is adjusted, and their citizens cannot leave their territory. It is the most complete boycott ever conceived in a public document, and I want to say to you with confident prediction that there will be no more fighting after that.

They averaged over four hundred miles a day, rarely spent more than a half-day in a single state. Sleeping through the night on the train became increasingly difficult for Wilson, which alarmed both Grayson and Edith as Woodrow had always found sleep a great restorative. Grayson sprayed his throat, diagnosed asthma, headaches, and fatigue. The crowds and the reporters knew nothing of it. Anti-League senators were following Wilson on his journey and were speaking to packed houses. Wilson felt pursued.

In Bismarck, Starling flushed two hoboes from under the cars and asked them to take another train. One hobo asked the president to shake hands with him, and Wilson did. So did Edith. The president even offered them a lift, but they declined, saying they wouldn't add to his burdens. He watched them go wistfully, and Starling thought that Wilson envied the bums.

As the days went by, reporters were saying the president's speeches were getting better and better, and the crowds were growing. He told people how the treaty and the League would protect them, brought to bear one of the most formidable oratorical talents in American history:

> Nothing brings a lump into my throat quicker on this journey I am taking than to see the thronging children that are everywhere the first, just out of childish curiosity and glee, no doubt, to crowd up to the train when it stops, because I know that, if by any chance, we should not win this great fight . . . it would be their death warrant. They belong to the generation that would have to fight the next war, and in that final war there would not be merely seven and a half million men slain. The very existence of civilization would be in the balance. . . .
>
> I do not hesitate to say that the war we have just been through, though it was shot through with terror of every kind, is not to be compared with the war we would have to face the next time. . . . Ask any soldier if he wants to go through a hell like that again. The soldiers know what the next war would be. They know what the inventions were that were just about to be used for the absolute destruction of mankind. I am for any kind of insurance against a barbaric reversal of civilization.

In Billings, Montana, several small boys ran after the train. One had a small American flag which he begged Edith to give to the president. She took it from him. His companion didn't have a flag, but he wanted to give the president something. Starling leaned over as far as he could and took the boy's offering. It was a dime. The president took it with deep feeling and put it carefully into his pocket.

Back in Boston, the great police strike began, and many people believed it heralded the onset of a Bolshevist revolution. There was so much ignorance that Wilson had to work hard to dispel. Some people, a newspaper reported, thought the League of Nations would be a third circuit in American baseball; one woman in Birmingham was actually swindled into buying stock in the new enterprise.

As Wilson reached the Pacific Northwest, his fatigue became more pronounced. In Spokane, reporters noticed that Edith had to steady the president, but he still spoke with passion. In Tacoma, Wilson talked about the little boy who had given him the dime, a token of all he had to offer and, in terms of the boy's wealth, an enormous amount. Such trust, Wilson believed fervently, must not be misplaced or misled. Then they came to Seattle, scene of the year's first and to date most celebrated strike, the January General Strike. In early September when the IWW, the Wobblies, announced that they wanted to give Wilson a petition about releasing political prisoners such as bomber Tom Mooney, who were being held in federal jail, Mayor Ole Hanson said he wouldn't let them near enough to annoy the president. In answer, the Wobblies planned an unusual demonstration during Wilson's visit.

It was Saturday. Businesses were closed, bands were playing, there was a lot of cheerful noise on jammed streets. Motorcycles surrounded the open car where Wilson stood and waved his hat while Edith sat beside him. All of a sudden Wilson came to a block where everything was quiet, filled with silent Wobblies, men and women from the entire state, laboring men standing with their arms folded and looking, not at Wilson, but past him as if he didn't exist. No cheers, no sound, no movement. Returned servicemen formed their front ranks, and all had hatbands saying "Release Political Prisoners." Wilson was smiling when he entered the block; he lost his smile in an instant, seemed flabbergasted, his hat hung in his hand by his side. When the terrible silence continued for four more blocks, Wilson sat down heavily. Even when the hurrahs began again the president did not get up. It was as if he had been shot.

After the parade the Wilsons went on with their planned activities, visiting the Pacific fleet with Navy Secretary Daniels. The Wilsons' launch collided with another boat and shipped water before they got to the *Oregon*, which took them around the bay. In the evening Wilson made two speeches in different halls. Later he sat with Edith on the roof garden of their hotel and looked out at the bay and the lights of the fleet, a magnificent and romantic sight. They had a moment's calm there, but later the president again could not sleep, kept awake by sailors and other revelers. Edith had a new maid on the trip who was good at giving Swedish massages to help her relax, but nothing seemed to help Woodrow. In the morning he had a headache.

That morning a delegation of Wobblies arrived, specially invited by Wilson, who was angered by the mayor's actions in trying to prevent them from airing their grievances. To the men, Wilson appeared haggard, leaning on a table for support. When he answered their statements his voice shook, and so did his hand which grasped his lapel. Organizer Jack Kipps recalled,

> I thought to myself that Wilson, in his fine cutaway coat and striped pants, and we, in our working clothes, were just the opposite poles of the same mess. . . . I had no feeling against him. I only thought what a mess he was. A goddamn tragedy—the President of the United States, the most powerful ruler on earth, but unable to do anything for us—the workers—although I don't doubt now that in his heart he was for us. . . . I felt like two cents for pulling that demonstration the day before.

More and more Wilson was showing the cumulative effects of the journey. Grayson, concerned that the president was not eating enough, prescribed predigested foods for him. Wilson complained about the cigar smoke and his asthma. He dictated to Swem with his head lying back on a chair. Edith worried about his lack of exercise, for they had spent nearly all of their time on the train. Wilson had not wanted to take time off for golf, believing perhaps that the public should not see him at leisure when important matters hung in the balance.

Although the crowds were becoming increasingly pro-League, when the president asked people if they had written their senators to tell them so, only a small percentage—in one place, one out of four hundred—said they had.

Disturbing news came from Washington. Young William Bullitt, a minor official who had resigned from the American delegation to the peace conference, testified before Lodge and other Republicans on a day the Democrats of the Foreign Relations Committee were absent. Bullitt told the senators that Secretary of State Lansing had admitted to him privately that he did not believe in the League or in the efficacy of the treaty. Lansing immediately sent Wilson a telegram attempting to explain, but the president didn't believe him. Were he in Washington, Wilson told Tumulty, he would immediately demand Lansing's resignation: the man had constantly sought to undermine him in Paris, and this telegram confirmed it. It was, he said, practically unthinkable for this to come from a man whom he had raised from a subordinate to secretary of state. Nevertheless the president continued to work through Lansing in Washington for the time being as if nothing had happened.

He roused four audiences in two days in San Francisco then, in one of the first speeches in the country given through amplification, he talked to fifty thousand people in San Diego. "They mean so well," he told Edith of the well-wishers, "but they are killing me."

In Los Angeles, Wilson tried to track down a girlhood friend of Ellen Axson's, a woman who had shared her room for years, and who had corresponded with Ellen for a long time. She was not at home, and was eventually located by the Secret Service at the train station, where she had gone to try and catch a glimpse of Woodrow. The Wilsons spoke with her briefly aboard the train. Then Edith left to go ahead to the Hotel Alexandria. Some time later Wilson followed. At the hotel another guest awaited him. It was Mary Hulbert.

She was wearing the same gown she had worn to see the president in the White House in May of 1915. Mary, Woodrow, Edith, and Grayson went to lunch. The women sized each other up. Edith thought Mary sweet but faded; Mary decided Edith was Junoesque but had a charming smile. Starling couldn't for the life of him imagine how such an innocuous, middle-aged, drab-looking woman as Mary Hulbert could have been thought of as a romantic figure. The talk at lunch was of churches, of the California climate, of how well the president looked. To Edith it seemed evidence of how little Mary Hulbert knew about Woodrow now. Afterward they went back to the suite to chat. From time to time Grayson would announce "Converts, sir," and Wilson would excuse himself to visit with groups. During these interruptions the women would talk. They were both good at light banter, and it saw them through awkward moments. At last all the visitors were gone, and Woodrow asked Mary Hulbert what had befallen her in the past four years.

A tale of woe, near-poverty, intrigue, and persecution came tumbling out. People had been after her to buy Wilson's letters, to have her testify at impeachment proceedings; her rooms had been searched—in sum, she had been hounded because of her relationship to Wilson. The president was amazed, wondering why various people she had named had done the things she related. Mary Hulbert said she didn't know, that he would have to discover those answers for himself as she had neither the time nor the inclination. The president smiled wanly, said,

"God, to think that you should have suffered because of me." Edith made a bad joke: "Where there's so much smoke there must be some fire."

"Then perhaps," Mary retorted, "you *were* von Bernstorff's mistress!"*

There was an impasse. To change the subject, they discussed the League, and Wilson's hurt at all the "venomous personal animosity" came out; he believed, for instance, that the League would be instantly passed by the Senate if his own name was not so prominently associated with it. The personalities were having more to do with passage than the issues. Hearing of Wilson's larger troubles, Mary forgot her own. Edith kept steering the conversation into channels unlikely to upset Woodrow further. Mary felt Edith to be a powerful personality much greater than herself.

When it was time to go, Woodrow laid his hand on Edith's shoulder and wondered if there was something they could do for Mary. When Edith pointedly remained silent for an instant, Mary broke in and said she wished nothing. Edith left to get Mary's wrap, and Mrs. Hulbert turned to Wilson, alone. He did not know how much she had counted on him, did not know that she kept still in a chest at her home the lace for the dress she had planned to wear at her White House wedding. And she did not know what she had done to alienate Wilson. Was there anything he might do? She told him he could try to help her son Allen, and Wilson dutifully took down the New York address. They walked along the hall and, theatrical as ever, Mary Hulbert quoted, "With all my will, but much against my heart, We two now part." In another moment she was gone.

News came of a congressional resolution to look into the royal shower of gifts the Wilsons had received in Europe. Emphasis was laid on Edith's, as if she had done something wrong. This hurt her. Both had tried to avoid these gifts, but had found themselves forced to accept them lest they be rude to their hosts. There was no mention in the congressional investigation of the monies the Wilsons had laid out personally to reciprocate.

The tour turned eastward, tracing a circular route back toward Washington. In the Sierras, forest fires irritated Wilson with their smoke, and their heat blistered the sides of the railroad cars and made them hot. The tunnels were especially suffocating. Changes in altitude and the heat of the desert affected him even more. The nervous twitch-

*Possibly an apocryphal retort.

ing in his face became worse. As he was about to speak at the Mormon Tabernacle in Salt Lake City, he was so faint that Edith had to hand him a handkerchief with lavender salts to clear his head.

The speech in Salt Lake City summed up Wilson's arguments against reservations to the treaty, which he believed would negate its purpose. For him there was but one way: "Instead of wishing to stand aside, get the benefits of the League, but share none of its burdens or responsibilities, I for my part want to go in and accept what is offered to us, the leadership of the world."

Afterward Wilson left the platform soaked with perspiration, and when he changed the dry clothes were soon wet. Later that night Edith and Grayson asked him to rest for a week. "No," he replied, "I have caught the imagination of the people." He told Edith it would all be over soon, and then they'd have a vacation. To those newsmen who were worried about his health he said, "My constitution may be exhausted, but I ought to get along for a good while on my by-laws."

And it was true: he did seem to have caught the people's imagination, and the crowds were growing more responsive to his arguments. In Cheyenne, in Denver, he made good speeches and, an analysis of newspaper sentiments before and after shows, changed many minds. In Denver he was met by his cousin Hattie Woodrow, now a middle-aged married woman. They chatted until after midnight, and then he could not get to sleep. At nine-thirty the next morning he gave a speech in an auditorium where the acoustics were so bad that he had to shout. By eleven they were on their way to Pueblo, Colorado, where he was scheduled to take a trip around the fairgrounds before making a speech. When he learned of the plan he angrily said, "Who authorized such an idiotic idea?" Tumulty showed him his own "okeh" and Wilson grumbled, "Any damned fool who was stupid enough to approve such a program has no business in the White House." But he went anyway, standing in a car going around the fairgrounds where 10,000 people cheered. Afterward, on the way up the steps to the auditorium where he was to speak, he stumbled and Starling had to assist him. On his way to the stage he told the reporters he'd make it short, and jested they must be tired of hearing his arguments over and over.

But when he reached the podium and began, the words wouldn't come out for a moment. A reporter looking at Edith believed her terrified. Starling thought Wilson ready to collapse, but the president mustered his strength and went on. He told the audience of his experience in Suresnes cemetery, of the dead boys from America. He wished his Senate opponents could have been there, because then they would not block the treaty. Tumulty saw people in the audience beginning to cry, then saw that the president himself was in tears. "I wish," he said, "that they could feel the moral obligation that rests upon us not to go back on those boys, but to see the thing through. . . . nothing less depends upon this decision, nothing less than the liberation and salvation of the world."

Now newsmen who had heard these sentiments many times were crying. Wearing his uniform of the heart, Wilson came to the climax and conclusion of his speech:

> Now that the mists of this great question have cleared away, I believe that men will see the truth, eye to eye and face to face. There is one thing that the American people always rise to and extend their hand to, and that is the truth of justice and of liberty and of peace. We have accepted that truth and we are going to be led by it, and it is going to lead us, and through us the world, out into pastures of quietness and peace such as the world never dreamed of before.

There was a moment of silence. Then the audience realized that the president was done, and as he turned away the applause began and did not stop for a long time. His eyes, full of tears, met Edith's, also wet, and they stumbled away from the platform.

In the late afternoon, rolling on toward Wichita, Kansas, Grayson asked if he wouldn't like to stroll in the open air. Yes, Wilson said. So Woodrow, Edith, Grayson, and the ever-present Starling stopped the train and went out into the Colorado air. It was prairie country with no houses in sight. The four saw the small Arkansas River from a wooden bridge, and walked on. A farmer driving by stopped and gave them a cabbage and some apples for their dinner. They took the gifts, thanked him, kept wandering. In a little while they saw a house some distance off the road, with a soldier in uniform sitting on the porch. "That fellow looks sick to me," Wilson said. The doctor agreed. Climbing over the fence, they started for the house. It was nearly sunset, and six years since Grayson and Wilson had stopped by a house on a country road to put out a fire. It was September 25, 1919; they had traveled over 8000 miles, and the president had made thirty-seven formal speeches plus numerous rear-platform talks in twenty-two days.

The boy on the porch was a private who had indeed come back from the Great War. His parents and brothers came out for a few minutes and talked respectfully to the visitors. There was something poignant, almost pleading in the president's manner, as if he were looking for reassurance from these people. After a few moments' chat, though, he was ready to return to the train. When they came within a short distance of the tracks, Grayson and Wilson both broke into a trot, and raced each other to the platform. The president was smiling as they went in, said his headache was much better.

At 11:30 that night, Edith was getting a massage from her Swedish maid when the president knocked on the door between their compartments and asked her to come to him as he was ill. Dressing quickly, Edith went in and found Woodrow sitting on the side of his bed with his head resting on the back of a chair in front of him. The pain was unbearable, he said; she must call Grayson. When the doctor came, it seemed there was nothing he could do. Wilson said the sleeping compartment was too stuffy and cramped, so they moved to a room used as a study, piled pillows on a chair, and Woodrow tried to rest with Edith and Grayson watching. It was five in the morning before he fell asleep. Edith sent Grayson to get some rest. She breathed as quietly as she could and hoped all would be well when her husband awoke. But she knew what Woodrow had been through, how this illness had been coming on him for so long, and knew with what effort of will he had kept it at bay for this long. She also knew, or believed she knew, what would be best for him and for her and for everyone around Woodrow, now:

> As I sat there watching the dawn break slowly I felt that life would never be the same; that something had broken inside me; and from that hour on I would have to wear a mask—not only to the public but to the one I loved best in the world; for he must never know how ill he was, and I must carry on.

The president awoke about seven, went to his room to shave, saying he had to get ready to speak at Wichita. He was weary, but—at least to himself—he didn't seem badly hurt. He had none of the symptoms of illnesses with which he was familiar. He managed to shave himself. He wanted to make this next speech, continue the trip. Edith, Tumulty, and Grayson tried to decide what to do. It was obvious to them that Wilson could not continue, even when he appeared, dressed and shaved, in the middle of their conference and vetoed the suggestion that the rest of the trip be canceled.

Now, though, he spoke with great difficulty, one side of his face fallen, and tears streaming from his eyes. This had never happened to him before, he told Tumulty, and he didn't know what to do, but believed he had to keep on or else Lodge and his bunch would say the trip was a failure and that he was a quitter. Tumulty took both Wilson's hands in his own and pleaded for cancellation. Joe loved the man as a father, and the emotion came through. Wilson tried to answer, but now his body refused to respond to his commands, and he could not speak. Grayson told him firmly he must rest; Wilson agreed, but only to a twenty-four-hour postponement. It was left to Edith to be brutally frank and to tell him that whether he liked or not, the trip was over. It was the hardest task she had ever faced, but she did it, and in her words, Woodrow "accepted the decree of Fate as gallantly as he had fought the fight." The rest of the trip was canceled, and the train started for home.

With a pilot engine running ahead to clear the track, the train raced the seventeen hundred miles toward Washington. Woodrow and Edith sat in a compartment together. Edith knitted, tried to divert Woodrow with small talk. Grayson had forbidden him either to talk or to read. It was agony. He endured another bad night, the blinds drawn in the car, but still he was unable to sleep. At about 2:00 A.M. Edith sent for Starling, who was due to leave the train at St. Louis to visit his mother, who was also ill. Edith told him the president did not want his illness to interfere with Starling's plans. Then she took Starling back to say good-bye to the president, who was reclining on a couch, a dressing gown wrapped over his suit. The Wilsons gave Starling a beautiful shawl and two boxes of candy to take to his mother, and told him to remain at home until the mother's illness was resolved.

At three in the morning, Starling got off with his presents at St. Louis, and was met by a friend. He watched the Presidential Special pulling away to the east, the red lights glowing in the darkness as it disappeared down the track, and felt his friend's hand on his shoulder.

"What's the matter?" asked the friend.

"What do you mean, what's the matter?" Starling replied.

"You're crying, you damn fool!" said the friend, and took him to get a drink.

13

IF WE DO NOT KNOW
COURAGE

As THE PRESIDENTIAL Special sped toward Washington, news of 300,000 steelworkers out, and violence escalating on both sides of the picket line, shared the headlines with Grayson's first medical bulletins about the president's condition. The steel strike looked as if it were going to last a long time, and it was viewed as a mammoth clash between the reactionary forces of the steel industry and the Communist-tinged steelworkers. Wilson had pleaded with them all to wait until his scheduled October industrial conference had a chance to settle the differences, but Samuel Gompers had been unable to persuade the radical elements to do so. Now the strike was on in earnest.

Grayson was telling reporters that Wilson's condition was due to overwork and dated back to the "influenza" attack in Paris. Nevertheless, he held, Wilson's condition was "not alarming," although it would be necessary for the president to have rest and quiet for some time. Some reporters thought the president had been defeated on the tour, and was hiding behind his illness, but the majority of the reporters accepted the doctor's diagnosis, for they had seen the president overtaxed. Grayson said he thought the president was not seriously ill, and that he would soon recover.

Miraculously, it seemed that the prognosis was precisely that, for when the train arrived in Washington on a Sunday morning, Wilson emerged from his coach smiling and walking naturally, to be greeted by Margaret, who had hurried home from a visit to Connecticut. They linked arms and Wilson walked quite a distance to the waiting car.

Photographers covered the whole scene. At lunch Edith's brother John Randolph Bolling joined them. He had started to keep a scrapbook of the Wilsons' peregrinations on the western trip; earlier, while the couple was in Europe, he had handled their financial matters, getting things in a bit of a mess which Edith had to straighten out. After lunch the Wilsons and Bolling took a drive in the open car- through Rock Creek Park and Chevy Chase. Things seemed alright.

But that night the president could not sleep, and his headache made it impossible for him to work or read. His eyesight, already much impaired on one side, was now probably entirely gone in that eye. He roamed the corridors on the second floor. Edith, never much of a sleeper, tried to keep him company. Illness was nothing new to the White House. Wilson had been ill before; so had Edith. Everyone kept quiet, and most appointments for the next few days were postponed.

On Monday Edith entertained ten of the reporters who had been on the western trip. It was a sort of farewell which the Wilsons had not had time to give during the rush of the journey. Edith joked with the reporters, telling them how she had mistakenly bowed to a cow, thinking its call just another cheer. Wilson, she said, was too ill to join the tea party. During the day he kept his activities to a minimum, dictating a few letters, signing several bills.

On Tuesday Sir William Wiseman, head of British intelligence in New York, and a close confidant of Colonel House, sent word that he had important information to convey directly to the president. Edith asked him to come at eleven, and when he arrived told him Woodrow was ill and that she would receive his information and have a reply ready by two o'clock. She had never liked Wiseman, and was glad when Wilson told her that his information was not important enough for further consideration. This was the only time, Edith later insisted, where she acted as an intermediary between the president and someone else on an official matter, except when directed to do so by a physician.

On Wednesday evening, October 1, after a movie in the East Room, Wilson said he felt so well that he would read aloud to Edith from the small khaki soldier's Bible. Standing in her room, his voice was strong and vibrant. When he finished reading they chatted for a while, then Wilson went to his room. Edith noticed he'd left his watch, and went to deliver it to him. "That worries me," he said, "to have left that watch there. It is not like me." Edith made light of it.

Since his initial collapse, she had been sleeping only in small naps, getting up every hour or two to see how Woodrow was doing. In the early morning hours of October 2, she got up and found Wilson sleeping

soundly, but when she went in again shortly after eight in the morning
he was sitting on the side of his bed trying to grasp a water bottle and
having difficulty doing it. His left hand hung limp; he had no feeling in
it, and wanted her to rub it, but first he wanted to go to the bathroom.
She helped him in. Every move brought spasms of pain. Alarmed, Edith
asked Ike Hoover to call Grayson. Then she heard a slight noise and
rushed back into the bathroom to find Woodrow unconscious on the
floor. Her first thought was to keep him warm; she snatched a blanket
from the bed and a pillow for under his head. While she was arranging
these, he stirred and asked for a drink of water, which she also got him.
She later wrote, "I did these things automatically, for I was utterly
devoid of feeling. I had a curious sensation of having lived through this
thing before—and so knew how to act, and act quickly."

When Grayson arrived, he went up the stairs and tried to get into the
presidential suite. The door was routinely locked; he banged hard, and
Edith opened it. Ike Hoover stood in the hall, thought he saw blood on
the president's face as if from a fall. (Edith later denied there had been
such a fall.) Together Edith and Grayson came out and told Hoover,
"My God, the president is paralyzed," then sent him for additional help.
Within hours three doctors had arrived and examined Wilson, much to
the patient's distress: Dr. F. X. Dercum of Philadelphia, a noted neu-
rologist; Dr. Sterling Ruffin, for many years Edith's friend and a
well-respected Washington physician; and Dr. E. R. Stitt of the Washington Naval Hospital. All agreed that the president had had a stroke
which had paralyzed the left side of his body, and that Grayson's
suggestion for recovery, absolute rest, was essential and, under the
circumstances, all that could be done for the president.

The medical bulletin given to the press said that the president was "a
very sick man" who must have absolute rest for some time. The word
"stroke" was never mentioned. Inside the sick room, however, it was
acknowledged that the president was in grave danger. Edith believed his
life hung in the balance.

On October 3, the president's second collapse made the headlines, but
so much was happening in the world that this event could not crowd
other matters wholly to the side. The French Chamber of Deputies
overwhelmingly ratified the Versailles Treaty, as had the British earlier,
and a report from Paris cautioned that statesmen there were suggesting
"even in delay the United States Senate assumes an enormous responsibility which holds in the balance the affairs of the whole world."

The Senate killed twenty-five amendments to the treaty proposed by
Senator Fall, giving credence to Hitchcock's charges that Republicans
were delaying action because they knew they would lose. In an anti-

League speech in Oklahoma, Senator Reed was pelted with rotten eggs. Violence continued widespread in the steel strike; martial law was declared in Omaha after a lynching; six were killed in riots in Arkansas and the governor only narrowly escaped death. King Albert and Queen Elizabeth of Belgium landed in New York and were welcomed in Wilson's name. They telegraphed the White House that they would change their plans and travel quietly during the president's illness.

Grayson spent most of the night at Wilson's bedside and the president got a bit of untroubled sleep. Rumors raced through Washington about the president's condition. It was syphilis, contracted from a prostitute in Paris; it was a heart attack; it was poison. A tearful Tumulty told Daniels, "We must all pray."

The Washington weather was unbelievably hot, which added to Wilson's discomfort. Edith only left his side for brief periods when either Margaret or a nurse would take over. The several doctors were "unanimous in agreeing that [Mrs. Wilson] has a peculiarly good effect on him," being able to anticipate his requests, relaxing him. The doctors admitted that Wilson was a difficult patient who had at first been unwilling to concede he was seriously ill. Now Edith and Grayson had persuaded him it was necessary to rest. He tried to do as he was told—rid his mind of executive problems—but the fate of the treaty and other great problems kept worrying him. He had many questions about them. Grayson felt these must be answered or the president would worry still more. Some information was allowed to trickle into the sickroom. Dr. de Schweinitz, an oculist who had been treating Wilson for many years, came to see the president. Special medicine was ordered shipped to the White House from Boston.

While these consultations went on upstairs, Tumulty was having a stormy meeting with Secretary of State Lansing. The cabinet officer had brought with him a text of the Constitution, and was reading aloud the passages which stated that in the case of removal of the president from office by death, resignation, or inability to discharge the powers and duties of the office, "the same" should devolve upon the vice-president. Tumulty heard him out, then said, "Mr. Lansing, the Constitution is not a dead letter with the White House. I have read the Constitution and do not find myself in need of any tutoring at your hands of the provision you have just read."

Who, Tumulty challenged Lansing, should certify to the president's disability? Lansing said either Tumulty or Grayson could do it. Tumulty countered, saying, "You may rest assured that while Woodrow Wilson is lying in the White House on the broad of his back I will not be a party to ousting him. He has been too kind, too loyal, and too wonderful to me to receive such treatment at my hands."

Grayson walked into the room just at this moment, and Tumulty asked whether he would certify Wilson's disability. Grayson would not. Tumulty then blasted Lansing, said if anyone other than the White House inner circle attempted to say Wilson was incapacitated, Tumulty and Grayson together would repudiate such an opinion. He added that if Wilson were in condition to know of this episode, he would no doubt "take decisive measures." Lansing's response was to summon an extraordinary session of the cabinet for Monday at eleven.

Saturday's bulletin said Wilson was improving slightly but that Grayson believed they were still "skating on thin ice." Reporters noted that the admiral seemed more cheerful than he had, and left the White House in the company of Bernard Baruch. Tumulty met David Houston by chance, and they agreed it would be one of the great tragedies of the age if Wilson were to remain incapacitated. Tumulty was probably thinking of the insurrection brewing in Lansing's mind. He swore Houston to secrecy about the nature and extent of Wilson's illness. When Houston met Secretary of War Newton Baker—who did not know—Baker said, "I am scared literally to death."

Senator Hitchcock told reporters that Senate Democrats working on the treaty were hampered by not being able to confer with the president. Four bills, including one on prohibition, were being sent to the White House for signature. They would become law in ten days if Wilson did not sign or veto them.

Sunday the president asked for his stenographer, but Grayson joked that he should be a better Presbyterian and not work on the Sabbath, and deflected that impulse to work. The admiral told his nominal superior, Secretary Daniels, that Wilson was completely paralyzed on the left side. Daniels was so distraught at this information that he could not bring himself to tell his wife. David Houston had his oath to Tumulty sorely tested on Sunday when he met Vice-President Marshall having lunch at the Shoreham Hotel. Marshall, Houston later noted,

was evidently much disturbed and expressed regret that he was being kept in the dark about the president's condition. He asked me if I could give him the real facts, which I was unable to do. I could not even repeat what had been told to me, because it had been said in confidence. The Vice-President expressed the view that he ought immediately to be informed; that it would be a tragedy for him to assume the

duties of President, at best; and that it would be equally a
tragedy for the people; that he knew many men who knew
more about the affairs of the government than he did; and
that it would be especially trying for him if he had to assume
the duties without warning.

There were more rumors: the president had lost his mind, that's why
a "nervous" specialist had been brought in; the president was about to
be operated on for a blockage in his breathing apparatus, perhaps a
polyp; McAdoo was going to take over the management of the executive
departments.

On this Sunday, October 5, 1919, how sick was the president? From
all available evidence, Dr. Edwin Weinstein now concludes that Wilson
had had a massive stroke, was paralyzed on one side, was totally blind in
one eye. His mental processes were disturbed. One of the manifestations
of this kind of stroke is that the sufferer often does not have the capacity
to acknowledge the seriousness of his illness; in particular, he does not
see that he is not thinking normally.

Was there hope for recovery? At this point the doctors thought so,
and it was on this judgment that Grayson, Tumulty, Edith, and even the
president himself based their actions. All believed Wilson to have great
powers of recuperation. Equally important, his associates believed him
the greatest man in the world and the only one capable of leading the
country at this moment, even if he was physically impaired. As the
Daily Chronicle of London was writing, "It is not too much to say that
no sickbed in our time, or perhaps in any other time, has commanded
such universal sympathy." This was perhaps, the paper said, because
Wilson was "The pillar of a people's hope/The centre of the world's
desire."

Europe believed that the passage or failure of the Treaty of Versailles
in the United States Senate was at stake, and all recognized that the
president's hand in what would happen to the treaty was crucial.

On Monday at eleven the cabinet meeting came to order. The secretary of state chaired the meeting, and put the problem squarely to his
colleagues—it was up to them to decide whether or not they should
continue to carry on the government, as there was nothing to guide them
on who could decide on the president's ability or inability to discharge
the duties of his office. They agreed to call Grayson, and while waiting
for him they discussed the legal situation. Garfield had lain incapacitated from July 2 to September 19, 1881, while his secretary ran the
government and there had been no crisis—but Congress had been out of
session then and no great business was pressing.

When Grayson and Tumulty came in, Grayson said there had been some improvement over the weekend, but that the scales might tip either way. He added that if the president were harassed by business matters, they might tip the wrong way. He would not specify what was wrong with Wilson and said, with a sort of twinkle in his eye (according to Houston), "The President asked me what the Cabinet wanted with me and by what authority it was meeting while he was in Washington without a call from him."

This warning shook Lansing, and he immediately backed down, while other cabinet members said that they were just taking up routine business as they had while the president had been in Paris, and were meeting to extend their joint sympathy to him. On this note the meeting ended, and Lansing's attempt at *coup d'etat* was defused. Privately, he talked of resigning.

In the president's bedchamber, Edith took down one of the first of her dictated notes, to Daniels, a request to see all dispatches referring to navy movements in the Adriatic or Mediterranean. The newspapers had been getting incomplete details on an American incursion into Italian space, and it was causing some small alarm. Edith took the dictation standing up near the bed, writing rapidly so Woodrow would not have to repeat himself. Later in the day, in response to a Daniels inquiry about something else, she sent the navy secretary a note saying this particular matter would not have to be submitted to Wilson at all because it was "finished business."

On Monday as well, Senator Hitchcock told Tumulty that the treaty situation in the Senate was not bad enough as to cause the president immediate concern. It would be, Hitchcock said, two weeks or more before the vote, and he was beginning parleys with moderate Republicans. This news, submitted to Wilson through Edith—and possibly exaggerated a bit at two times remove—cheered the president enormously. Unfortunately, it was incomplete and half-false news, since the treaty's foes were actually gaining strength.

Across town, Lord Grey of Fallodon, a special envoy from England charged with the delicate mission of breaking through the United States' partisan deadlock over the treaty, was told by Lansing that no questions could be submitted by Grey to the president for at least two months. On the strength of this, Grey decided to see if he could not sway Lodge. Lansing's statement, made in pique, was perhaps a premature judgment, but the White House inner circle was indeed saying that, although out of immediate danger, the president would need an extended period of recuperation. Edith asked the doctors to be frank with her. Dercum said there was every reason to believe Wilson would recover completely, and cited Louis Pasteur as a man who had done his most brilliant work after recovery from a stroke. But there would be no recovery unless Wilson the man could be released from the problems of Wilson the president.

"How can that be?" she asked, for everything that came to the president was a problem. "How can I protect him from problems when the country looks to the president as the leader?"

Dercum said she could have everything of importance pass through her own hands and decide what could be acted upon without bothering Wilson, and what he absolutely must see. "Always keep in mind that every time you take him a new anxiety or problem to excite him, you are turning a knife in an open wound." Dercum added that Wilson's nerves were crying for rest.

"Then had he better not resign, let Mr. Marshall succeed to the presidency, and he himself get that complete rest that is so vital to his life?" asked Edith.

Dercum said no, that resigning would have a bad effect not only on the country but on Wilson's chances for survival, since the impetus to get better would be removed. Dercum maintained that Wilson's mind was "clear as crystal," and that he could do more with a maimed body than anyone else could. Moreover, Wilson trusted Edith completely, and that would enable her to do what was necessary. She agreed to go ahead. And from then on,

> I studied every paper, sent from the different Secretaries or Senators, and tried to digest and present in tabloid form the things that, despite my vigilance, had to go to the President. I, myself, never made a single decision regarding the disposition of public affairs. The only decision that was mine was what was important, and what was not, and the *very* important decision of when to present matters to my husband.

In later years Edith assigned the responsibility for her assumption of the role of steward to the doctors. Dr. Edwin Weinstein believes, however, that Mrs. Wilson may have invented the whole scene with the doctors as an excuse for her own actions. Evidence suggests that she was a willing, rather than a reluctant participant. In her mind there must have seemed really not much choice. There was no one else in the White House or out of it whom she could trust to act totally on Woodrow's behalf, and since she would merely be screening things from him and not acting on her own initiative, she believed it would be best for all concerned. Grayson would help her, would deal with reporters and the staff while she would deal with business, and the president's sacred interests—primarily the treaty—would be protected as he himself wished to have them protected. This last is important, for Wilson almost certainly concurred with the plan, or at least did not offer any alternatives. He did not want to resign, and felt he would shortly recover; therefore whatever arrangements were made would be for only a finite and endurable period. He had been away in Europe and things had not fallen apart; now he would be in Washington but working at a slight remove. It appeared a practical way for the Wilsons to achieve those goals which they both wanted. Edith would take care of Woodrow, take dictation, see people with notes from him in front of her, and act as a shield for him for all things which would tax him or be unpleasant intrusions upon his recovery.

In this plan, the roles the Wilsons had set for themselves in 1915 did not materially change. The knight being sorely wounded, the lady would watch over him until such time as he would reemerge with his powers intact. The guardian of the private trust would come more to the fore, but only because that private trust, which included the nurture of the mind of Wilson, was seen as more essential than ever to the maintenance of the public trust which was the leadership of the country.

How can we understand this extraordinary situation? One avenue is through the work of sociologist Erving Goffman on the ways in which people perceive each other in various situations. In Goffman's terms, Woodrow Wilson at this stage in his life was more than an individual, he was a public figure with a certain public personality to maintain, a persona. The mask of the *persona* must be maintained, since it is vital to the conception a person has formed of himself and of his place in the world. In this sense the mask is the truer self, the self one would like to become completely. Wilson the man must continue to be Wilson the president, strong and whole and capable of leadership—or his inner being would crumble. Holding up and honoring such a mask exacts a heavy toll. For, as George Santayana put it,

> Whether the visage we assume be a joyful or a sad one, in adopting and emphasizing it we define our sovereign temper. Henceforth . . . we do not merely live, but act; we compose and play our chosen character, we wear the buskin of deliberation; we defend and idealize our passions. . . . Under our published principles and our plighted language we must assiduously hide all the inequalities of our moods and conduct, and this without hypocrisy, since our deliberate charac-

> ter is more truly ourselves than is the flux of our involuntary
> dreams. The portrait we paint in this way and exhibit as our
> true person may well be in the grand manner . . . but if this
> style is native to us and our art is vital, the more it transmutes
> its model, the deeper and truer art it will be. . . . Everyone
> who is sure of his mind, or proud of his office, or anxious
> about his duty assumes a tragic mask.

The idea of Wilson maintaining his hero's mask goes a ways toward explaining his attitude and those of the people around him during his illness. The family, too, must maintain the mask, and not allow the outside world to know that the man inside of it is frail and human. As Goffman points out in a study of behavior during illness, it is natural for the family to encourage the patient to believe he will soon resume his former role:

> Since the patient's spirit and will and intentions are those of a
> loyal and seemly member, his old place should be kept wait-
> ing for him, for he will fill it well, as if nothing untoward has
> happened, as soon as his outer behavior can again be dictated
> by, and be an expression of, the inner man.

As long as the patient does not *will* to be demanding and useless, is grateful for the attentions paid, belittles his discomfort, the family will work on his behalf. Woodrow Wilson did all of these things—tried hard to be accommodating, belittled his pain and discomfort, and was grateful to those who helped him. And Edith worked hard for him.

But, in the case of Wilson, the scenario for recovery was perhaps unreasonable, and in fact the patient refused to acknowledge that his brain function was impaired, and that his mind was no longer what it had been. Dr. Edwin Weinstein, who has examined the problem of "denial of illness" in general, and who found in Wilson a perfect case in point, points out that denial is common in patients who have suffered a stroke or brain injury:

> In this condition, the patient denies or appears unaware of
> such deficits as paralysis or blindness. . . . Patients com-
> monly talk of their incapacities in the "third person," as if
> they were occurring in someone else. . . . To casual observ-
> ers [such] patients may appear quite normal and even bright
> and witty. When not on the subject of their disabilities, they
> are quite rational; and tests of intelligence may show no

deficit. The syndrome . . . is most marked in persons who, like Woodrow Wilson, have habitually perceived the physical manifestations and consequences of illness in the context of principles and values, and as separate from the real self, who are highly work and efficiency oriented, and who have been accustomed to the overcoming of physical indispositions by force of will and character.

Dr. Weinstein holds that neither Edith nor Woodrow—or, for that matter, Grayson—would admit that Wilson's brain had suffered damage and that he was at least partially incapacitated. This was, perhaps, because he would banter with them, make up limericks, and be occasionally witty. Not enough was known by medical science at the time of Wilson for the doctors to understand how, and by what amount, his brain function had been impaired, and the plan for stewardship proceeded on the assumption that Wilson's brain was, as the doctors said, "crystal clear."

As the inner circle at the White House began to feel its way toward a *modus operandi*, Edith spent most of her time with the president, but tried to limit official problems to ten or fifteen minutes of his day. Most business was transacted without recourse to the president—or to Edith. Departments and cabinet officers made their own decisions. Federal troops under General Leonard Wood were sent to help put down the riots in Omaha. Wilson would probably have approved this. President Poincaré's cabled request that he see Ambassador Jusserand went unfulfilled, but Wilson probably didn't want to see him since he was undoubtedly carrying messages urging Wilson to compromise to get the treaty passed.

Meanwhile the newspapers reported that there was a test of wills in the White House, Grayson wanting Wilson to rest while the president wanted business as usual. Grayson's comment at this oversimplification was "The sooner the story gets off the front pages and on the back pages of the papers the more satisfied we will be."

A phonograph was installed in the sickroom for Wilson's relaxation, but a band playing a block away from the White House was asked to mute its noise and heavy trucks were routed away from the area. On October 11, reporters finally broke through Grayson's defenses and wrung from him an admission that "long bed rest" would be required. He had never said "long" before, and for the hungry press it was a revelation.

A discussion was sparked by this about Wilson's ability to carry out his duties and how—if necessary—would presidential authority be transferred. To begin with, no one knew whether the vice-president was ever supposed to be more than acting president if disability were proven. The Constitution said that in case of disability to discharge the powers and duties of the office, "the same" would devolve on the vice-president. Did "the same" refer to the office, or only to its temporary powers and duties? Also, who might call the vice-president to take over? It wasn't clear which branch had the authority—if any. A cabinet had at least once notified a vice-president when a president had died. There might be a resolution introduced in Congress to call for him, as if there were a deadlock in the electoral college. Or the Supreme Court might act, but the Court could only do so after the constitutionality of a law signed by the vice-president acting as president had been brought up for review.

The man who was vice-president, Thomas Riley Marshall, had said nothing since the president had become ill. Indeed, he didn't know the extent of Wilson's illness, and had not wished to call and find out lest he be thought to be grasping after his chief's post. Tumulty and others in the White House thought Marshall must be advised about the possibility of Wilson's dying, but they didn't want to do so officially, and so asked *Baltimore Sun* correspondent Fred Essary to quietly inform Marshall about the president. The journalist found Marshall at his desk, and when he told him of Wilson's condition, Marshall said nothing, just put his head in his hands and stared, as if a great weight had been placed on him. Essary left him sitting there, silent.

Outside the White House no one knew what Wilson's medical condition really was, but Senator George Moses of New Hampshire answered a constituent's inquiry by telling him that Wilson had had a cerebral lesion and that "There is no possibility that Mr. Wilson would be able to perform the functions of his office in the immediate or remote future." This letter was splashed over many newspapers, and was said to represent the thinking of most of the Senate. It was not said where Moses (who was not a doctor) might have gotten his medical information, but other senators started calling him Doc. The president's physician, Grayson, refused to comment on the allegation, saying that if he had to answer each rumor he'd have no time to get the president well. In fact, Grayson had been asked by both Wilsons not to reveal the nature of Woodrow's illness. Hitchcock finally told the press that the president had decided on several matters in the past ten days, and that his judgment was not impaired.

Other senators scoffed and went over Wilson's recent signatures with microscopes to see if they could prove forgery. On October 13 Lodge, Fall, and other Republicans engaged in acrimonious debate over the president's condition on the Senate floor. Reporters brought the substance of this to Grayson on the fourteenth, told him the Foreign Relations Committee was considering a proposal to obtain information from Wilson on the treaty, and asked him how he'd react to such a request if it came. If such a proposal were to come at this time, Grayson said, he'd ignore it, and continue to devote his time to restoring the president's health. Smarting from attacks from even friendly papers saying that nothing enlightening had been forthcoming about Wilson's condition, Grayson told reporters that nothing would be kept from the public if the president's illness became critical.

The papers noted on October 15 that the president, though sick, had remembered Edith's birthday and would give her a present that he had instructed someone else to buy her several days before. The press also reported that medical bulletins from the White House said that the president's prostate was swelling and making him uncomfortable.

Alarmed by the swelling, Grayson had called in Dr. Hugh Young from Johns Hopkins and Dr. H. A. Fowler of Washington, both specialists. The prostate swelling was putting pressure on and constricting the bladder. Dr. Young found Wilson's abdomen hugely distended. Within forty-eight hours this had blossomed into a full-scale medical crisis. Dr. Young tried repeatedly to dilate the muscles so the bladder could function normally, but on the morning of October 17, all elimination ceased.

Edith helped as nurses applied hot-packs to Wilson's bladder area. His pulse had slowed; now it speeded up and his temperature rose. Grayson, Ruffin, Stitt, Dercum, Young, and Fowler held a conference and agreed: if the president were not relieved of wastes soon, his body would be fatally poisoned by them.

About what happened next there are several reports. The first, an Edith Wilson–Admiral Grayson story. After the conference Grayson took a walk around the block to steady himself, then asked Edith to step into her room with him, alone. They stood looking at the Washington Monument. Overcome with emotion, he could say nothing for a while, but at last told her that all of the other doctors were agreed that the condition could not be relieved without an operation, but "I feel an operation will be the end. Therefore, while I hate to put the responsibility on you, there is nothing else but for you to decide."

Edith felt a chasm open at her feet, but had no hesitation. She believed Wilson had great powers of recovery and that nature would take care of things. She vetoed the operation. In a moment Grayson was back with Dr. Young, who drew diagrams trying to convince her that the operation was absolutely essential. Trusting to faith, and to her mystic feeling about herself and the president, Edith held her ground.

The nurse came to say Wilson was asking for her. As she started to go to him, Dr. Young called after her, "You understand, Mrs. Wilson, the whole body will become poisoned if this condition lasts an hour or at most two hours longer." The suffering president greeted her with a smile, as always, and his hand gripped hers, and they waited for death or salvation.

The second report is from Dr. Young. The famous surgeon, who had worked extensively with the wounded in France, had in the wartime *Manual of Military Urology* strongly advised against operations in cases like Wilson's—and he did so now, believing the bladder's tremendous internal pressure would soon force open the obstruction. In Young's memoirs, *A Surgeon's Autobiography*, he describes Edith's version of the incident as being the result of her distraught condition. He recommended *no* operation.

In any case, Edith went in to sit with Woodrow and hoped for a miracle. She sat watching the coming and going of the hot-packs, feeling as if her own life hung suspended. She talked quietly to Woodrow, whose temperature kept rising, told him, perhaps, how the Shantung amendment, to the surprise of the anti-treaty forces, had been defeated in the Senate just now, and how the last of the Fall amendments had gone down to defeat as well. The clock crept on. After two more hours, when the tension was near unbearable, the president's muscles finally relaxed and his bladder relieved itself. His temperature slid downwards and Wilson slipped over into sleep.

Nature and a lot of hard medical work had won. The crisis was over and the president lived, convincing both Edith and Grayson that they were indeed doing the right thing, pursuing the best possible course. "If we do not know courage," the president had said, "we cannot accomplish our purpose." It had taken courage to resist the overwhelming advice of the doctors, but they had had courage and faith and an intimate knowledge of the patient, and they had won—and so the stewardship would go on.

14

STRUGGLING WITH THE DREAM

COLONEL HOUSE HAD been anxious to get to the president on many matters. His letters since mid-September had gone unanswered. He had his wife write to Edith and tell of his own illness, but the letter arrived on October 17, while Wilson was near death. Some time during that trying day, Edith wrote to Mrs. House that when the president got better she would tell him of the colonel's message, "but as we keep everything from him (which it is not important to have his advice about and which would annoy or distress him)—I have not yet told him of the Colonel's illness or that he has left Paris." Next day the newspapers reported that House had offered to come to Washington to testify before Lodge and the treaty's enemies as to what, precisely, had happened in Paris, but that Lodge had told him he need not appear. This item probably only stiffened Edith's resolve not to tell Wilson much, if anything, about House at that time.

Daily Edith would read Woodrow the headlines—he was nearly blind—and sometimes a complete story or two. She took turns watching over him with Margaret.

Edith's power as guardian of the door was immense, but it was only a negative power. That is, she could say no to many things, but believed she had no latitude to make positive decisions. She made no policy. Mostly she referred items back to appropriate cabinet members (even when they had come from those same officers), or let issues of minor importance slide. She showed to Woodrow only those items which needed action and which were obviously important, and only those she was sure would not upset him. She firmly believed that the possibility of another stroke hung over them, and would occur if Woodrow became unduly vexed. Far better that she should suffer criticism, personal attacks, and immense indignities, than that the most important man in the world should move nearer to death.

And so, as the month moved on, the rules of the sickroom remained unchanged. A visitor, either on paper or in person, could come in, but could only say certain things. If one accepted Edith's right to protect her husband—and most men in the society at that time did so—then everything had to be done by her rules.

The recent defeat of Fall's amendments had given the Democratic leadership false hopes about ratification. Hitchcock said baldly that seventy senators favored no amendments, and the worst that could happen to the treaty was that certain interpretations would be written into the resolution of ratification. Two days after the president's illness, Hitchcock was forced to concede that some compromise might be necessary.

Around the nation, labor unrest continued to crowd the treaty for space on newspaper front pages. After much violence, a force under General Leonard Wood had gone into Gary, Indiana, and had rounded up "agitators" in the steel strike. Wood's investigators found that the people who incited the Gary violence were neither steelworkers nor regular union organizers; rather, they were card-carrying radicals. "Kill radicalism as you would a rattlesnake," Wood yelled, sounding again like a presidential candidate. On October 19, Congress sent Attorney General Palmer an urgent request to proceed with finding and deporting undesirable aliens.

During the height of the Gary disorders, the president's National Industrial Conference had convened in Washington. Secretaries Lane and William Wilson had tried to get the three major factions—labor, capital, and "the public interest"—to agree, but the deck was stacked, as Judge Gary of U.S. Steel and John D. Rockefeller were on the public-interest committee. On October 21, shortly after the president's medical setback, Samuel Gompers, head of the American Federation of Labor, advanced a resolution to have the conference uphold "the right of wage earners . . . to bargain collectively . . . in respect to wages, hours of labor, and relations and conditions of employment."

This was a position which President Wilson had previously upheld. In fact, the demands of the steel strikers had been for those modest gains which the Taft committee had endorsed during the war—such things as the eight-hour day and a minimum wage. However, the public interest combined with business votes and killed Gompers's proposal in the conference. The labor leader was ready to go. The *Chicago Tribune* trumpeted, "Labor Quits, Capital Flits, Public Sits!" Secretary Lane announced he had a six-hundred-word letter from the president, which he read and released to the press. It asked the conference to continue, pleading the necessity of conciliation.

Many thought the president's statement inferior Wilson; in fact it was drawn up by cabinet members and merely agreed to by the president. It had no effect, for Gompers led his men out anyway and the conference disbanded.

A handful of bills had come to the White House for signature. Many were let ride but, in a surprise move, Wilson vetoed a prohibition enforcement bill with a message that labeled it confused and possibly unconstitutional. Congress passed it over his veto within one day, something that had rarely been done while Wilson was well.

Coal miners, led by John L. Lewis, had also made little or no progress during the war. Now, with food prices up 86 percent since 1913, they called a strike for November 1. Tumulty gave written reports to Edith for the president, and secretary Wilson brought both sides together in Washington to try and head off the strike. While Lewis publicly emphasized the distance between his goals and those of the steelworkers, mine operators circulated reports that "Moscow gold" was financing the proposed "insurrection." Another presidential statement was issued (this one written by Tumulty): in the face of approaching winter, with the nation still technically at war and dependent upon coal to move supplies and soldiers, we could not tolerate a coal strike. It would be "a grave moral and legal wrong . . . unjustifiable . . . unlawful."

Such a statement, though filled with moral fervor, was a pale substitute for personal intervention, which Wilson had used to such good effect in August of 1916 to head off the nationwide railroad strike. Just at a time when his leadership seemed most demanded, Wilson found himself unable to exert it.

On October 29, in a final attempt to head off the coal strike, Attorney General Palmer was summoned to the White House to see Wilson. Palmer's house had been bombed, and he had narrowly escaped assassination; the current crises had confirmed his thoughts about Reds and radicals. He knew what he wanted to do before he entered the sickroom and saw the pathetic figure lying in bed with a shock of white beard upon his face. All he needed was the nod to go ahead—in fact, he'd already started so much in motion that he was more nearly reporting his actions than asking for direction.

The president, Palmer said, must enjoin the miners from striking so that the country's economy and fuel supply would not be compromised. Wilson agreed or acquiesced—it's hard to know which, as Josephus Daniels later wrote that if Wilson had been well he would have acted differently—but in any case the president did not stop Palmer. The Fuel Administration was reactivated, Palmer applied to an Indiana federal judge for an injunction against the walkout based on the wartime Lever Act, and on October 30 a temporary restraining order was issued. Gompers cried that labor had only agreed to the Lever Act upon personal assurances from Wilson that it would never be used to interfere with legitimate grievances of labor. It was the truth, but the deed was done.

As the country waited to see whether the miners would walk out anyway, King Albert and Queen Elizabeth of Belgium waited to see the president. Vice-President Marshall was entertaining them (and becoming annoyed because his expenses were not being reimbursed). Now they were going to see Wilson, which even Marshall himself hadn't been able to do. Before the royal visitors arrived, the following dialogue was reportedly held between Tumulty and Wilson:

> Tumulty: I am going to see the king of Belgium.
> Wilson: The king of the Belgians.
> Tumulty: I accept the amendment.
> Wilson: It is not an amendment, but an interpretation.

It seemed that the president had not lost his sense of humor.

The royal couple brought gifts: an eighteen-plate set of china showing Belgian scenes, for the president; a fan decorated with diamonds and sapphires and lace, for Edith. The king and queen chatted for a few minutes with Wilson, who was wearing a dressing gown, after which Edith showed them about the White House. Then the queen wanted to introduce her seventeen-year-old son to the president, and they went back to the bedroom. Wilson had exchanged his dressing gown for an old Scottish sweater, and was studying the scenes on the gift plates through a magnifying glass. When the couple left the White House they were besieged by a phalanx of reporters wanting to know about the president's condition. The queen remarked that he had had on a worn sweater, but reporters thought she said "torn," with the result that letters poured into the White House chastising Edith for letting the president wear ripped clothing.

Edith was faring badly at the hands of the press and the public.

"Petticoat government" was the charge. Senator Fall actually said she was president, others called her "Presidentress" and Woodrow "First Man." This was difficult to bear but she would bear it because her husband needed her to do so. In fact she refused all opportunities to make decisions in his place.

For example, there was a tangle about a group of ships taken from Germany. The shipping board wanted to keep them in retaliation for the fact that Great Britain had kept others that were supposed to have gone to America. Lansing and the cabinet wanted to give the ships back to Great Britain. Tumulty suggested Edith have Wilson decide on a compromise—to return the main ship, *Imperator,* and hold a half-dozen others for trading purposes. Edith could have taken any of the three suggestions as her own, or as Wilson's own and, since all the positions were well backed, no one would have ever been the wiser. She need not have told Wilson at all. But across the bottom of Tumulty's note, in Edith's hand, was the following message: "The President says he does not know enough about this matter to act upon it. . . . that no action be taken until he is well enough to act upon it." The same course was followed on many other matters.

Both Edith and Woodrow Wilson firmly believed that his condition was stable and improving, that his mind was clear. People had been in to see him; he had made some important decisions and his staff was taking action on several fronts. Josephus Daniels pleaded with Admiral Grayson: "If you would tell the people exactly what is the matter with the President, a wave of sympathy would pour into the White House, whereas now there is nothing but uncertainty and criticism." But Grayson just said the Wilsons had made him promise not to give out such information, fearing it would encourage the League's detractors and might even result in Wilson's ouster from office.

Continuity seemed essential, for the country was in acute domestic uproar. Despite the injunction, 394,000 coal miners walked out on November 1, and the army kept order while scabs shipped some coal coming for the approaching winter. Unemployment and prices were still rising.

And there was still the treaty. Stephen Bonsal, one of Wilson's interpreters in Paris, visited Washington and wrote in his diary that people were saying the president was dead but Edith and Grayson weren't admitting it. At House's request, Bonsal met with Lodge. The vote on the treaty was nearing, and House wanted to see if there was any way to reach a compromise with its opponents. Lodge and Bonsal went over much of the League's Covenant, the heart of the treaty, word for word, the senator making alterations which he said might smooth the way to ratification—about forty words changed, another fifty inserted, changes which

> It seemed to me [Bonsal wrote] . . . were more concerned with verbiage than with the object and intent of the instrument. In my judgment they were complementary to, rather than limiting, any substantial purpose of the Covenant. In this they differed sharply from the Reservations Lodge had introduced into the Senate.

In other words, Lodge was being publicly strident while privately more restrained in the changes he wanted. As an English composition, the senator told Bonsal, the treaty was abominable: "It might get by at Princeton but certainly not at Harvard." The whole discussion may have been sophomoric jibing, for Lodge and Bonsal sparred—and missed—each other's points about Article X, the heart of the Covenant. In any event Bonsal took the paper Lodge had annotated and sent it next morning to House, who then supposedly sent it to the president. House and Bonsal both later expressed the view that Edith or Grayson never showed it to Wilson. However, the document is not in the Wilson papers, nor does a copy exist in the House papers, even though House was in the habit of copying important papers before he sent them to the president.

Convinced that he and only he could get compromise effected, House kept trying to reach the president. He sent notes; Edith answered coolly. Going by Woodrow's attitude toward House since the break between the men, and knowing House to be the bearer of compromise proposals, Edith was afraid the president would be upset by House's notes. The colonel waited for an invitation to come to Washington and straighten out the world in the first weeks of November. It never came. On November 6, Lodge's committee sent fourteen reservations to the Senate floor. It particularly pleased Lodge to have fourteen reservations to Fourteen Points. The next day another was added, a particularly noxious one that would require three of the four cosigning countries to accept the Senate's reservations before the treaty would be binding upon the United States. The compliant Lodge who had bantered with Bonsal had vanished, the battler had resurfaced. Perhaps it had all been a ruse.

Believing Lodge to have the upper hand, Senator Hitchcock went to see the president that same day. As floor leader, Hitchcock had been fighting a losing battle all summer and fall. He had somewhat untruthfully given positive smoke signals, but now, with only a few days remaining before a vote was taken, he had to tell the president that the Democrats could not count on even a bare majority for ratification without reservations. When he went in to see Wilson, Hitchcock too was shocked by the white beard and changed face, and felt constrained to come right to the point. He told Wilson the probable count on the vote, and suggested "it might be wise to compromise." "Let Lodge compromise!" Wilson said with indignation.

The president believed he had compromised quite a bit already himself—he had fought the Allies for the changes Republicans had wanted; he had admitted the treaty's inadequacies forthrightly during the summer; he had given to Hitchcock some reservations which he could accept. Now it was Lodge's turn to bend. It appeared to Wilson that Lodge had never budged an inch during all the time of debate, and that he might very well—as he had in the past—now ask for more concessions if Wilson appeared to give in.

"Well, of course he must compromise also," Hitchcock said of Lodge. "But we might well hold out the olive branch."

"Let Lodge hold out the olive branch," Wilson commented.

In the two weeks before the vote both Wilson and Lodge were under pressure to compromise. Colonel House wrote the president that "To the ordinary man the distance between the treaty and the reservations is slight," that Wilson should accept the reservations and let time give the world a workable League. Tumulty sent notes to Edith advocating compromise. So did McAdoo and others. Edith ignored much of this importuning, but some got through to the president. Wilson could not bring himself to believe, however, that men of good conscience would let something as important to the world as the treaty go down to defeat when push came to shove. He was counting on public opinion to force the Senate to a reasonable position.

But the country was bored with the treaty and distracted from the fight over it, beset by a devastating coal strike which affected the railroads, factory production, and schools, as well as people's homes. The steel strike violence still continued at a low level, and the specter of Bolshevism was rampant. Armistice Day 1919 found the nation in turmoil, with a blizzard exacerbating the coal situation, with cordons of soldiers guarding public buildings in several cities from the fear of radical attack. In Centralia, Washington, members of the IWW, believing American Legionnaires were about to wreck their headquarters, fired on the marchers, killing four people. Later that evening one of the suspects was lynched. And all President Wilson could do to personally commemorate the day's significance was sit up in a wheelchair.

On the thirteenth, with the treaty vote a week away, the young Prince of Wales came to tea with Edith and was then taken up to see the president. Edith hadn't wanted him to go, but the young man had been insistent, and he was royalty. Mrs. Jaffray, the housekeeper, peering in on the meeting, noted that the president was having difficulty with his speech. While the prince fretted nervously, Wilson told in halting words that he was lying in the bed in which Abraham Lincoln had slept. The prince's grandfather had also slept in the bed one night, Wilson continued, and had slipped out the window for a private social event. The prince wanted to know which window.

With the treaty vote so near, the Democrats were in a bind. They knew the treaty without reservations would not pass. So, Democrats could either vote against the treaty-with-reservations which Lodge proposed—and cause it to fail—or they could vote for it, and get some kind of a treaty even if it was not the one they or the president wanted.

More people came to the White House to urge compromise, understanding the Democrats' bind. Bernard Baruch, knowing his advice to be unwelcome, nevertheless advised concession; Wilson thought him "true to the bone," but wrong. (This, when there was grumbling from Colonel House that Baruch had too much influence with Wilson.)

On November 17, Hitchcock returned to see the president and get orders on which way he should advise Democrats to vote. Edith asked him out of Woodrow's earshot if he were there to urge compromise. Hitchcock pleaded with her that some treaty was better than no treaty at all.

It was a crucial moment for Edith. The long, drawn-out fight over the Versailles document was eating into her soul. She agreed with Hitchcock. Motioning the senator to wait, she went in to Woodrow's bedroom alone. "For my sake," she said, "won't you accept these reservations and get this awful thing settled?" He took her hand and answered,

> Little girl, don't you desert me; that I cannot stand. Can't you see that I have no moral right to accept any change in a paper that I have signed without giving to every other signatory, even the Germans, the right to do the same thing? It is not *I* that will not accept; it is the nation's honor that is at stake.

His eyes were wet with emotion, and Edith felt he was right. He concluded, "Better a thousand times to go down fighting than to dip your colors to dishonourable compromise." Edith told Hitchcock she would never again ask her husband to give in.

Hitchcock now went in himself. The president wanted the revised preamble about three out of four signers deleted, or else he would pocket veto a treaty-with-reservations. But rather than vetoing the treaty and giving Lodge the pleasure of saying Wilson had killed his own creation, the president supported a plan which Hitchcock outlined and on which he had already done considerable work. The Democrats would vote against the amended treaty, and then the Senate would recess with the treaty itself still pending. The senators would then go home, hear the overwhelming voice of public opinion which wanted the treaty unblemished, and would then return and pass the treaty without reservations.

The senator left the president the draft of a letter to Democrats advising them how to vote. Lodge's proposal, it said, did not "provide for ratification but rather for defeat of the treaty." Wilson changed "defeat" to "nullification." The letter went on to urge friends of the treaty to vote against the Lodge proposals, so that "the door will probably then be open for a genuine resolution of ratification." Edith and Woodrow went over this text until they were satisfied, then it was sent back to Hitchcock and released to the press. Later, in his wheelchair, Wilson was taken outside for the first time since his illness.

On November 19, the Senate finally voted on the Treaty of Versailles. A two-thirds vote was necessary for ratification. With Lodge's reservations attached, it was defeated, 55 to 39. Hitchcock now moved for adjournment so he could work out some compromise with "mild reservationists." Earlier Lodge had told him he would allow this, but now, with a majority of Republicans, Lodge defeated the motion to adjourn. Vice-President Marshall then ruled the treaty was open to any substitute resolution, offering Hitchcock his opportunity for compromise—but again Lodge objected, saying that only *his* resolution was before the Senate and that all else was out of order. Marshall was overruled by the majority.

The vice-president was overruled twice more when he tried to take other compromise resolutions to a vote, in what the *New York Sun* called "the most amazing parliamentary tangle that anyone could remember." Blocked from compromise, the Democrats were being herded down a narrow path whose end, it seemed, only Senator Lodge knew. Even a motion to get Lodge and Hitchcock together to draft a new resolution of ratification was defeated. Lodge allowed a second vote on his motion, which was defeated 51 to 41. Then Senator Underwood moved the unconditional ratification of the treaty as brought back from France, and Lodge's trap closed. In the gallery, Alice Roosevelt Longworth felt a shiver of anticipation; she who had been "The Commander of the Battalion of Death" against the League had been waiting for the kill for a long time. Lodge said he'd have no objection if the vote on the unvarnished treaty were taken at once. It was.

With 53 nays to 38 yeas and four abstentions, the treaty was defeated. Lodge then introduced a resolution calling for a separate peace with Germany, which was referred to his committee for consideration, and the Senate adjourned at 11:10 P.M. Lodge, Fall, Harding, and a few other senators, went home with Alice Longworth to celebrate. Mrs. Harding cooked the eggs.

It was near midnight when Edith Wilson brought the sad news of the treaty's defeat to her husband's bedside. She was afraid the shock might kill him, but knew she had to tell him. Woodrow Wilson was silent for a few moments, then said, "All the more reason I must get well and try again to bring this country to a sense of its great opportunity and greater responsibility."

15

INTERVENTIONS

VICE-PRESIDENT THOMAS RILEY MARSHALL, who had worked hard for compromise on the treaty vote, had been a successful reform governor of Indiana, a man who consistently hid his intellect behind homespun jokes, such as his famous line, "What this country needs is a good five-cent cigar." He was a good vice-president, even if Wilson and most of the cabinet considered him a lightweight.

In the early months of Wilson's illness some Democrats tried to get Marshall to wrest the presidency from Wilson, saying he'd be filling the void and could compromise on the treaty (a position he was known to favor, privately), but they didn't push hard. Four Republicans jointly told him he would have the support of the congressional majority if he would make his move. He refused. "I could throw this country into civil war," he told his wife, "but I won't." Nevertheless, Marshall's secretary, Mark Thistlethwaite, insisted he must prepare himself for assuming the presidency in case of Wilson's death. If reporters came with bad news one night, Marshall ought to say he'd continue Wilson's policies. Marshall disagreed, said there were many things he'd change. The secretary told him to change all he wanted—but first to announce a continuation of the past. Marshall scoffed at the thought of obtaining the presidency, telling his adviser, "I am not going to seize the place and then have Wilson—recovered—come around and say 'get off, you usurper!' "

A few days after the treaty was defeated, the genial Marshall was in Atlanta to make a speech when a man came up on the platform and

whispered to him that Wilson was dead. Marshall bowed his head and
was overcome. He asked that the band play "Nearer My God to Thee,"
and during the hymn left the stage. Later the report was denied.
Marshall told Josephus Daniels that when he thought he was president,
"There was no sense of elation but rather the contrary. I was stunned,
first by grief for my dead chieftain and second by the awful responsibility that would fall upon me. I was resolved to do my duty but I can
truly say that I dreaded the great task." The perpetrator of the hoax
was never found.

Now that the defeat Lodge had planned had occurred, many people
wanted to start anew on compromise plans. Lord Grey was one of these.
He tried to get evidence to the White House that a treaty with some
reservations might not be totally unacceptable to England. But this
information he was unable to convey personally. Then his position was
further damaged when his aide, Major Charles Kennedy Craufurd-
Stuart, slurred Edith Wilson at a dinner party. News of this reached
Edith and Woodrow, and Lansing was asked to inform Grey that
Craufurd-Stuart was *persona non grata* and should be sent home. Grey
refused to send him. Lansing insisted, at Grayson's urging, that the
major at least be severed from Grey's official mission—or else Grey
himself had best go home. While all this was being resolved, Grey had
no access to the president and his attempts at compromise were frustrated.

Another who tried was Colonel House. On November 24, House
wrote Wilson suggesting the treaty be turned back to the Senate so
Republicans would bear the responsibility for passing it in a form
acceptable to other signatories. He enclosed the letter in one to Edith
which said, "You can never know how long I have hesitated to write to
the President about anything while he is ill, but it seems to me vital that
the Treaty should pass in some form. His place in history is in the
balance." Edith, who worried about bothering the ill president every
day, decided that her husband's place in history was already assured.
House's letter went unanswered. Three days later he wrote again,
altering his plan so that the burden of acceptance of reservations would
be not on the president but wholly on the other signatories to the treaty.
Again, there was no reply. By December 2, though, the colonel had
changed his mind once more and now believed the treaty should not be
returned to the Senate at all until two-thirds of the senators were
committed in advance to vote for it with mild reservations.

Margaret Wilson visited House in New York and, knowing how upset he was by her father's silence, told House how she thought his behavior had offended her father. In his own defense House maintained he had acted only out of concern for Wilson's basic goals. When Margaret returned and told this to her father, he sighed. House hadn't stood up to the pressure, wasn't the man Wilson had once thought him to be. Rather, he was closer to what Edith had thought of him from the first, a sycophant of small caliber. Could they meet and be friends again? The president thought not: it would be embarrassing for them both.

While the anti-treaty forces, fueled with money from Mellon and Frick, intensified a campaign to reject the treaty altogether, Hitchcock and others were trying to find ways to bridge the gap to Republican mild-reservationists. Senator Underwood, who was contesting the minority leadership with Hitchcock, wrote Wilson, "the treaty is not dead in the Senate." Hitchcock himself wrote, "we will have 81 who favor or pretend to favor ratification." The president and Grayson clashed over the patient's Thanksgiving dinner, Wilson wanting turkey, the doctor something lighter. They compromised on quail.

The president's appetitite was returning, and not only for food. He wanted work. He dictated longer notes now to various cabinet officers, asking them to put off certain decisions until he was better and had more information. These notes, in Edith's shaky handwriting, went up and down the sides and bottoms and top white spaces of official letters, and along the backs of envelopes. Decisions were being made on some matters—they weren't the best, but they were Wilson's own, and that was what counted. The most important task confronting the president was the annual message to the opening of the winter congressional session. This couldn't wait. So Tumulty asked Charles Swem, the stenographer, a man who knew Wilson's writing style well, to put together various reports and departmental requests and to draft a message. This was done, and the resulting document sent into the sickroom for approval.*

Edith and Woodrow went over it together. In the copy of the message in the Wilson Papers, an opening section about the importance of passing the treaty has been crossed out; so have portions dealing with the railroads, civil service, and merchant ships; thereafter, only a few words have been changed. The revisions are in Edith's handwriting but show unmistakable Wilsonian preferences for certain turns of phrase— for instance, such-and-such an act must be "adopted," not "passed."

---

*It was considered close to scandalous at the time. Now presidents do this routinely. There were no paid speechwriters for the Wilson White House.

The president's mind, not yet razor sharp as it once had been, nevertheless was showing signs of returning agility. Every day they did a bit more, and the more Woodrow did, the easier Edith breathed.

Around the beginning of December a crisis loomed from an unexpected quarter. The affair had begun in Mexico in October when a consular official in Mexico, Herbert Jenkins, had been kidnapped. A clamor started, led in the Senate by Albert Bacon Fall, for the United States to intervene. For years, Fall said, we had stood the provocations of the Carranza government; now, with the war in Europe over, we had to do something about them.

Jenkins was ransomed and freed, and then, curiously, the Mexican government itself arrested him. From jail Jenkins called for the United States to get him out. The press, fed information by Fall, shouted for immediate action.

In truth Fall had personal reasons for wanting war with Carranza. He had invested heavily in Mexico, and was beholden to an even heavier investor, oilman Edward Doheny. Doheny had spent hundreds of thousands of dollars to document abuses of power in Mexico, such as attempts to abrogate his oil leases. He had sponsored a lobbying organization for foreign oil producers with offices in major cities. In 1918 he'd given Josephus Daniels a plan for protesting Carranza's activities; Daniels said it would result in war with Mexico while we were still fighting in Europe, and rejected it. Doheny kept trying. In 1919 he hired former Secretary of the Treasury McAdoo to do some legal work, and made overtures to Interior Secretary Franklin K. Lane, offering him a job if he would leave the cabinet.*

On November 12, 1919, Carranza had begun to seize all oil wells drilled in Mexico which did not have required government permits. Doheny feared confiscation was just around the corner. Senator Fall told the Senate that Mexico was responsible for the Communist propaganda that was "causing" the strikes and civil disorder in America. He talked about introducing a proposal for intervention. Lodge backed it. So, too, did Lansing. On November 28, the secretary of state threatened Mexican Ambassador Bonillas: if Jenkins were not released, there would be a break in relations and troops might have to be sent in. On December 1, Lansing and Fall met and exchanged papers on Mexico,

---

*Around this time Lane was pushing Wilson to sign legislation allowing private producers to lease government oil lands. Wilson refused. It was just this scheme which later resulted in the Teapot Dome scandal in the Harding Administration involving Doheny—and Fall.

and the secretary told Fall that he was acting on his own initiative and without consulting the president.

News of all this filtered to the White House, where Tumulty convinced Edith that the president must be informed. Tumulty called Lansing to account. The secretary of state said he hadn't informed Wilson about the Jenkins matter because it was minor. He said he had it well in hand, that in fact Jenkins was about to be released, and that he would submit the whole business to Wilson "when it gets critical."

At the very least, several deceptions were being maintained. There was some evidence that Jenkins had arranged his own kidnapping and ransom as a pretext for getting the United States to intervene in Mexico, and that was why the Mexican authorities were holding him. In addition, Lansing was actively cooperating with Fall, though he denied this to Tumulty, and after their meeting delegated future dealings with Fall to a subordinate.

On December 3, Fall introduced his resolution to sever relations with Mexico. During the debate on the resolution in the Foreign Relations Committee, the question became—courtesy mostly of Senator Lodge—not whether to go into Mexico with troops, but whether or not President Wilson was competent to handle the crisis which Fall's resolution would inevitably bring about. When, late on December 4, Secretary Lansing testified that he had not discussed Mexico or any other matter with the president since Wilson's return to Washington, the fat was in the fire. Straightaway a special subcommittee was appointed to go and see Wilson and find out if he was competent to guide the United States through the coming crisis with Mexico and, if they found he was not, to tell that fact to the Senate—after which the Senate might possibly open to debate the entire question of unseating the president.

Fall and Lodge assumed that the president would refuse to see the subcommittee, and then action would be taken on the basis of the refusal. To their surprise, the White House agreed to see Senators Hitchcock and Fall midafternoon on December 5.

In the interim Tumulty talked to Lansing and to Daniels, obtaining much background information on Fall's work, and a promise to push hard for resolution of the Jenkins problem. Lansing, who actually thought war with Mexico would cure the United States' current domestic problems, bragged to Tumulty that he had diverted the committee's attention *to* the Jenkins matter because it was so minor, and that once solved it would remove any rationale for further action by the Senate.

Grayson, fearing deception, went around Lansing to get other advice from the State Department. Senator Key Pittman gave Grayson a letter outlining strategy for the Fall meeting; Wilson should, the senator suggested, kick Fall "in the slats" once and for all. Robert Wooley, the Democratic party's publicity head, was called in to set up the props for the meeting, such as a copy of Fall's resolution close to the president's good hand, and the chair in which Fall should sit. It was going to be quite an interview.

Performances, sociologist Erving Goffman contends, whether private or public, are controlled by those who are already in a room, rather than by those who enter. The insiders act as a team, keeping their own secrets, managing the flow of information, knowing far better than those who enter just what it is they want to have happen, and working in a rehearsed way to achieve their goals.

In the early afternoon, what Wilson called "the smelling committee" came to the White House, and for the first time since the illness the gates were opened to reporters. More than a hundred waited to grill the senators when they left the president. Grayson told Fall that, within reason, there would be no time limit to the visit.

Edith escorted them into the sickroom. The president sat in his bed wearing a brown sweater, the bedding pulled up to cover his entire left side. He gathered all his strength to give Fall a hearty handshake with his good right hand and waved him to a chair. He had been freshly shaved, and was smiling. "How are your Mexican investments getting along?" the president asked. Nonplussed, Fall took the chair designated for him and said, "We have all been praying for you, Mr. President." "Which way, Senator?" Wilson shot back. Edith was already writing down everything that was being said. "You seem very much engaged, Madam," Fall said to her. "I thought it wise to record this interview so there may be no misunderstandings or misstatements made," she answered.

Hitchcock remained in the background like a bit player. Fall asked Wilson if he knew about the resolution to sever relations with Mexico. Wilson waved his copy and quipped that Senator "Doc" Moses would be disappointed to see that his right hand was still useful. He told Fall he'd been following the Mexican situation in a general way, and wanted to know what Fall had found that was new. It was immediately obvious that Wilson knew quite a bit about the situation, and could not be considered incompetent. Outmaneuvered, Fall blundered on, telling the president he had "proof" that the coal strike was connected to a Carranzista plot to recover territory lost to the United States in 1848. At that moment Grayson left the room to take a phone call. Fall talked about Jenkins's kidnapping. Grayson returned to say that the State

Department had just been informed that Jenkins had been released from jail.

"That seems to have helped some," Wilson said. It was the crowning blow, but Fall didn't even seem to know it. He went on telling the president how adoption of his resolution would strengthen the administration's hand in dealing with the Mexican problem. Wilson dismissed him by courteously asking that all of Fall's arguments be sent to him in a memorandum so he could comment to the Senate before the committee voted on the resolution on December 8. He ended the interview by quoting Peter Finley Dunne's Mr. Dooley: "Sure, with Mexico so contagious [contiguous], we'll be takin' it soon whither we want it orr not."

Outside the reporters gathered about the two senators. Fall had to admit that he had found Wilson competent, able to joke about his health, and reasonably informed as to the situation in the Senate and in Mexico. Hitchcock added that Wilson looked better than when he had seen him last, was easily understandable in his speech, and had given a hearty handshake.

On Monday, after receiving Fall's memo and other materials from the State Department, the president ordered an investigation into the department's handling of the Jenkins case, and wrote a sharp note back to Fall. The Fall resolution, Wilson said, would put the Senate into the driver's seat in foreign policy, and

> would constitute a reversal of our constitutional practice, which might lead to a very grave confusion in regard to the guidance of our foreign affairs. . . . The initiative in directing relations of our government with foreign government is assigned by the Constitution to the Executive, and to the Executive only.

Having read this letter and having met with the full Foreign Relations Committee, Senator Lodge ruefully announced that the Fall resolution was dead. The crisis, too, was over: from this moment on, there was no more serious talk in Washington about attempting to remove the president from office.

Wilson was paying more and more attention to affairs of state, including the coal strike. On December 6, Palmer and Joe Tumulty met with UMW officials and presented a Wilson statement which would give the miners a 14-percent wage increase now, to be absorbed by the producers and not passed along to the public, if they would return to work and accept arbitration that might result in a further increase. In the face of this offer—and contempt proceedings—John L. Lewis accepted the president's plan, and the coal strike ended on December 10.

The great fall strikes had a tremendous effect on the public mind, increasing the fear of domestic Bolshevism and the determination on the part of big business to resist unionization. As faith in the patriotism of the workers dried up, the general hysteria over communism took over. People who stood up to strikers and who moved on radicals, became heroes. None was more lionized in the press than Attorney General A. Mitchell Palmer. He was seen as "running the administration." Though Wilson had warned Palmer against excesses, while ill the president seemed unable to resist him or his measures. By early December, Palmer had 249 "undesirable aliens" ready for deportation aboard the army transport ship *Buford*, which the press dubbed "the Red Ark." Few of these aliens had criminal records or had been directly connected with terrorist acts—most were guilty only of membership in the Union of Russian Workers, which professed anarchy. Belabored and over-taxed, influenced by the constricted and biased flow of information available to him in the White House sickroom, Wilson did not seem to know enough about the situation to counter it.

As the undesirables got ready to leave against their will, so did Viscount Grey. He had not seen the president, and he could not budge Lodge. Lansing sent a request that Grey be allowed, unofficially, to come and say good-bye to the president, but the White House denied this last favor.

On December 18, the Wilsons' wedding anniversay, Tumulty sent Edith a list of matters to be brought up to the president when that seemed most possible. The list included deciding what to do with the railroads and when; the recognition of Costa Rica; the selection of a commission to settle the miners' grievances; the appointments of the secretaries of the treasury and the interior, the assistant secretary of agriculture, and two dozen more minor appointments at home and abroad. Edith and Woodrow went over the list and, one by one, ticked off what was to be done. A message on the railroads would go out Christmas Eve; the miners' commission would be set up with a few recommendations; try McCormick for this position, ask Houston to suggest for that one, etc. Choices were made for most, if not all, of the appointments. Costa Rican recognition would have to wait, though, until Wilson knew more about the situation there.

Of old, Wilson would have disposed of all of this in a morning. Now he could not do that; he did a bit here, a bit there, and originated nothing. His job was still to get well. Christmas came, the Bolling and Wilson families gathered, but there was no tree in the White House. Edith and Grayson went out to give candy and presents to the hundreds of children who lined the president's old pleasure-ride and golfing routes. Wilson's sixty-third birthday brought a small flood of cards and telegrams. At New Year's no one put a leg up on one table.

The night of January 2, 1920, Palmer's federal agents went on the rampage, raiding Communist haunts in thirty-three cities across twenty-three states, rounding up over four thousand people. Civil liberties were flagrantly violated, many innocent people were detained, some given the third degree, some held without bail. In a day or two about half the prisoners were released without apologies, but several thousand were held for deportation hearings. The attorney general was again celebrated as the savior of the age. Liberals looked to the White House for guidance and response, but neither was forthcoming. Either the president did not know what Palmer and his cohorts were doing or the president had nothing to say.*

If the crisis of leadership seemed so apparent at this moment when Woodrow Wilson was ill, it was because his actions had been so strong during the previous decade. He had accomplished a rare thing in American politics—had crystallized people's thoughts and had actually led their minds with his questing vision—and when he was removed Americans were not used to the void at the top and missed his strength. If Taft had been similarly incapacitated in his time in office, there would have been less of a vacuum. But Wilson's silence left the country fatherless. No one of stature emerged to take his place.

Exacerbating the problem was the fact that the country was in a roiling, seething time of change, a time characterized by the rejection of those values, icons, and standards of service and sacrifice which were associated with Wilson during most of the previous decade. The world had gone up in flames. No one could truly comprehend the magnitude of what had been destroyed: it was a time when the passions of cupidity, revenge, and protection ran rampant, when people shrank from a future they did not want to know.

A leader is a man whose insights pierce the shroud of the future and make it knowable to the present. Wilson had done this for the country in the past. "Principles, as statesmen conceive them, are threads to the labyrinth of circumstances," he had said thirty years before. Now the labyrinth was overwhelming, and he had not the soundness of body nor

---

*Later evidence upholds the theory that Wilson may never have been told about the January 2 raids at all.

mind to find the thread. Wilson had always believed that reality was shaped by God's hand and by men's dreams, that experience was as much a creation as a happenstance. As he later told Raymond Fosdick, "The world is run by its ideals. Only the fool thinks otherwise."

The awful truth was that, as 1920 began, the mind of Wilson was no longer supple enough to create new ideals for the world. He believed he had helped to create one great ideal, the League of Nations, and surely that ought to be enough, but it was not carrying the day in the United States. Still, he was enthralled with it. Years ago, he had warned against undue reliance on one such lofty principle:

> The captain of a Mississippi steamboat had made fast to the shore because of a thick fog lying upon the river. The fog lay low and dense upon the surface of the water, but overhead all was clear. A cloudless sky showed a thousand points of starry light. An impatient passenger inquired the cause of the delay. "We can't see to steer," said the captain. "But all's clear overhead," suggested the passenger, "you can see the North Star." "Yes," replied the officer, "but we are not going that way." Politics must follow the actual winding of the channel of the river: if it steer by the stars it will run aground.

At the beginning of 1920, Wilson had run aground.

In the early mornings the president would be put into his wheelchair to do some work. There were times when he would drift off in the middle of a sentence, and dictating to Swem was difficult, but some business was being transacted. Later in the morning he would watch a film, a new one every day, shown without musical accompaniment in the East Room. To the film's projectionist, to members of the White House staff who had admired him in better days, Wilson was only a shadow of his former self. He was particularly fragile emotionally. Good news about the treaty's progress would make him exorbitantly happy. On the other hand, when Edith was reading to him in the early evenings, he would begin to cry for no apparent reason. The strain of being unwell was almost more than he could bear, and it was extremely hard on Edith.

The First Lady was a woman of average but not soaring intelligence who had relied throughout her life on her instincts and on her emotions of the moment. Until now she had little feeling for the sweep of history. But now her job was clear: to champion Woodrow's ideals until he could again do so himself. She lived from day to day, without too much foresight or planning as to what the future might bring. If she made mistakes, well, she was learning, and would guard against making the same error twice. That was the best she could do.

Most women of her day lived in this manner; without authority in a male-dominated world, they had shut off their own faculties of concentrated thought and speculation, leaving those domains to the men. There are many stories of this time about women whose husbands had had disabling illnesses, and all have the same pattern as the story of the Wilsons.

Perhaps because the times were difficult and the tasks seemingly insoluble, the relationship of Edith and Woodrow grew into another dimension. They left the physical behind; they had now to trust to one another's spirits. Many relationships, subjected to this sort of stress, break down. Theirs was cemented. While all about them was crumbling, they would not retreat from their bond together.

People would remark how tenderly Edith cared for the president, how she spent her every waking moment looking after him and trying to coax him back to vigor. She kept the promise of returned health before his eyes. He would always smile when he saw her and respond to her charm, tremendously grateful for her loyalty and her labors. On a scrap of memo paper—one of the few items of a personal nature written in Wilson's hand after his stroke—is this deeply felt note:

> My Darling:
> Whenever I fail to live up to the great standards which your dear love has set for me a passion of sorrow and remorse sweeps over me which my self-control cannot always withstand.
>
> Your own
> Woodrow

I love you! I love you. I love you.

16

TROUBLED ON EVERY SIDE

WILLIAM JENNINGS BRYAN had sent Christmas cards to thousands, which he had not done since he was last a presidential candidate. In his latest speeches, he was saying that the treaty must be immediately passed in some form or other so that the United States could help make the League of Nations into a workable body. Obviously Bryan was trying to take the torch from the failing Wilson. The Great Commoner planned to open his campaign with a talk at the annual Jackson Day dinner. Hearing of this, Wilson sent a letter of his own to the diners. "The United States enjoyed the spiritual leadership of the world until the Senate of the United States failed to ratify the Treaty," it opened. Wilson contended the Senate was wrong, that the treaty must be passed "without changes that alter its meaning." If there was any doubt on what the electorate felt about this matter, the next presidential election should become "a great and solemn referendum" as to what part the country would play in the settlement of the world's affairs. He had no objection to interpretations, and some compromise would be possible as long as it did not abrogate the treaty's basic tenets.

The reading of this strong letter effectively blunted Bryan's drive for the nomination. But it also pointed up a lot of questions. Was Wilson aiming for a third term? Would he compromise on the League? What would happen next?

Senator Hitchcock proclaimed that the Senate was now stimulated by Wilson to greater efforts on the treaty. On January 12, the *New York Times* announced that "Twenty Democrats Plan a Compromise."

Next to that story was one about the recent experiments of Robert Goddard, "Believes Rocket Can Reach Moon." In 1920 many people had more faith in the possibility of compromise on the treaty than in the possibility of rockets reaching the moon. Although the president's message acted as a spur to Democrats, it hardened the posture of the mild-reservationist Republicans and drove them toward immovability. As Dr. Arthur Link points out, the Jackson Day message

> destroyed Wilson's leadership among the various segments of elite opinion makers who had heretofore been his strongest supporters—religious leaders, educational leaders, publicists, editors, and politically active professionals. A reading of their correspondence, journals, editorials, and resolutions reveals a sharp and sudden turn in their opinion. In their view, Wilson was a petulant and sick man and now the principal obstacle to ratification.

In mid-January, while compromisers were meeting on both sides of the Senate aisle, Wilson conceived a plan to reach boldly over the heads of the senators to finally ratify the treaty. He would challenge those senators who opposed the treaty to resign their offices and take immediate steps to seek reelection based on their positions. If a majority of them were reelected, Wilson himself would resign, along with Marshall, and would turn the government over to the opposition. It would be a grand plebiscite, a true taking of the electorate's pulse. This idea echoed his plan to resign in 1916 if Hughes had won the election.

Edith bustled about seeking advice. She asked Palmer to draw up a statement on the legal effects of the resignation of senators in thirty-five states. Burleson was asked for a hard-core list of those who opposed the treaty; so was Hitchcock (even as Wilson was refusing to aid the senator in his fight to retain minority leadership). Within days, Wilson learned there were difficulties facing his plan. First, he had no power to compel senators to resign; second, not all the governors had the authority to make interim appointments; third, Wilson could not be sure the governors would schedule elections to assist him. Edith met with Vice-President Marshall, who agreed to go along since the president wished him to do so. Grayson was known to be in favor of the plan: the president prepared a letter naming fifty-seven senators who should resign. It also told the public:

> I have, as you know, repeatedly professed my adherence to the principles of referendum and recall, and I could wish both

that you might have an early opportunity at the ballot box to
express your sovereign wish with regard to the Treaty, and
that you might, if you desire, also have an opportunity to
recall your commission to me to act and speak in your name
and on your behalf.

The burden of acting in a responsible manner was put on the senators.
Although many of Wilson's advisers seemed willing to go along with the
plan despite its legal difficulties, the letter did not go out. It appears
that Edith vetoed the letter, believing the plan would subject Woodrow
to possible ridicule and defeat. She would not have that.

Meanwhile in the Senate compromise seemed near. Taft, Lowell,
Bryan, and other opinion leaders were calling for it, pressuring Lodge as
well as Wilson. Lodge and Hitchcock actually began going over, point
by point, the Lodge reservations and Hitchcock's substitutes (previously
discussed with Wilson) and were making some progress. Wilson sent
Hitchcock a long letter about compromise, agreeing to yield on a good
many points and interpretations, but refusing to accept a rewording on
Article X which would have, as the president understood that rewording,
gutted the treaty and League.

The president believed firmly that the power of the League lay
basically in its capacity to impose sanctions—primarily economic ones,
but military ones if necessary—against aggressive nations. Lodge
wanted the United States to be unable to commit to such sanctions
unless specifically approved in each case by Congress. Wilson believed
Lodge's strictures would hamper the power of the League to prevent
war by subjecting each case to the same sort of Senate debate that had
held up the Treaty of Versailles for these many months.

This fundamental difference between Wilson and Lodge brought all
possible compromise to a halt. It seemed then an either-or choice. Either
the U. S. would consent to sanctions, or it would not. Either Wilson's
reading of Article X, or Lodge's substitute. Republican "bitter-enders"
threatened to abandon the party, form an independent bloc, and cause
Lodge to lose his leadership of the Senate if Lodge compromised at all
on Article X. Lodge canceled his compromise meetings and issued an
ultimatum saying there would be no compromise on either Article X or
the Monroe Doctrine.

In the light of sixty years later there seems little but semantic
differences between the two sides in the wording of the changes (rather
than the complete intent). The president in actual practice would have
to consult with the Senate before making any commitment to economic
or military sanctions, and Wilson knew that. Just as surely, Lodge knew

it, just as he knew that the Monroe Doctrine had already been guaranteed. Changes making the policy more explicit would weaken the League, which even he publicly professed not to want. As January drew to a close both Lodge and Wilson turned their backs on compromise.* The president continued to hope for public pressure to change Lodge's mind, or at least the minds of some still-wavering senators. There were demands for aid to those starving in Poland, Austria, Armenia, and other places—aid which was being held up in the Senate by those also holding up the treaty—and the senators were being deluged with mail demanding the obstructionism stop. The pressure worked in the case of aid to the starving nations. Could the same thing happen with the treaty? Wilson still hoped so.

At this moment Lord Grey published a letter in the *London Times* which caused enormous controversy. It said that the Allies would have to accept the United States into the League with treaty reservations, since without the United States there would be no effective League. Grey hoped his letter would provide Wilson a bridge to the Senate and make compromise a reality. It had precisely the opposite effect.

Because it appeared in such an establishment paper, Grey's letter was widely assumed to have the backing of the British government, and quite possibly to have been discussed with the French government before publication. And what Grey said seemed to give the lie to a number of Wilson tenets. It declared that reservations would *not* nullify the treaty or mean renegotiation, and destroyed Wilson's public position for refusing to compromise any further. There were many in Europe who disagreed with Grey, and his letter did not have the stamp of authority many took it to have—but the European press came out overwhelmingly in back of Grey's stance. Wilson reacted in fury. He dictated a letter to Edith which expressed surprise at a foreign ambassador's attempt to influence this country's policy: "It may be safely assumed that had Lord Grey ventured upon any such utterance while he was still at Washington as an Ambassador . . . his government would have been promptly asked to withdraw him." Grayson and Edith persuaded Wilson not to release this letter. Instead, Hitchcock belatedly gave the press Wilson's letter urging compromise—but a lot of damage had been done.

Further damage was caused almost immediately when the president's ire turned to Lansing. He wrote to the secretary of state asking if it were

*Modern Wilson scholars believe that had the president been in better health, or had he realized the extent of his own mental impairment caused by his strokes so that he might have allowed others to carry on his work, an effective compromise might well have been made.

true that Lansing had called cabinet meetings while he had been ill. Lansing answered that he had, just as he had called meetings when the president was away. Wilson then asked for his resignation on the grounds that this was an intolerable usurpation of presidential power. The real reason, of course, was Lansing's long record of personal disloyalty, but the public knew nothing of that. All the voters got to see were Wilson's query, Lansing's reply, and the firing notice, which Lansing made public. A storm of outrage filled the headlines. One paper went so far as to call this firing "Wilson's Last Mad Act." Even the president's friends and major supporters who believed Lansing should have been fired objected to the timing and the manner of his dismissal.

The fact that, about this time, Edith brought the offer of secretary of the treasury to D. F. Houston, and had tea with other prospective cabinet appointees, coupled with the Lansing business, gave the public reason to wonder whether Edith was doing more than acting as a messenger for her husband.

Also contributing to the atmosphere of mistrust was the publication of an interview with Dr. Young in the *Baltimore Sun.* Dr. Young thought he was doing the president a favor talking of how bravely he was recovering. But during the interview the doctor publicly stated for the first time that Wilson had had a stoke in October. Though the bulk of the Young interview was very positive about the president's recovery and the clarity of his mind, it was the revelation of the stroke which other newspapers headlined when they picked up the story.

There was no similar coverage of the fact that the president was resuming personal command. Little space was given to his reception of a delegation of railroad men, and his actions in sending sharp notes to Europe over an Adriatic matter were shamelessly misinterpreted for several weeks, until it was belatedly discovered that the president had been in the right and that the French had been carefully hiding some important facts in the matter. Neither the press nor the wavering senators were privy to Wilson's now daily correspondence with Acting Secretary of State Polk, notes which show Wilson's old courtesy and inquisitiveness, and which make firm decisions on international affairs. Whereas Wilson could no longer work with Lansing, he did very well with Polk. All the undecided senators could see was, a few weeks later, the surprising nomination of New York lawyer Bainbridge Colby to succeed Lansing. Nobody knew who Colby was, and he appeared to have no experience in foreign affairs.

By this time many Democratic senators had decided to defect from the party ranks and vote for the treaty with Lodge's reservations. They could then go home and say they had indeed voted for a League, but that a Wilson veto was to blame for everything. Lodge was hoping for such a scenario, as a prelude to a later Wilson-Lodge showdown at the polls, with the voters repudiating Wilson and putting Lodge at long last into the White House.

That Lodge hadn't much of a prayer for the Republican nomination was not yet clear. Leonard Wood was the front runner. Herbert Hoover's name had been bandied about, but nobody was sure whether he was a Democrat or a Republican. On the Democratic side, front-runner Palmer was losing his edge as liberal voices objected to his excesses. Then there was McAdoo, who privately said he wanted the nomination but only if Wilson was not going after it. Friends entered McAdoo's name in Georgia but, as Mac wrote to Grayson,

> Of course the President's silence makes it very awkward for me, even if I had an inclination to stand for the Presidency— which, as you know, I have not, but it is not possible to resist the demands of one's friends to state either that they may proceed or that they may not. In the latter case I should have to say flat-footedly that in no circumstances would I permit my name to be so considered. . . . It seems hardly fair to do this now with so many uncertain elements in the situation. . . . Any suggestions you may have to offer I shall appreciate. I am really very much perplexed.

Grayson—as well as Nell—advised Mac to withdraw his name, which he did, saying in a public letter that he was *not* a candidate, but that if he were drafted by the Democrats it would of course be his duty to accept. Wilson commented to Tumulty that Mac had the right attitude.

Edith's attitude at the time is unknown, but most likely she may have believed, in the face of some evidence that Wilson was getting better, that a third term was possible. This feeling—if it were ever there—soon faded.

But the president believed in his own recovery and his potential. One day in early March, with the treaty vote near, a number of Wilson's friends met at the Chevy Chase club: Homer Cummings, Baruch, Colby, Tumulty, Houston, Burleson, Glass, Palmer, McCormick, and Daniels. Staring them in the face was a note from the president: "What part should the writer play in politics in the immediate future?" Nobody had the temerity to write back "None," though all but Burleson objected to Wilson's running again. They not only thought he should not run, but that he should accept the Lodge reservations and take the country into the League. Yet not a one of them would volunteer to bring back to the sick man the unpalatable news that he ought not to run in 1920. Perhaps they believed the truth would kill him—or maybe they were simply afraid of his wrath.

As the treaty vote neared, the world seemed to be going rapidly to pot: riots in Germany, armies clashing in Russia, starvation in Poland and Armenia, rearmament in France, revolution in the Adriatic. Pressure on Wilson to compromise was very great, but he told Burleson, "I will not play for position. This is not a time for tactics. It is a time to stand square. I can stand defeat. I cannot stand retreat from conscientious duty." The bitter-enders would not compromise either, and those pushing for a middle ground finally gave up. Wilson knew what was coming. "I am very well for a man who awaits disaster," he told Tumulty.

Edith sent Ray Stannard Baker in to see the president, believing in her heart that accepting the modified treaty was best, but Wilson couldn't agree with her emissary. He told Baker, "If I accept [the Lodge reservations], these Senators will merely offer new ones, even more humiliating." Of course that was what had happened in the past, and Baker could not gainsay Wilson's logic.

On March 8, Wilson sent Hitchcock another letter about reservations. Many of the new substitutes suggested by other senators were worse than Lodge's travesties. Didn't anybody understand that Article X was a moral obligation and a pledge of good faith? He had known of reservationists and mild reservationists, but couldn't see a hair's breadth of difference between a "nullifier" and a "mild nullifier." Either the United States should go into the League with its head high, or it should walk away completely. Senate reaction was intense. The last of the middle-ground senators had their good will smashed by this letter.

On March 19, the treaty with the Lodge reservations attached came up for the Senate's vote and was defeated, 49 yeas to 35 nays. An analysis shows that twenty-eight Republicans and twenty-one Democrats voted for it, and twenty-three Democrats and twelve Republicans opposed. Had it passed, the president would probably have vetoed it. The Treaty of Versailles, said Lodge, was dead. The newspapers noted that Clemenceau, Orlando, and Wilson had now all been defeated on votes of confidence, and that Lloyd George was predicting his own downfall within six months. The Welshman said that no one who had tried to bring peace to the world at Versailles was going to remain untouched.

That evening the president was unable to sleep. Grayson stayed with him. "Doctor," Wilson said, "the Devil is a busy man." At three in the morning the president asked Grayson to read to him from Second Corinthians: We are troubled on every side, yet not distressed; we are perplexed, but not in despair; Persecuted, but not forsaken; cast down, but not destroyed.

Wilson let the Bible verses roll over him and was in some ways comforted. He told Grayson, "If I were not a Christian, I think I should go mad, but my faith in God holds me to the belief that He is in some way working out His own plans through human perversities and mistakes."

17

NORMALCY ASCENDANT

AFTER THE LONG, unhappy winter, the White House began to show signs of life again in the spring of 1920. With the treaty's defeat over, other work could proceed. There was less than a year left in Wilson's presidency; most expected he would not attempt to run again—in the House of Representatives a congressman who declared Wilson should renounce any possibility of a third term was roundly applauded by Democrats as well as Republicans—yet the president was still determined to do business. In April he met with his cabinet for the first time since his stroke.

The meeting took place in the study near his bedroom. Wilson was helped into his chair early, and as each secretary came in he was announced by Ike Hoover. This made Secretary Daniels wonder if Wilson were blind. In fact, the president's vision was severely limited, and the introductions helped him to orient himself. The cabinet as a whole was shocked by the change in the president's appearance; his left side still wouldn't do what he wanted it to, his voice was soft, his attention flagged easily. He seemed content to let others take the initiative in a discussion of railroad problems, and stayed mostly out of a heated argument between Palmer and Labor Secretary William Wilson over Palmer's harsh treatment of radicals and aliens. Several times during the hour-long meeting Grayson peeked in, and at last Edith came in and suggested the meeting be ended. It was, said the president, "an experiment," and he ought not to stay long. The following week he chaired another meeting. Afterward Bainbridge Colby wrote him, "You cannot fully realize the tonic effect upon us all of personal contact with you, and I thought your conduct of the two recent meetings, and particularly the last was luminous and invigorating." Wilson's older friends considered Colby a latecomer and a sycophant who told the president what he wanted to hear. The truth was less palatable: Wilson was still a very sick man, a shadow of the former self who had made cabinet meetings crackle with the excitement of his own presence.

Mostly the government limped along, cabinet members such as David Houston moving swiftly into the forefront by drafting messages and sometimes vetoes for the president's signature. It was not a time for new initiatives, because progress was effectively stalled by the Republican Congress until the November election.

In the afternoons the president and Edith would sit out on the portico watching the sheep, occasionally joined by two-year-old Gordon Grayson, who often arrived in a pony cart. The president and the toddler were buddies. Wilson liked to give the boy the cookies which accompanied his own milk. Starling arranged for circus parades to march near the White House so the duo could watch them. At times Wilson would tell the elder Grayson that he saw himself resigning if he proved unable to perform the duties of his office; at other times he contrarily hinted he would like a third term. He still harbored the feeling that the 1920 election must be turned into a referendum on the League of Nations. Under the doctor's guidance he tried walking with a blackthorn stick, but his left side wasn't coming around and he was unable to take more than a few steps before sinking into a wheelchair. Starling, who had returned to the White House after a long absence, grieved to see the president so helpless. When the Wilsons went out for a ride, Starling organized a group to stand at the gate and cheer as they came back. The first time this happened the president turned to Edith with tears in his eyes and said, "You see, they still love me!"

What affected the president most on these rides was the sight of a soldier or sailor. Invariably he would try to salute. He felt he owed these boys his allegiance forever. Starling found the chief increasingly irascible. Once he insisted on going in a horse-drawn carriage, the guards following by automobile. He also insisted that no vehicle should go faster than his own leisurely pace, so whenever a car passed his he would order the Secret Service to pursue it and bring back the driver for questioning. Starling always told him the car was going too fast to be overtaken. In his frequent letters to his mother, Starling noted that Mrs. Wilson was as sweet and gracious as ever during these trying times.

On May 14, Edith wrote to her "precious one" on a sample of a new White House writing paper that she loved and adored him. He penciled back, in his still-shaky hand, that the paper was "almost fine enough for the loveliest woman in the world, whom I love to distraction." Ten days later, she wrote another note to tell her own "precious boy,"

> what a day of gold this has been despite its gray sky, for I have felt your dear love, expressed in tender ways, ways that cost effort and sacrifice, which in spite of your suffering and heartache you did for me! Dear Little boy, I can not express the love and gratification this thrills me with, but I believe you know, and because you know, you will struggle on and on until this valley of sorrow is over and together we will stand on the height and look back upon it, both stronger for the lesson it has taught, and sure of our great love.

> Remember I want to share everything with you, and that it will make it easier to see beyond the cloud and doubt. Keep a stout heart under your jacket, little boy lover, and we will win!!

The language echoed notes of five years earlier, when they had been courting. Then Woodrow had assured Edith they would get over the difficult times; now it was her chance to tell him they would prevail.

The future centered on the 1920 election. Some months earlier, Democratic front-runner Palmer had predicted mass murder on May Day, and called for more action against subversives. When the Communist holiday came and went with no uproar, Palmer's star began to sink. A poll found the Democratic choice to be McAdoo, followed closely by the president. Meanwhile Bryan campaigned against Hitchcock in the Nebraska primary and said that the party's platform must contain *no* endorsement of the unrevised treaty. A quick message from Wilson pushed the state's convention to endorse the League anyway. Throughout May, Wilson tried to get other states to endorse the League with varying success. In national affairs Wilson's hold was difficult to assess. One day the Senate defeated a plan he backed for a mandate over Armenia; soon afterward it sustained his veto of a Knox proposal to unilaterally end the war with Germany. Nearing the end of the term, Wilson still appeared to hold the party's leadership.

The Republican convention in May picked Warren Harding and Calvin Coolidge for president and vice-president. The senator from Ohio uttered the phrase which made him famous: "America's present need is not heroics, but healing; not nostrums, but normalcy; not revolution, but restoration . . . not surgery, but serenity." Harding's remarks were widely taken as an indictment of Woodrow Wilson. Lest anybody mistake their intent, Harding's booster Henry Cabot Lodge put it even more plainly: "Woodrow Wilson and his dynasty, his heirs and assigns, or anybody that is his, anybody who with bent knee has served his purposes, must be driven from all control, from all influence upon the government of the United States."

At the end of May, Homer Cummings, Democratic national chairman, came to the White House and found the Wilsons on the south portico. The president was tired and looked old, but he was lucid. He encouraged the chairman to try and get Bryan to drop out of the race, and to do other things that would enhance his own influence over the party's platform. Reading over Cummings's proposed speech, he objected to lines saying he had been at the point of death last fall. Edith made a face behind Wilson's back at Cummings, as if to say Wilson never believed how ill he had been at the time. The president did not bow out of the race himself, nor did he name a successor. Basically he directed Cummings to keep any possible Wilson candidacy in abeyance, and gave him a secret code with which to communicate with him during the convention. It had been House's, but Wilson said the colonel wouldn't need it anymore.

Did Edith actively question his position on a third term? Had he his own doubts? One can only wonder what engendered the request from Woodrow that made her respond in this note of June 5, 1920:

> When you asked me if I had faith in you it was like asking if I believed the sun gave light. You are to me the tangible evidence of all that is strong, fine and true! I trust you unquestioningly and have faith in you beyond words to express.
>
> Sometimes you tell me I am strong, or, as you put it, "great"—don't you see little boy that it is the contact with you and your greatness that lifts me up and if there is merit in me, it is because I am your mirror in which your fineness is reflected. You are so splendid yourself that the very fact makes you blind to itself and I would not have it otherwise.
>
> Always remember dear one that you are not only strong yourself but that by your example you make us so—and that any one who is with you as I have been absorbs all wholesome things and became better from the inspiration.

In mid-June Tumulty proposed that Louis Seibold of the *New York World* be allowed to do an in-depth interview with the president. Edith accepted on the condition there be no questions about the election.

Tumulty, who had wanted the interview so that Wilson could disavow definitely plans for 1920, wrote angrily on Edith's note that she could go straight to hell for what she was doing—but Seibold came anyway. He spent four hours with the Wilsons and was amazed by the president's vitality, "mental vigor," and by his "saving sense of humor." The article Seibold wrote gave the impression of a man well able to bear the strains of his office not only then but—it hinted—in the future. Adding to the impression was the picture the White House now gave out of Wilson seated at his desk, with Edith standing and assisting him.

Immediately after the Seibold article appeared, McAdoo asked his supporters to switch to Carter Glass and said he was withdrawing. But the next day Glass told the president McAdoo's statement did not say he would not accept a draft. Wilson agreed with that estimate. He and Glass talked of other candidates. The president said Palmer's nomination would be futile. Weeks ago, when Palmer had proposed getting an injunction against harbor strikers in New York, Wilson had rebuked him, saying, "Every lawyer knows that is an abuse of the writ." The president also appeared to have given up on the candidacies of Newton Baker and David Houston, believing they would be good presidents but could never be nominated. As for Cox, Wilson said his nomination would be "a joke." He said nothing about his own nomination.

Grayson and Tumulty grabbed Glass on the way out—did the president mention a third term? Grayson knew Wilson wished somehow to be drafted—the president had even told Grayson he would run, get the treaty ratified, then resign—so Grayson begged Glass, "If anything comes up, save the life and fame of this man from the juggling of false friends."

Edith's attitude seems to have echoed the doctor's and that of Wilson's closest friends: she believed that her husband's reputation—and his health—would be best served if he were *not* renominated. She was convinced that his place in history was secure, but would suffer if he were somehow to be nominated and to go down to defeat or die during the campaign. Woodrow wished renomination to vindicate the past and to go out fighting; he believed that the last act had just begun. Edith knew the climax had already come, that tragic heroes do not go to the audience and ask retroactive blessing. He had been the grand playwright of an extraordinary life; now she knew it would be better for him to gracefully retire, and she worked on helping him to shape the right curtain line. And so she humored him, let him feel her faith in him intact, but guarded the door against opportunities for him to declare himself openly.

The convention opened with an enormous flag being slowly pulled up to reveal a huge portrait of the president. There was a great demonstra-

tion in honor of him. New York State's delegates sat on their hands
until Franklin Delano Roosevelt forced them to join in by his own
example. Behind the scenes at San Francisco, the Bryan and Wilson
factions were at war on almost every issue including the treaty, prohibition, and the world in general. In several speeches the old orator
received great applause, but adroit maneuvering by Wilson's people
beat him back on most issues. The platform committee recommended a
plank calling for ratification of the treaty without reservations but
leaving the door open to interpretations.

On July 1, Colby leaked to the *New York Times* a scenario that
would have Wilson nominated by acclamation following suspension of
the convention's rules. On July 2, Colby telegraphed the president that
neither Palmer, McAdoo, nor Cox had enough votes individually to win.
Wilson did not discourage Colby, but replied only that he would await
events.

And, indeed, the candidates were deadlocked. McAdoo was so personally confused by Wilson's nonsupport that he was in the odd position
of having his supporters disavow his own statements in order to place his
name in nomination. Palmer couldn't get the administration united
behind him. Cox, who had started slow, was gaining—he had solid Ohio
support and, perhaps more importantly, had little to hold politically
against him. Observers noted that the same thing had been said at the
Republican convention about Harding.

While waiting for a resolution of this impasse, Wilson composed a
"Solemn Referendum and Accounting of Your Government," which he
apparently planned to publish (or use as the basis for a statement) if he
became a candidate. It asked the electorate:

1.   Do you wish to make use of my services as President for
     another four years?

2.   Do you approve of the way in which the Administration
     conducted the war?

     CHIEFLY

3.   Do you wish the Treaty of Versailles ratified? Do you, in
     particular, approve of the League of Nations . . . and
     do you wish the United States to play a responsible part
     in it?

This was never sent out. In San Francisco, Cummings, Glass, Burleson, Daniels, and other leaders summoned Colby to their hotel room on
July 3. Glass said he'd rather vote for Wilson's corpse than for any man

alive, but that he would have no part in a scheme that would kill the president and be bad for the party. Colby said they were making him feel like a criminal. If Wilson should have been renominated, the men in the room said, they would have seen to it, and it would not have required the services of Bainbridge Colby. They told Colby to send Wilson a message and begin to let him down gently.

They also sent messages to the White House hinting that delegate support already pledged was too firm to dislodge. Next day the same group told Colby to step up the pressure, and he cabled the White House that sufficient votes could not be commanded to nominate Wilson, and that the placing of his name in nomination and a subsequent turndown by the convention would be interpreted as disapproval of the League of Nations. It would therefore be better if his name were not entered at all. This argument bore fruit with Wilson. With a heavy heart, he acquiesced. There would be no third term. Next day Tumulty pleaded with Edith that Wilson at least endorse one of the candidates, but got no answer.

After numerous ballots, the deadlock broke on July 6 and Governor Cox was nominated. He got the nod because he was an outsider, something of a dry, not a southerner, and because the delegates had repudiated McAdoo, who seemed too closely allied to Wilson. When news of Cox's nomination reached Wilson, his valet, Brooks, heard the president utter an uncharacteristic string of curses. But even if Cox's nomination was anathema to Wilson, they would have to meet. As Wesley Bagby points out in a study of the 1920 election, "Although he had been given the nomination by Wilson's enemies, Cox could not hope to win the presidency without the hearty support of Wilson's friends, and had to do his best to conciliate those who felt defeated." Primary among these was Wilson himself.

During the summer Cox and vice-presidential nominee Franklin Roosevelt came to the White House. They found Wilson in his wheelchair on the south portico, a shawl draped across his shoulders. Cox whispered to Roosevelt that Wilson seemed a very sick man. When Wilson said he was very glad they had come, FDR noticed tears in Cox's eyes. The nominee said he had always admired Wilson's fight for the League. "Mr. Cox," said Wilson, "that fight can still be won." Roosevelt was not so sure of this but, also affected by the sight of Wilson, he kept silent. The three men had lunch with Edith.

They talked of many things. Edith had taken Eleanor Roosevelt along with her on some charity expeditions in Paris; FDR had in the past sent autographs from his collection to the president. One subject broached was of a circular that had surfaced in the San Francisco area which "proved" that Harding had Negro blood. Tumulty had suggested that if the Democrats took advantage of it, this might lead to a victory by Cox. But Wilson would have none of it and ordered Burleson to seize and destroy such flyers if they came through post offices; a quarter-million were intercepted in the San Francisco area alone. Cox agreed with Wilson's actions on the flyer, and summed up the lunch by saying, "Mr. President, we are going to be a million percent with you and your administration, and that means the League of Nations." Afterward Cox gave a statement to the press: "What he promised I shall, if elected, endeavor with all my strength to keep." Cox told Tumulty no one could talk with the president about the League and not come away a believer.

Harding was not a believer. At the campaign's outset he seemed favorably disposed to a treaty—with reservations, of course—but by late summer he made an open denunciation of "Wilson's League," and only a vague promise of a new "association" for world cooperation. Late in the campaign many prominent Republicans still were saying Harding's election would ensure the country's going into the League. When he refuted this, the *New York Times* ran a cartoon showing bad boy Harding stomping on a hat labeled "The League" while indulgent father Taft was saying, "The little darling, he doesn't mean it."

The League faded somewhat as an issue over the summer. More important were the economic matters. In June there was a precipitate drop-off of production in business. Farm prices began to slip, new construction faltered, workers were laid off, and unions weakened as unemployment started to climb. Inflation kept prices high, and incomes were not climbing to match the prices. It was the onset of a depression. Because of the suddenness of the downturn, many Democrats believed that the depression was an organized Republican conspiracy designed to win the 1920 election.

Though Wilson took very little part in the campaign at first, he was vitally interested in it, noting carefully those primary victories in which pro-League men won. He also worked to promote the passage of women's suffrage, knowing it had been women who had helped reelect him in 1916 and believing more female votes would help Cox. Late in August, the last of the two-thirds of the states necessary ratified the amendment, and women's suffrage became law.

Edith took Harding's campaign theme of "normalcy" as a personal slur; she believed she had made things as normal as possible during the past year. Wilson was now walking a bit, dictating daily to Swem, insisting that correspondence come to him directly as it had prior to his illness. He stayed out of the campaign because he did not want to appear to be running it: he knew that Cox had to distance himself from the Wilson administration in order to have a fighting chance. Nevertheless, late in September, Cox's strategists were begging the White House for a weekly Wilson statement to boost their candidate's failing campaign.

On October 3, the statement Cox's advisers had wanted came out of the White House, and in it Wilson said that the coming election was to be, after all, a national referendum, a choice between isolation and leading the world. A few days later he came out fighting and refuted a charge that he had promised to send American boys overseas to defend European boundaries. Late in October a group of fifteen pro-League Republicans came to see him, and he read them an address warning that the supreme issue of the campaign was in danger of becoming obscured, and that "I suggest that the candidacy of every candidate for whatever office be tested by this question: Shall we or shall we not redeem the great moral obligations of the United States?"

As the election date neared, the recession dominated all other issues. By early November some steel plants in Pennsylvania and Ohio were operating at only 50 percent of capacity, and some woolen mills had gone to a four-day week. Wesley Bagby observes that "nationalists, dry's, anti-southerners, liberals, reactionaries, hyphenated Americans, Wilson-haters, and business interests . . . all added up to a vast determination to have a change."

On election day Wilson told his cabinet that Cox would be chosen since "a great moral issue is involved," but these were only brave words. By early evening the sweep of Harding's victory over Cox was evident, long before the president went to bed.

The returns showed Harding with sixteen million, Cox eight; Harding 404 electoral votes, Cox 127. Republicans increased their majorities in the House of Representatives to 172, and in the Senate to 22. The *New York World* said the election reflected the "stored up resentment for anything and everything" people had had to complain about for the past eight years. FDR wrote of a "kind of total flow of discontent and destructive criticism" as a result of the war. Later statistical studies show that interest in reform had all but vanished; the discussion of correcting social abuse had been replaced by pro-business articles in magazines; research in pure science had faded; patents were down; publication of books had dropped to its lowest point in fifteen years. As a contemporary observer saw it, the United States was "tired of issues, sick at heart of ideals, and weary of being noble."

For a short time the president was despondent. When Starling said a friend of his would follow Wilson wherever he wished to go, the president replied there was no place left to go. But within days Starling noticed that Wilson was more cheerful than at any time in recent months. He told the story of a man who had lost his donkey but nevertheless rejoiced: "I thank the Lord I was not on him because I would have been lost too."

Edith was glad to have the decision completed, for now they could turn their minds to the future. When Stock Axson came for a visit and watched Edith ministering to Wilson, he was glad it was Edith, rather than his sister Ellen, who was around now to care for Wilson, because Edith was by far the better warrior.

Wilson plunged back into work with a vigor uncharacteristic of a lame-duck office holder. He fixed European debts, agreed to a conference with Russia, arranged funds and food for war relief, and recognized a new government in Mexico. He also arranged a South American swing for Colby and proposed a sweeping budget reform measure. In his annual message to Congress, Wilson pleaded the causes of governmental economy, simplification of tax laws, care for veterans, and independence for the Philippines. To Newton D. Baker, the president "still showed that he saw more clearly and decided more impersonally than any of us or indeed all of us."

On November 15, the first assembly of the League of Nations opened formally in Geneva. In early December the Nobel Peace Prizes for 1919 and 1920 were awarded to Woodrow Wilson in recognition for his work as founder of the League. Jan Smuts wrote later that it had been humanity, not Woodrow Wilson, who had failed at Paris.

A film of the Versailles adventure was being shown when Ray Stannard Baker came to visit the president. Watching Wilson shuffle over a floor from which the carpet had been pulled back so he would not slip, Baker was at first shocked, then vastly cheered by the incredible determination of Wilson. Here, Baker thought, was a man whose will was unconquerable. After watching the film, Baker wrote of the strange experience of seeing the glory of 1918 in the fading, gray days of 1920:

> We were in another world, a resplendent world. . . . There was the President himself, smiling upon the bridge, very erect, very tall, lifting his hat to shouting crowds. . . . There he was again . . . driving down the most famous avenue in the world. . . . And there was the President, riding behind

magnificent horses with outriders flying pennants, and
people shouting in the streets. . . .

Baker was very moved by the contrast between the past and the present,
but the president seemed not so romantic as the writer. He was more
aimed at the future.

Woodrow and Edith had from time to time spent hours rating cities in
which to spend their retirement, on the bases of "Climate, Friends,
Opportunities, Freedom, Amusements, and Libraries." New York got
the best overall score, but in the end they chose Washington, for that
was Edith's home and Woodrow would have the Library of Congress for
his research. For weeks Edith, her brother Wilmer, and Starling
searched the Washington area for a suitable house. After many disap-
pointments Edith saw one in the 2300 block of S Street that was neither
too large nor too small, had space for the president's thousands of books,
and had room to put in an elevator.

She told Woodrow about it before going to a concert one afternoon.
On her return, she found Woodrow in the Oval Room with the deed to
the house in his hand. Ten friends, including Baruch, Dodge, Cyrus
McCormick, and others, had helped him purchase it. On December 14,
they went to look at it together. Wilson had Brooks dig up a piece of sod
and, placing the key upon it, presented both to Edith in an old Scottish
ceremony. Four days later the couple celebrated their fifth wedding
anniversary.

Edith invited Mrs. Harding to tea. It was a strained meeting; Edith
thought the woman talked too much, wore too much makeup, and was a
bit rude to Mrs. Jaffray, who was detailed to take her about the
mansion. She was still jawing with the cook in the evening when Edith
returned after some errands. Christmas and New Year's were quiet.
The Wilsons distributed candy and gifts to the children along their auto
routes. The president's sixty-fourth birthday occasioned little celebration.

In early 1921 Edith found Woodrow busy at his typewriter. When he
pulled the paper from the machine and handed it to her she saw that he
had dedicated to her the book on the philosophy of politics he had long
held in mind.

> I dedicate this book [to E.B.W.] because it is a book in which
> I have tried to interpret life, the life of a nation, and she has
> shown me the full meaning of life. Her heart is not only true
> but wise; her thoughts are not only free but touched with

> vision; she teaches and guides by being what she is; her unconscious interpretation of faith and duty makes all the way clear; her power to comprehend makes work and thought alike easier and more near to what it seeks.

It was understood that he would work on the book when they moved into the new house.

At the end of January, Palmer recommended that the President commute Eugene Debs's sentence to expire on Lincoln's birthday, February 12, as Debs believed himself closely allied to Lincoln in spirit. The Supreme Court had unanimously upheld Debs's conviction, but public sentiment was for a pardon (which Debs professed not to want as it would seem admission of his guilt) or for commutation. Wilson, in response, told Tumulty that he would not pardon Debs while he was president, for Debs had stood "behind the lines, sniping, attacking, and denouncing" the boys who had gone to "vindicate the cause of civilization" on the bloody fields of Europe. The denial of the request for commutation was all over the newspapers on February 1.

That evening, the Wilsons went to the theater together. With assistance the president managed to walk across the stage behind the curtain, then was lifted up to the box seat he had not inhabited for eighteen months, to see John Drinkwater's *Abraham Lincoln*. The audience did not know he was there until after the first act. He had been denounced in the papers for his decision on Debs, but when he was recognized there were no boos, just a tremendous applause. Edith was heartened by this: he took strong stands and, yes, they loved him still.

Three days later, the Wilsons took possession of the house on S Street. Ten days after that, the president managed the six-hundred-yard walk to the executive wing of the White House for a cabinet meeting, letting photographers get a few shots on the way.

At private lunches with the cabinet members, Wilson went over old times and discussed what each might do in the future. With Secretary of State Colby he speculated about opening a law partnership together in Washington. "I can't face a life of idleness," he told Colby, who leaped at the chance and soon afterward set up the partnership with the help of Edith and Grayson.

At the last full cabinet meeting on March 1, Wilson was asked how he was going to spend his time. Would he, for instance, write a history of the administration? (Lane, Lansing, Houston, Daniels, Tumulty, and others were already sharpening their pens.) No, the president replied. He was too near to the events to have any perspective. But, he added, "I

am going to try to teach ex-Presidents how to behave. There will be one
very difficult thing for me to stand, however, and that is Mr. Harding's
English."

Colby said how much they had all been inspired by the president's
example, and then tears rolled down Wilson's cheeks and his lips
quivered. "Gentlemen," he whispered, "it is one of the handicaps of my
physical condition that I cannot control myself as I have been accustomed to do. God bless you all." The men got up and shook his hand as
they went out; they considered calling another meeting to send him a
tribute but, mindful of the example of Lansing, they did not. Instead
they composed a joint letter to him:

> The final moments of the Cabinet on Tuesday found us quite
> unable to express the poignant feelings with which we real-
> ized that the hour of leave-taking and official dispersal had
> arrived.
>
> Will you permit us to say to you now, and as simply as we
> can, how great a place you occupy in our honor, love, and
> esteem?
>
> We have seen you in times of momentous crisis. We have
> seen your uncomplaining toil under the heavy and unremit-
> ting burden of the Presidency. We have had the inestimable
> privilege of sharing some of your labors. At all times you
> have been to us our ideal of a courageous, high-minded,
> modest gentleman, a patriotic public servant, an intense and
> passionate lover of your country. You have displayed toward
> us a trust and confidence that has touched us all, supporting
> and defending us, when under partisan attack, with staunch
> and untiring loyalty, and placing at our command, always in
> the most considerate way, the wisdom of your counsel. His-
> tory will acclaim your great qualities. We who have known
> you so intimately bear witness to them now.
>
> We fervently wish you, dear Mr. President, long life and
> happiness that you so richly deserve and have so abundantly
> earned.

On the day of Harding's inaugural Wilson put on a cutaway, gloves,
and a high hat. It had been suggested he forego the ceremonies,
pleading his illness, but he would have none of that. He had even tried to
argue with Grayson that he should walk, but finally agreed to ride.

Tumulty came in to plead that his last act in office be to pardon an old man in a federal prison. Wilson turned him down, saying "the country needs the spectacle of a stable, just, and righteous government more than that old man needs a pardon or I need an act of mercy."

Edith came in wearing orchids and said that Harding waited in the Blue Room. Yesterday the Hardings had come and the president-elect had sat in a chair and casually thrown his foot over the armrest, while "Duchess," his wife, chattered and called him "Wurr'n." It had been suggested to Wilson that he act in such a way as to put Harding "in a hole," but this he refused to do, despite Harding's gaucheries, because he said the country's situation was too serious to play petty games and the presidency was more important than either of them personally.

Harding offered to help Wilson into the car, but Woodrow thought that would be improper, and had more familiar hands do it. As the women got into a second car, Harding's wife chattered continually and waved gaily to reporters, whom she called "my boys."

It was a blustery day with a promise of spring not far beyond. Harding talked on the ride of pets, said he'd always wanted to own an elephant, then told a story of a dying elephant who put his trunk around his keeper. When Harding looked over at Wilson he saw the president was weeping. Did Wilson find the story a vicious parallel of Harding's offer to help him to the car? Or was it just the emotion of the day, his feeling of the asininity of his successor? At length the president wiped away his tears and the public mask descended once more. Tradition was important; ceremony, not personality. In the car with them was Uncle Joe Cannon, a congressman who had helped nominate Lincoln.

Harding bounded up the steps of the Capitol with the vigor of a man in full possession of his physical powers, while Wilson took the elevator. The obvious contrast made Edith furious. In the president's room Edith watched as Woodrow signed some bills passed during the last hours of Congress, shook hands with the cabinet. He excused himself to General Pershing for not rising, and begged off going to see the Coolidge swearing-in. Then Henry Cabot Lodge came in as head of a joint congressional committee, and told Wilson that Congress's work was done and that the houses were prepared to receive any further communication from the president. For a moment Joe Tumulty thought Wilson would say something violent, but Wilson's face kept its mask and he said, with dignity, "I have no further communication. I would be glad if you would inform both houses and thank them for their courtesy—good morning, sir." Lodge looked at his watch, said "It's time we're moving," and then went out.

Harding came in to tell Wilson it would be fully understandable if he did not attend the swearing-in or the inaugural speech; Wilson was grateful for his concern and wished Harding "all the luck in the world." In a few minutes the next president would tell the crowd,

> We must strive for normalcy to reach stability. . . . I pledge an Administration wherein all the agencies of Government are called on to serve, and ever promote an understanding of Government purely as an expression of the popular will. . . . There are a hundred millions, with common concern and shared responsibility, answerable to God and country. The Republic summons them to their duty, and I invite cooperation.

Harding's last words were this echo—perhaps conscious, perhaps not— of the clarion call Wilson had uttered eight years earlier. No one mentioned it this day. however, Harding went out of the room along with the host of functionaries, leaving Wilson and his small party of family and friends alone.

The clock tolled twelve times. Wilson ceased officially to be president. He reached up for the scarf pin with the president's seal upon it. He and Edith had had the pin fashioned from the gold nugget which had also yielded their wedding rings. He took it off and put it in his pocket. He would never wear it again.

18

CONFIDENT OF HEAVEN'S APPLAUSE

THE WILSONS BROUGHT the mementos of a crowded life to the house on S Street. There was a replica of the Lincoln bed; the Pierce Arrow which the Wilsons bought from the government and repainted orange and black, the Princeton colors; a large oak table from the Wilson home in Princeton; Ellen's madonna; snapshots of the grandchildren and of the Wilsons with the crowned heads of Europe; the lamp Woodrow used while a student; a desk with a secret drawer; the khaki Bible; the brass shell casing of the first shot fired by American artillery in Europe in 1917; a portrait of Edith as First Lady.

They took most of their meals together and alone, played twin games of solitaire, answered the voluminous mail, took slow auto rides. Woodrow refused to be called Mr. President, though occasionally a visitor would slip. Grayson allowed only one caller a day. The doctor himself was graciously given permanent Washington duty by President Harding so he could attend his most famous patient, and he kept Wilson at the exercises prescribed by the renowned Dr. Mayo.

Wags called the place "the Bolling alley" because so many of Edith's relatives were about, principally John Randolph Bolling, a curious man who functioned as the Wilsons' secretary, writing letters declining honorary memberships and requests for assistance and photographs—except for those asked for by wounded servicemen, who got notes signed "Your War Comrade." The Sayres were in Massachusetts, the McAdoos in California, Margaret slid from job to job in New York as her music career faded.

There was plenty of legal work for the partnership of Wilson and Colby to discuss, offers from oilmen Sinclair and Doheny, from the government of Ecuador seeking a loan, from the Western Ukrainian Republic seeking a favored position with the League of Nations. All were turned down: Wilson would not peddle his influence with the United States government. At the end of a year Colby, who had taken all the expenses on himself, and whose main wish was to occupy his former chief agreeably, was in the red many thousands of dollars, and Wilson had made only enough to buy Edith a car she had wanted. But, as Colby wrote, "It's a fine game and worth the candle as long as we can hold out."

Wilson the writer was offered the chance to do book reviews, biographies of Burke and of Jesus, a weekly column, a record of his work in Paris. He wanted only to start his *Philosophy of Politics*, and so turned these down, but the great book would not take shape. He had not the persistence of mind for it; the dedication to Edith remained the only page of it ever written. As for his memoirs, he joked, "There ain't gonna be none." As he explained to Norman Davis,

> What I have done and stood for is of record, and any consequent interpretation or explanation that I might make would not affect the event, nor would it be a contribution to history. So far as I am concerned, I have done the best I know how. My conscience is clear and clean. I am confident that what I have fought for and stood for is for the benefit of this nation and of mankind. If this is so, I believe that it ultimately will prevail, and if it is not, I don't want it to prevail.

So there was silence. Which also pleased Edith, who had always been a very private person. She was less gay than in former years, people noted, but that was to be expected. As guardian of the private trust when the public trust was gone, she came in these years to be much in her prime, going to debates on Capitol Hill with her friends, playing games of cards, above all organizing her husband's life and attempting to ensure his place in history.

When Woodrow saw that Edith was spending too much time taking care of him, despite his joy in her presence he secretly arranged for a friend to invite Edith out to play bridge once a week. She needed to have a bit of fun away from him. She was only forty-nine, still a woman full of physical and mental energy, and he was an old man who at times felt he was dragging her down with his infirmities.

In the summer of 1921 the Wilsons invited Ray Stannard Baker to S

Street and gave him access to files Wilson had kept of his work in Paris. Woodrow deciphered his own shorthand notes on secret memoranda and answered most questions about his work at the peace conference. Robert Lansing's personal narrative of that time was in the works, and others were publishing similarly angry books about the conference, so Wilson felt Baker should be allowed access to his version of what had happened.

By summer the tenor of the Harding administration was known: lavish parties given by the "Duchess," open bottles of liquor all over the family's upstairs rooms. Harding was rumored to have made love with his mistress in a White House closet; there was a scandal in the Veterans Administration and rumors of one involving Interior Secretary Fall.

At Campobello that summer Franklin D. Roosevelt was afflicted with polio. Earlier FDR had become national chairman of a group which wanted a Wilson memorial. The ex-president didn't like the idea, since it presumed he was already dead, and suggested the word "foundation." When FDR fell ill, Wilson responded immediately and generously. There would now be, he wrote to Franklin, a race to see which of them would recover enough to play golf first. Wilson wore a cape rather than a coat since it was easier for an invalid to put on; soon FDR would wear the same kind of garb.

A special plea to Harding allowed Wilson to take part in ceremonies on Armistice Day 1921, honoring the Unknown Soldier. The funeral procession was an impressive parade of men and horse-drawn carriages. Dignitaries from all over Europe came to decorate the unknown warrior with their countries' highest honors. The crowd was hushed and silent, but when the Wilsons were spotted in their carriage, cheers started to grow for the war leader as surely fallen in the Great Crusade as the doughboy who had served under him and whose body had just rolled by on its caisson. The applause grew and grew, and Wilson grimly reached up to lift his high silk hat once to acknowledge the crowd's cheers. As the Wilsons left the procession to return to S Street they were followed by thousands who came to their door and cheered "the greatest soldier of them all." Wilson hobbled to shake hands with three disabled young veterans. When an admirer told him "your work will not die," he was overcome. Cheeks wet with tears, he whispered, "I wish I had the voice to reply." Flowers strewn before his path, he grasped Edith's hand— she, too, was crying—and they went inside. Behind them the crowd sang a patriotic hymn.

People gathered near his house on days of importance from then on—on his birthday, Flag Day, July Fourth, Armistice Day. On his rides, Wilson would salute all soldiers in uniform, and take his hat off whenever he spotted an American flag waving. In Washington there were many flags. He began to go out more, especially to the theater on Saturday nights, to Keith's. Seats near theirs were sold at a premium, and Wilson was often applauded. The management had to get a policeman to keep order, and the performers would give him bouquets of flowers to take home.

Those who could keep dignified silence with him were rewarded with continued friendship and mutual support. Those who could not, or who made a mistake—even an unintentional one—were cut off. Prominent among the casualties was Tumulty, who gave a message at a Democratic rally that he believed Wilson had endorsed only to have the ex-president disavow his actions in a letter to the *New York Times*. Woodrow was upset by the misunderstanding, and Edith never allowed Tumulty near the house again.

His former opponent Charles Evans Hughes was secretary of state, his avowed enemy George Harvey was ambassador to London, his nemesis Henry Cabot Lodge virtually ran the new administration's foreign policy. Yet when important visitors from abroad came to the United States, they came to see Wilson. Clemenceau and Lloyd George both made the journey to S Street. As with Wilson, they too had been cast down in the post-war reaction.

In early 1922, spurred by his old beliefs and by the deteriorating spirit he saw in the United States, Wilson began to compose a political platform which might serve as the basis for a future candidacy, either for himself or for some as-yet unknown Democrat. Drafts were sent to Colby, Newton Baker, Houston, Baruch, Justice Brandeis, all of whom were invited to S Street to discuss it. Wilson was not clear as to what would be done with this document, and eventually it was laid aside, a statement of philosophy that seemed to have too much of the quixotic about it to have relevance in a changed world.

In the fall Colby sadly suggested closing their joint law office, which was done with much grace on both sides, and a note to the public that Wilson had become too busy with other matters to support a legal practice. On December 28, 1922, Wilson's birthday, the officers of the new foundation came to tell him that they had raised nearly a million dollars for Woodrow Wilson Foundation Awards to those who had done "meritorious service on behalf of democracy, public welfare, liberal thought and peace through justice." A note accompanying one small check read: "From the family of Frank M. Thompson, who died in the World War for world peace, in gratitude to Woodrow Wilson for the faith he has kept for the dead." People understood! Tears came to Wilson's eyes; after the committee left he was upset that he had been too emotional to speak.

When Margaret visited, he tried to reassess the past. Perhaps, he said, it was for the best that the United States hadn't joined the League at the time he had come back from Europe. Startled, she asked why. Because, he answered, if it had happened then it would have been only a personal victory, but "Now, when the American people join the League it will be because they are convinced it is the only right time for them to do it." God's plan had better timing than his own, he said. If it had not been meant to be in 1919 and 1920, then that was God's will, and he must accept it as such.

He would have to live, as Wordsworth said of the happy warrior, "confident of heaven's applause." He knew now that his health was not going to return, said to visitors, "I am tired swimming upstream," or "the sands are running fast."

Albert Bacon Fall had just resigned as secretary of the treasury, facing grave charges of corruption; there were signs of dissipation throughout Harding's administration. Wilson wanted to say something far-reaching. Plagued by neuritis, unable to type with both hands, he dictated a short article to Edith, a sentence at a time, over a period of weeks. Sometimes a thought would come to him in the middle of the night, and he would have her awakened to take it down. She wanted it no other way. When it was done she sent "The Road Away From Revolution" to George Creel. Sadly Creel wrote back to Edith that it was not up to earlier Wilson standards, and that in other circumstances he would advise against publication completely. Knowing that would hurt the chief, Creel alternately proposed having it printed with as little fanfare as possible. He wrote a sham letter for Edith to deliver to her husband which suggested he not subject the piece to "cheap huckstering" that would come if they tried to auction it to the highest bidder.

It was not Edith's way to lie to Woodrow, so while riding one day with him and Stock Axson, she told him Creel said the article lacked body, that Woodrow should expand and revise it. When he was angry, she told him not to "get on your high horse." At home alone, Stock found Edith sobbing in the hallway. She was the strongest woman he knew, and it shocked him. "I just want to help and I don't know how," she cried. Axson went upstairs and edited the article in a way that Wilson found palatable. Then they sent it out themselves, without Creel's help. "The Road Away From Revolution" was printed in the August issue of the *Atlantic Monthly*, and argued,

* * *

our civilization cannot survive materially unless it be re-
deemed spiritually. It can be saved only by becoming perme-
ated with the spirit of Christ and being made free and happy
by the practices which spring out of that spirit. Only thus can
discontent be driven out and all the shadows lifted from the
road ahead.

Specifically this meant the social and economic order must be based on
"sympathy and helpfulness and a willingness to forego self-interest in
order to promote the welfare, happiness, and contentment of others and
of the community as a whole."

Just as this sermon was being read in the magazine, President
Harding died. Both Wilsons were astounded. They wrote a joint condolence note to his widow and attended the funeral. Afterwards, Edith was
persuaded to leave Woodrow for more than a day for the first time in
years. She took a short vacation with friends on Cape Cod. When she
returned she saw what she had not previously been able to admit: that
Woodrow was surely dying.

Baruch's daughter arranged for Wilson to give a short radio broadcast on the eve of Armistice Day 1923. Wilson insisted on standing to
read his few paragraphs, saying he spoke better when on his feet. After
it was over he was sure the thing had gone badly, but next morning the
papers said he had addressed the largest audience in history.

As they had been doing for several years, crowds gathered next
morning in S Street to pay tribute to Wilson. "Pilgrims," the papers
called them. There was a band paid for by Tumulty, who was not
allowed inside anymore. Woodrow went out to thank them, said that
they should give this adulation not to him, but to those who had earned
it, "the most ideal army that was ever thrown together." The crowd
cheered him anyway, and the band started playing a hymn. He was
about to go inside when he stopped and asked that the band be quieted
because he had something to say. Then he told the assembled crowd,
with all the old passion:

I am not one of those who have the least anxiety about the
triumph of the principles I have stood for. I have seen fools
resist Providence before, and I have seen their destruction, as
will come upon these again, utter destruction and contempt.
That we shall prevail is as sure as that God reigns. Thank
you.

* * *

They were his last public words.

On Christmas Eve the headliners at Keith's, Olsen and Johnson, arranged a large tribute for him at the theater. On his sixty-seventh birthday his old Princeton friends presented him with a magnificent Rolls-Royce.

The McAdoos came for the holidays and Woodrow begged Edith not to leave him alone in a room with Mac, for he was sure the son-in-law would ask for an endorsement for the 1924 election. During the same visit he told Nell he owed everything he had to her mother Ellen. One day he awoke from a nap, dreaming of old days when they had all been together. The McAdoos could not stay, went back to California. On January 20 Wilson repeated to Raymond Fosdick the words of a former president, "John Quincy Adams is all right, but the house he lives in is dilapidated and it looks as if he would soon have to move out." He went on to discuss the days at Princeton and the progress of the League; "The world is run by its ideals," he told Fosdick.

Then Edith had a fever and they kept apart from each other for five days, but Woodrow managed to hobble to her door to try and comfort her. Grayson went to Baruch's estate in the Carolinas to hunt; after four days Edith had to call him to come back, for it seemed obvious to her that Woodrow was dying. Grayson took the next train. When word leaked out that Wilson was failing the crowds began to gather in S Street, carrying candles, staying at their vigil through the night, praying the inevitable would not happen. Wilson was the man of peace to them, and peace must never be allowed to die. "The machinery is broken," Wilson told Grayson, "I am ready."

He hung on for three days, while the McAdoos raced from California, while hundreds of people important and unknown left their calling cards at S Street as if they were totems that would prevent his life from ebbing away. Grayson came out and told reporters that the former president's bravery was a model of a "game effort," that the equanimity with which Wilson was facing death almost "breaks one down." Wilson had taught men many things; now he would teach them how to die.

Joe Tumulty came and wanted to go in for a last look. A month ago Wilson had written him a letter endorsing Joe for a Senate seat from New Jersey, but now Grayson could not get him in to see his old chief. Edith guarded the door. She stayed by Woodrow's bedside along with the nurses, Grayson, her brothers, and Margaret, who had come from New York. Jessie and Frank were in Siam, unreachable.

"Edith!"—it was his whisper when she went out of the room for a moment, his last word. In the street people knelt as church bells sounded all over town. At 11:15 on a beautiful Sunday morning, with Margaret holding one hand and Edith the other, Woodrow Wilson reached, in Edith's words, "the peace which passeth all understanding."

Though she had been prepared for it, Edith was devastated by Woodrow's death. Standing with Altrude in the downstairs room where his body lay in state, she whispered, "Oh, the majesty of death!" Cary Grayson quietly had Wilson's blood analyzed to put to rest the lie that the former president had had syphilis and died of its ravages. He felt he owed his friend that.

When the McAdoos arrived, it was to headlines not only of Wilson's death, but also of the revelation of McAdoo's relationship to Edward Doheny. The oilman, in a desperate attempt to distance himself from the spreading Teapot Dome scandal, told how he had for a time engaged McAdoo as a lawyer. The pairing of the two events was threatening to doom Mac's chances for the 1924 nomination. Mac sent out telegrams saying "skunks" and "calumniators" were trying to smear him. Nell was frantic. Edith lashed out in rage at them both, feeling such talk of the future over the dead body of the world's greatest man was sacrilege. Edith could not stop weeping, said things that forever estranged her from Nell. And when Margaret went about babbling Christian Science platitudes that death was an illusion, Edith would have none of her, either. Grayson told Edith she was in shock.

When Henry Cabot Lodge was appointed to a Senate committee designated to attend the services, Edith penned him a vicious note that he was not welcome. He replied he would not come and embarrass her. Within a year he would be dead, too. Colonel House, uninvited to the funeral, heard the memorial service for Wilson as broadcast over a loudspeaker, while he was standing in the rain in New York.

The light of Edith's life, the reason for her being had gone. Distracted, not caring about her appearance, Edith would visit the grounds of the National Cathedral where Woodrow's body lay interred in the crypt. Cleaning up his room and putting away his clothes a few weeks later, she was pained: each garment evoked a memory, was a requirement for more courage. In the pocket of one of his suits she found, carefully wrapped in tissue paper, the dime a small boy had insisted Woodrow take as their train had pulled away from Billings, Montana.

She worked slowly to make a life for herself, now that the mainspring was gone. No longer did she have to keep the same hours, or worry about going out and leaving him alone. It took a while to get used to that sad freedom. She would have preferred to be still bound. The Democratic convention of 1924 approached, and she wanted to go in Woodrow's memory; it was several months after he had died, but Grayson told her no, she was yet in shock. At the convention McAdoo lost to a man whom Bryan contemptuously called "J. P. Morgan's lawyer," John W. Davis. Edith was glad because Davis was a sincere proponent of the League of Nations. Coolidge was elected, however, hands down.

By late 1924, she was better, coming out of the acute phase of her grief. With intimates she was heard to laugh, the good humor deep in her soul bubbling up to assure that life would, indeed, go on. Death could take Woodrow away, but love lived on and surpassed death. She would have and know and be that love always, no one could take it away from her. *Love lives*: it was the secret that kept her heart going, that comforted her as she went to sleep alone in a house nearly too redolent with memories to bear.

She began actively to help Ray Stannard Baker work on his massive opus of Woodrow's life, reaching out to Wilson's former associates and friends for letters and thoughts which must go into the books. She rigorously refused to let anyone else publish so much as a single letter from Woodrow, claiming they were her property as his heir. Baker would publish them, and his would be the only authorized biography. However, she withheld from publication all Woodrow's love letters; they were too close to the core, too admissive of the secret which quickened her life. She would not let the public have them until she herself was dust. What was important were the ideals, the accomplishments of Woodrow Wilson. Baker told her he was grateful for even being able to see the love letters, because, he wrote to her, they made him understand so much more about his subject, but he made no plaint to her about publishing them for he knew she would never agree.

She began to go again to Europe in the summers, with Baruch's daughters or her own female relatives, very much as she and Altrude had gone in the years before the World War. The hotels, the trains, the flutter of travel were much the same, but now she was treated as the widow of the world's hope. Stopping at the League of Nations headquarters in Geneva, she was applauded, but the cheers did not swell her head because they were not for her, nor even precisely for her dead husband—they were for the ideals he championed.

At times her preference for the legend distorted her perception of events. Largely uncritical of Baker's treatment of Wilson's early years, she objected to his chronicling of the difficult period just after Ellen's death. She didn't like it, she wrote, it was not up to his usual standards, didn't capture the Woodrow she knew. Baker pointed out that the evidence of letters to friends, particularly of those to Mrs. Hulbert (purchased for the biography by Bernard Baruch from the near-destitute woman) documented his view; nevertheless Edith forced him to cut back on the depth of sorrow he found in late 1914 and early 1915.

She carefully monitored other books on Wilson as they came out, taking notes on where they were inaccurate and—more important to her—insensitive. She particularly disliked those which became mawkish about the president's illness, for neither she nor Woodrow had ever asked to be pitied. Charles Seymour's arrangement and annotation of Colonel House's *Intimate Papers* angered her so much with its glorification of House's role that she began immediately to set down her own thoughts for a memoir. That was in 1929, a year in which she went around the world.

The Crash and subsequent Depression gave her a difficult time, for Galt's, the jewelry store which still provided some income for her, had lean years at that time. But she worked on her memoir steadily, from 1929 onward. With Herbert Hoover's ascension to power she was invited again to the White House, and became a regular there when Franklin Roosevelt assumed office. Both men were great admirers of Woodrow's. She went to political conventions and became a familiar figure in the Senate's gallery, in company of Mrs. Brandeis and Mrs. Borah. Woodrow had often disagreed with Borah but had never impugned the integrity of the senator's motives, so it was alright for the women to be friends. Edith had a bitter laugh when the Senate put reservations on the United States' willingness to enter the World Court—and then the World Court rejected those reservations. Wilson memorials sprang up even as the clouds of fascism and imperialism darkened the world's horizons and emasculated the League of Nations. Edith traveled to Poland to accept homage for Woodrow and see a statue of him, which she hated; she worked tirelessly on the Wilson birthplace at Staunton, Virginia; she attended meetings of the Woodrow Wilson Foundation in New York.

Jessie died after an operation in 1933. McAdoo divorced Nell and remarried a younger woman. Margaret took off for India to study under a holy man. Edith's sister Bertha died in 1935, and Cary Grayson died in 1938. It was a decade of loss.

My Memoir came out in 1939, serialized first in the *Saturday Evening Post,* and was avidly read. With war on the horizon, echoes of Wilson were everywhere. Baker shipped Woodrow's papers to the Library of Congress, but Edith restricted their use. Scholars had to get past her scrutiny before they could see them. On December 8, 1941, Franklin Roosevelt, with his genius for gesture, invited Edith to sit next to Eleanor as Congress was asked for a declaration of war. Within weeks Edith was busy sewing again for the Red Cross, a sixty-nine-year-old tornado. McAdoo, seventy-seven, died that year; Margaret passed away in India in 1944. Edith worked on, as active as ever until, in 1944, she had what she called a "nasty spell" with her blood pressure while vacationing at Baruch's. Nineteen forty-four saw also the premier of the Hollywood version of Woodrow's life, thoroughly sanitized to Edith's liking, but which she nevertheless thought did little justice to Wilson.

During the 1944 campaign, a worker asked a member of President Roosevelt's family why FDR was running again—surely the war was going to be won, and he was a sick man who could retire on his laurels. "He is haunted by the specter of Wilson," was the answer. There was a peace yet to be won, a peace as important as the war. Roosevelt did not live to see it. When peace came, and the birth of the United Nations, only Jan Masaryk mentioned aloud the name of Woodrow Wilson, though Wilson's spirit was as evident in San Francisco as it had been at Versailles.

Edith grew more gracious and charming, lost her stoutness even as her tastes became more luxurious. She was a *grande dame*; young men never minded sitting next to her at parties because she had such fascinating stories to tell. Unlike Eleanor Roosevelt, unlike Alice Longworth, she was unique in her devotion to her husband. The name of Woodrow Wilson was for a time hated, then admired—the cycle of repudiation and then resuscitation seemed complete. When someone would inquire, "Really now, didn't you run the White House in 1919?" she would be incredulous: there could have been no thought of doing so, for she was married to the greatest man in the world. When a new generation of scholars rediscovered Wilson, Edith watched and aided their work. Woodrow's hundredth-birthday year of 1956 seemed to find his reputation at a high point; she was the centerpiece attraction of many of the ceremonies.

History, Edith could attest, was as Joseph's storied coat, of many colors but of only one weave. The luminous thread that was Woodrow Wilson connected many disparate men and influences in the American twentieth century: Herbert Hoover, Franklin Roosevelt, the Second World War, the United Nations—even the new president, John F. Kennedy, had written a laudatory account of Woodrow in his book *Profiles in Courage* and invited Edith to ride in his inaugural parade in early 1961. That day, a small old lady, Edith went unrecognized.

A few months later, she sat beside President Kennedy in the White House as he signed a commission to design a suitable memorial to

Woodrow Wilson and handed her the pen with which he made the signature. "I didn't dare ask you for it," Edith said, and everyone laughed because it was so out of character for her to be meek.

Her life was ebbing. Wilmer and Randolph were gone, and during 1961 Altrude died. By Christmas Edith was failing, but there was to be a dedication of the Woodrow Wilson Bridge over the Potomac River on the one-hundred-fifth anniversary of Woodrow's birth, and she made plans to be there, despite icy weather, despite her age, despite everything. She would go, because it was for Woodrow: *love lives*.

During the early morning hours of December 28, 1961, Woodrow's birthday, Edith slipped quietly into her final sleep.

ACKNOWLEDGMENTS

A writer on the Wilsons has many debts to pay. I have noted some in the Sources, below. In addition I must especially thank Drs. Arthur S. Link and David W. Hirst of the staff of The Papers of Woodrow Wilson for sharing their lifelong study and enthusiasm for Wilson with me. My associate Carl Kaplan's insights proved always good and helpful. Interviews with Katherine E. Brand, Arthur Walworth, and Dr. Edwin A. Weinstein were valuable in assisting me to understand aspects of the complicated relationship of the Wilsons. Permission for access to, and quotations from, the Edward M. House papers was given by the Yale University Library. The staffs of the Manuscript Division of the Library of Congress, The Princeton University Library, and the Woodrow Wilson House in Washington, as well as the National Archives, aided me in obtaining important materials. I used the research facilities of the Wertheim Study of the New York Public Library, and acknowledge my gratitude to the Library for their shelter. I owe debts beyond the power of words to repay to Phyllis Grann, to Mel Berger, and to all the members of my family, all of whom sought to encourage and sustain me in a time of difficulty. All errors in the book are, of course, mine alone.

Tom Shachtman
New York City
February, 1981

SOURCES

The papers of Woodrow Wilson are the primary source for any study of Wilson. The main bulk is at the Library of Congress, and a related cache is at Princeton University. Edith Bolling Wilson's papers, some recently opened, are at the Library of Congress along with those of Ray Stannard Baker, William McAdoo, Josephus Daniels, Gilbert Hitchcock, and others of importance to the Wilson era. The Wilson Foundation and Princeton University Press are issuing *The Papers of Woodrow Wilson* in annotated volumes at the rate of several a year, and have reached through 1915, as edited by Drs. Arthur S. Link and David W. Hirst; these volumes are invaluable because they put the Wilson materials in insightful perspective.

Ray Stannard Baker's eight-volume *Woodrow Wilson, Life and Letters* and his three-volume *Woodrow Wilson and World Settlement* (all Doubleday, 1923 through 1939) still have great relevance, though they have been superseded by Dr. Link's wider scholarship and new interpretations in his books *Wilson: The Road to the White House; Wilson: The New Freedom; Wilson: The Struggle for Neutrality; Wilson: Crises and Confusions;* and *Wilson: Campaigns for Progressivism and Peace* (all Princeton Press, 1947–1965). Dr. Link's essays on *Woodrow Wilson: Revolution, War, and Peace* (AHM, 1979) bring this material more up to date. I have taken Wilson's speeches from the published versions in *The Public Papers*, edited by Baker and Dodd (Doubleday, 1920s). Arthur Walworth's two volumes *Woodrow Wilson: American*

Prophet and *World Prophet* (Longmans, Green, 1958) are especially good for personal details.

Edith Bolling Wilson's biographers include Alden Hatch, *First Lady Extraordinary* (Dodd, Mead, 1961), which was done with her cooperation, and Ishbel Ross, *Power with Grace* (Putnam's, 1975), quite exhaustive on Mrs. Wilson's life after the president's death. Gene Smith's groundbreaking *When the Cheering Stopped* (Morrow, 1964), the first study of the Wilsons during the time of the president's illness, is very good in some of its details, but highly biased. The tackling of *Thomas Woodrow Wilson* by Sigmund Freud and William C. Bullitt (Houghton Mifflin, 1967) has been discredited as inaccurate both historically and psychoanalytically; yet because Freud had a hand in it, it demands reading. Similarly Alexander and Juliette George's pioneer psychohistorical study, *Woodrow Wilson and Colonel House* (John Day, 1956), has been refuted recently in its conclusions by the work of Dr. Edwin A. Weinstein and Link, but remains interesting in its theories about the two men. Dr. Weinstein's forthcoming medical biography of Wilson, to be published by Princeton University Press, 1981, has made revision of this aspect of Wilson history a necessity. William Allen White's *Woodrow Wilson: The Man, His Times and His Task*, though often wrong and contradicted by later evidence, has always thought-provoking things to say.

Mrs. Wilson's *My Memoir* (Bobbs-Merrill, 1938) is readable and poignant, but at times wrong on the facts, and leaves out much. It is often hard to know what is pure invention and what may be verbatim conversations for which Mrs. Wilson remains the only scribe. This memoir must now be supplemented by her papers.

It might annoy or perhaps tickle Mrs. Wilson to know that much the same is now said for *The Intimate Papers of Colonel House*, edited by Charles Seymour (four volumes, Houghton Mifflin, 1926–1928), for it was these volumes which spurred her to write her own autobiography. The House papers at Yale contain much information left out of the Seymour volumes. Particularly useful were correspondence files with Grayson and McAdoo. Two books by Eleanor Wilson McAdoo, *The Woodrow Wilsons* (with Margaret Y. Gaffey, Macmillan, 1937), and *The Priceless Gift* (McGraw-Hill, 1962), detail the lives of Woodrow and Ellen Axson Wilson. Cary Grayson's *Woodrow Wilson: An Intimate Memoir* is less than that, but the best we have from the inscrutable physician (Holt, Rinehart and Winston, 1960).

Cabinet memoirs: Josephus Daniels's *Cabinet Diaries* (Nebraska Press, 1963) and *The Wilson Era* (North Carolina, 1944); David F.

Houston, *Eight Years With Wilson's Cabinet* (two volumes, Doubleday, 1926); William Gibbs McAdoo, *Crowded Years* (Houghton Mifflin, 1931); Robert Lansing's *The Peace Negotiations, A Personal Narrative* (Houghton, Mifflin, 1921) and *The Letters of Franklin K. Lane* (Houghton, Mifflin 1922). Personal secretary Joseph Tumulty's *Woodrow Wilson As I Know Him* (Doubleday, 1924) has many important details. So do Bernard Baruch's *The Public Years* (Holt, Rinehart and Winston, 1960), George Creel's *Rebel at Large* (Putnam's, 1947), Herbert Hoover's *The Ordeal of Woodrow Wilson* (McGraw-Hill, 1958), Edith Helm's *The Captains and the Kings* (Putnam's, 1954), Ike Hoover's *Forty-two Years in the White House* (Houghton Mifflin, 1934), Mary Allen Hulbert's *The Story of Mrs. Peck, An Autobiography* (Minton, Balch, 1933), Elizabeth Jaffray's *Secrets of the White House* (Cosmopolitan, 1927), and Lillian Parks in collaboration with Frances Spatz Leighton, *My Thirty Years Backstairs at the White House* (Fleet, 1961). Edmund Starling (with Thomas Sugrue), *Starling of the White House* (Simon and Schuster, 1946). Biographies of secondary figures include John Morton Blum, *Joe Tumulty and the Wilson Era* (Houghton, Mifflin, 1951); John J. Broesamle, *William Gibbs McAdoo, A Passion for Change* (Kennikat, 1973); Louis W. Koenig, *Bryan, A Political Biography* (Putnam's, 1971); Joseph L. Gardner, *Departing Glory, Theodore Roosevelt as Ex-President* (Scribner's, 1973).

I have used throughout the *New York Times, Washington Post, St. Louis Post-Dispatch*, the *Literary Digest*, and supplemented them with the remarkable *Our Times* volumes of Mark Sullivan (Scribner's, 1920s). A.J.P. Taylor's account of *The First World War* is my source for fact and military comment on the war (Hamilton, 1963). Henry Steele Commager, *The American Mind* (Yale, 1950); Eric F. Goldman, *Rendezvous with Destiny* (Knopf, 1952); Richard Hofstadter, *The Age of Reform* (Knopf, 1955); and William E. Leuchtenburg, *The Perils of Prosperity* (Chicago, 1958) were invaluable for the sweep of the Wilson era. Richard Sennett's *The Fall of Public Man* (Knopf, 1977) was helpful for the philosophic underpinnings for public man in Wilson's time, though it deals mostly with earlier eras.

The books and materials listed below supplement these here. In all, the listings are meant to be cumulative; that is, books mentioned under, say, Chapter 1, are also used later but have not generally been identified the second time around.

Chapter 1
Details of the wedding are from daily newspapers. Other White

House details from Bess Furman, *White House Profile* (Bobbs-Merrill, 1951); from Eleanor Wilson McAdoo's novel, *Julia and the White House* (NAS, 1946); as well as *My Thirty Years Backstairs at the White House*. A lengthy profile of Wilson at this time is in the March 28, 1914 issue of *Collier's*.

Chapter 2

Walter Lippmann quote is from *Drift and Mastery*, 1914, reprinted by Prentice-Hall, 1961.

Collier's, Atlantic Monthly, Current Opinion, the *International Year Book* edited by Frank Moore Colby (1914), along with Walter Lord's *The Good Years* (Harper & Row, 1960), give a good picture of the world in 1914. The Wilsons' correspondence in unexpurgated version is in the Wilson collection at the Princeton University Library. Readings on attitudes of southern men and women include Milton Rugoff's *Prudery and Passion* (Putnam's, 1971), Edward Carpenter's *The Drama of Love and Death* (1912), William H. Chafe's *The American Woman* (Oxford, 1962), Viola Klein's *The Feminine Character* (Routledge & Kegan Paul, 1946), as well as Ernest Groves's *The American Woman* (Emerson Books, 1944). Personal details on the Wilsons come from books cited in the general section and also from "The Romance of Woodrow Wilson and Ellen Axson" by George Osborn (*North Carolina Historical Review,* vol. 39, no 1, 1962), from Margaret Axson Elliott's *My Aunt Louisa and Woodrow Wilson* (North Carolina, 1944), and from Stockton Axson's article in the *New York Times Magazine,* "The Private Life of President Wilson" (October 8, 1916).

Background on Mexico is in Robert E. Quirk's books *The Mexican Revolution* (Indiana Press, 1960) and *An Affair of Honor* (Kentucky Press, 1962). Details about the opening phase of the war are from Barbara Tuchman, *The Guns of August* (Macmillan, 1962).

Chapter 3 and Chapter 4

Readings on grief and bereavement include Glenn M. Vernon, *Sociology of Death* (Ronald Press, 1970); Geoffrey Gorer, *Death, Grief and Mourning* (Doubleday, 1965); Peter Marris, *Loss and Change* (Random House, 1974); and especially C. S. Lewis, *A Grief Observed* (Faber & Faber, 1961). Wilson's grief is also discussed in James Kerney, *The Political Education of Woodrow Wilson* (Century, 1926), and general social conventions are treated in A. M. Schlesinger, Jr., *Learning How to Behave* (Macmillan, 1946). Much information on this period is gleaned from a close reading of Colonel House's diary at Yale. Lodge and Roosevelt letters are from *Selections From the Correspondence of*

Theodore Roosevelt and Henry Cabot Lodge (Scribner's, 1925). Wilson's letter to Jessie is taken from Frank Sayre's *Glad Adventure* (Macmillan, 1957). A long interview with Wilson was published in the *Saturday Evening Post* by Samuel Blythe on January 9, 1915, as "A Talk With the President," and gives a good picture of the man at the time of his grief. Wordsworth's poem is "She Was a Phantom of Delight" (1804).

Chapter 5, Chapter 6, and Chapter 7
Details of Edith Bolling Galt's life are from her book, *My Memoir*, and from materials in the Edith Wilson Collection. Her child's birth and death are revealed in the family correspondence files. The president's letters to Mrs. Galt and hers to him are now in the Woodrow Wilson Collection itself, though not, as with the majority of the collection, microfilmed for general use. Wilson's comments to Edith on foreign affairs, attached to government documents, are in the Wilson papers. George Sylvester Viereck's record of the Albert incident is quoted by Mark Sullivan. The books on feminine character, courting, and the social behavior of the times, mentioned above, were also used extensively for these chapters. Edith's correspondence with Colonel House is in a folder in the House papers. The *New York Times Current History of the War* published volume three in October of 1915. Edith's comments upon her honeymoon are contained in several letters written to her mother during the Wilsons' time at the resort.

Chapter 8
The description of the changed routine at the White House is from long interviews Tumulty gave to the press in early 1916. The president's actions at the Gridiron dinner are chronicled in *The President Speaks off the Record* by Harold Brayman (Dow Jones, 1976). Edith's jaunt to a club is described in Nellie M. Scanlan (writing as Anonymous), *Boudoir Mirrors of Washington* (Putnam's, 1923), and other incidents are from *The Mirrors of Washington*, also anonymous (Putnam's, 1921). Details about the nomination and campaigns of Charles Evans Hughes are from Merlo Pusey's biography, *Charles Evans Hughes* (Macmillan, 1951), and from Frank Sayre's book, mentioned above. The letter from Altrude to Edith is quoted in Ishbel Ross's *Power with Grace*. Details of Martin H. Glynn's speech are from "He Kept Us Out Of War" by E. Neal Clausen (*Quarterly Journal of Speech*, vol. 52, February, 1966). Articles on the campaign include "The Election of 1916" by James A. Huston (*Current History*, vol. 45, October 1964), "Irish Americans and the 1916 Elections" by Edward Cuddy *(Ameri-*

can Quarterly, 1969). The letter from the socialist candidate is in the House papers, sent to the colonel by Tumulty. A description of the closing phases of the campaign and election night are taken from Mrs. J. Borden Harriman's *From Pinafores to Politics* (Holt, 1923).

Chapter 9 and Chapter 10
Psychological studies of second and late marriages are rare. A few: Judson T. Landis, "Adjustments after marriage" (*Marriage and Family Living,* 1945, 9); Rosalind Dymond, "Interpersonal Perceptions and Marital Happiness" (*Canadian Journal of Psychology,* 1954, 8); E. L. Kelly, "Marital Compatibility" (*Journal of Social Psychology,* 1941, 13). Karen Horney's comments summarized from *Neurosis and Human Growth* (1950). The incidents about Tumulty and John Randolph Bolling are detailed in Blum. Barbara Tuchman's *The Zimmermann Telegram* (1958) tells of the events cascading to war. *Cobb of The World,* compiled by John L. Hester (Dutton, 1924), tells of the newspaperman's visit to Wilson. The war on Congress is exhaustively analyzed in Seward Livermore's *Politics Is Adjourned* (Wesleyan, 1966); a useful compendium is John M. Cooper, Jr., ed., *Causes and Consequences of World War I* (Quadrangle, 1972). Preston W. Slosson, *The Great Crusade and After* (Macmillan, 1930), and Edward Ellis, *Echoes of Distant Thunder* (Coward, McCann and Geoghegan, 1975), are more general. The ferment of the thinker is mirrored in Randolph S. Bourne's essays collected as *War and the Intellectuals* (Harper, 1964) and Harold Lasswell's famous *Propaganda Technique in World War I* (Kegan Paul, 1927; reprinted by MIT Press, 1971) details Wilson's work with words in disarming Germany. Edith's comments quoted in this period are found in her correspondence with Ray Stannard Baker in the Baker papers at the Library of Congress. L. P. Jacks's article "President Wilson's War Mind" was brought to his attention in *The Living Age* of July 1918.

Chapter 11
The great plethora of books about Versailles is as confusing as it is enlightening. Among them I have used primarily Paul Birdsall's *Versailles Twenty Years After* (Princeton University Press, 1941), Inga Floto's *Colonel House in Paris* (reprinted 1979, Princeton University Press), Harold Nicolson's *Peacemaking 1919* (Grosset & Dunlap, 1965) and, of the diaries, Stephen Bonsal's *Unfinished Business* (Doubleday, 1944), and consulted Lansing, House, Herbert Hoover, and Baruch. I have used biographies of *Georges Clemenceau* by Jean Martet (Longmans, Green, 1930), David Lloyd George's *The Truth about*

the Peace Treaties (Gollancz, 1938), and Winston Churchill's deroga-
tory *The World Crisis*, Volume Four (Butterworth, Ltd., 1929). For
color and background, there are Arthur Krock's *Memories* (Funk &
Wagnalls, 1969), *The Selected Letters of William Allen White* (Holt,
1947), Lincoln Steffens's *Autobiography* (Harcourt, Brace, 1931),
Harry Hansen's *The Adventures of the Fourteen Points* (Century,
1919), Elsa Maxwell's *RSVP* (Little, Brown, 1954). Allen Cranston's
The Killing of the Peace (Viking, 1945) is biased for Wilson but useful.
"Early Press Reaction to Wilson's League Proposal" is given in James
D. Startt's article in the *Journalism Quarterly* (no. 39, 1962). Dr.
Edwin A. Weinstein's articles include "Woodrow Wilson's Neurologi-
cal Illness" (*Journal of American History*, vol. LVII, 1970); and—with
James William Anderson and Arthur S. Link—"Woodrow Wilson's
Political Personality: A Reappraisal" (*Political Science Quarterly*, vol.
93, no. 4, 1978).

Chapter 12
    Robert K. Murray's *Red Scare* (Minnesota Press, 1955) has
influenced this and the next chapters about the national hysteria of the
immediate post-war period. Howard Teichman's *Alice* (Prentice-Hall,
1979) recounts the activities of Roosevelt's daughter during these times;
the James E. Watson story is from his *As I Knew Them* (Bobbs-Merrill,
1936). A good study is "President Wilson's Tour in September, 1919,"
an Ohio State University dissertation (1958) by David Henry Jennings.
"The Assassin of Wilson" by Louis Adamic appeared in *American
Mercury*, October 1930, recounting a story told the author by Jack
Kipps.

Chapter 13
    Readings on presidential disability include Richard Hansen's *The
Year We Had No President* (Nebraska Press, 1961), John D. Feerick's
From Failing Hands (Fordham Press, 1965), both of which summarize
many earlier books on the subject. Grey's mission is reviewed in "A
Fettered Envoy" by Leon E. Boothe (*Review of Politics*, vol. 33, 1971)
as well as in Jonathan Daniels, *Washington Quadrille* (Doubleday,
1968). Erving Goffman's work, which has greatly informed the writing
of this book, includes *The Presentation of Self in Everyday Life* (Doubleday, 1959), *Behavior in Public Places* (Macmillan, 1963), and
Relations in Public (Basic Books, 1971). The Santayana quote is from
Soliloquies in England (Scribner's, 1922). The bladder crisis is related
in Hugh Young, M.D., *A Surgeon's Autobiography* (Harcourt, 1940).

The story about Essary and Marshall is from Olive Ewing Clapper, *Washington Tapestry* (McGraw-Hill, 1946).

Chapter 14

Edith's letters to House are in the House papers at Yale. The correspondence on the *Imperator* group of ships is in the Wilson papers. The meetings with Hitchcock are detailed in the Hitchcock papers, Library of Congress, and the copy of his letter which the Wilsons amended is in the Wilson papers.

Chapter 15

Thomas Riley Marshall's *Recollections, A Hoosier Salad* (Bobbs-Merrill, 1925) is piquant but short on facts; the biography *Thomas Riley Marshall* by Charles M. Thomas (Mississippi Valley Press, 1939) is highly critical of Wilson. Much information pertaining to Senator Fall's visit is in "Woodrow Wilson and the Mexican Interventionist Movement of 1919" by Clifford W. Trow (*Journal of American History*, vol. 58, no. 1, 1971). The quotations from the president are taken from the commencement speech "Leaders of Men" given in 1890, as edited by T. H. Vail Motter in 1951 for the Princeton University Press. The quote to Raymond Fosdick is recounted in his "Personal Recollections of Woodrow Wilson" in the *Lectures and Seminars* volume on the centennial of Woodrow Wilson.

Chapter 16 and Chapter 17

Kurt Wimer's articles, "Woodrow Wilson and a Third Nomination" (*Pennsylvania History* XXXIX, April, 1962) and "Woodrow Wilson's Plan For a Vote of Confidence" (*Pennsylvania History*, XXVIII, July, 1961), inform these chapters. I have disagreed with Wimer on the date of the "plan for the vote of confidence," but agreed with him on his redating of the "Solemn Referendum" paper. Wesley M. Bagby, *The Road to Normalcy* (Johns Hopkins Press, 1962) is the other major reference about the election year. Ray Stannard Baker's visits are detailed in his memoir, *American Chronicle* (Scribner's, 1945). The account of the candidates' visit to Wilson is in James M. Cox, *Journey through My Years* (Simon and Schuster, 1946). The account of the Debs case is from *Eugene Victor Debs: A Biography* (originally entitled *The Bending Cross*) by Ray Ginger (Collier's, 1962). Accounts of the Hardings are from Francis Russell, *The Shadow of Blooming Grove* (McGraw-Hill, 1968).

Chapter 18

This chapter draws on Smith, Hatch, Ross, Grayson, Fosdick, Baruch, and others, as well as on Bainbridge Colby's pamphlet of his speech "The Close of Woodrow Wilson's Administration and the Final Years" (Kennerly, 1930). The story about FDR in 1944 was related to me by an acquaintance.

INDEX

287